HOBBES

Tom Sorell

London and New York

First published in 1986 by
Routledge & Kegan Paul
First published in paperback in 1991
by Routledge, 11 New Fetter Lane, London EC4P 4EE

Simultaneously published in the USA and Canada
by Routledge, a division of Routledge, Chapman and Hall, Inc.
29 West 35th Street, New York, NY 10001

Set in Linotron Garamond 10 on 12pt
by Input Typesetting Ltd, London
and printed in Great Britain
by T. J. Press (Padstow) Ltd
Padstow, Cornwall

British Library Cataloguing-in-Publication Data

Sorell, Tom
Hobbes. – (The arguments of the philosophers)
I. Title   II. Series
192

Library of Congress Cataloging-in-Publication Data
Sorell, Tom.
Hobbes.
(The Arguments of the philosophers)
Bibliography: p.
Includes index.
1. Hobbes, Thomas 1588–1679.   I. Title.   II. Series.
B1247.S63   1986   192   86–499

ISBN 0–415–06366–3

The Arguments of
the Philosophers

EDITED BY TED HONDERICH

*Grote Professor of the Philosophy of Mind and Logic
University College, London*

The purpose of this series is to provide a contemporary assessment and
history of the entire course of philosophical thought. Each book
constitutes a detailed, critical introduction to the work of a philosopher
of major influence and significance.

Already published in the series:

Augustine	Christopher Kirwan
J. L. Austin	Geoffrey Warnock
Ayer	John Foster
Bentham	Ross Harrison
Bergson	A. R. Lacey
Berkeley	George Pitcher
Butler	Terence Penelhum
Descartes	Margaret Dauler Wilson
Dewey	J. E. Tiles
Gottlob Frege	Hans Sluga
Hegel	M. J. Inwood
Hobbes	Tom Sorell
Hume	Barry Stroud
Husserl	David Bell
William James	Graham Bird
Kant	Ralph C. S. Walker
Kierkegaard	Alastair Hannay
Karl Marx	Allen Wood
Meinong	Reinhart Grossman
John Stuart Mill	John Skorupski
G. E. Moore	Tom Baldwin
Nietzsche	Richard Schacht
Peirce	Christopher Hookway
Plato	J. C. B. Gosling
Karl Popper	Anthony O'Hear
The Presocratic Philosophers	Jonathan Barnes
Thomas Reid	Keith Lehrer
Russell	R. M. Sainsbury
Santayana	Timothy Sprigge
Sartre	Peter Caws
Schopenhauer	D. W. Hamlyn
Socrates	Gerasimos Xenophon Santas
Spinoza	R. J. Delahunty
Wittgenstein	Robert J. Fogelin

available in paperback

Contents

Preface   page ix

Editions and Abbreviations   xi

I THE SCIENCE OF POLITICS AND THE UNITY OF SCIENCE   1

1. A project within a project   1
2. Teaching philosophy from the elements   4
3. The autonomy of civil science   7

II THE PARTS OF SCIENCE AND THE METHODS OF SCIENCE   14

1. A strained parallel   14
2. Bodies politic, natural bodies, and method   17
3. The methodological disunity of natural and civil science   21
4. The order of the parts of science   24
5. The parts of science and the concept of science   26

III KNOWLEDGE AND POWER IN FALLEN MAN   29

1. Ends, means and the limitations of experience   29
2. Reason, science and human improvement   33
3. The conditions of science   37
4. Logic-book science?   41

IV TWO PROBLEMS WITH DEMONSTRATIVE SCIENCE   43

1. 'Demonstration'   43

2. Science, truth and convention   45
3. Old logic, new science   50

V FIRST PRINCIPLES, FIRST CAUSES AND THE
   SCIENCES OF MOTION   55

   1. The disclosure of universal things   55
   2. Motion and the 'several parts of science' 59
   3. Universal things adequately defined?   61
   4. Geometry and motion   63

VI MOTION, PHANTASMS AND THE OBJECTS OF
   SENSE   68

   1. The explanation of appearance   69
   2. Sentient and insentient bodies   73
   3. Objects of sense   75

VII SENSE, THOUGHT AND MOTIVATION   82

   1. Phantasms and the succession of phantasms 82
   2. Sense, appetite and passion   87
   3. Difficulties with the reconstruction of the passions 91
   4. The succession of the passions and action 92

VIII THE PURSUIT OF FELICITY AND THE GOOD OF
    SURVIVAL   96

   1. Egoism   97
   2. War and the free pursuit of felicity   100
   3. Egoism and the avoidability of war   103
   4. Hobbes's sense of 'moral'   105
   5. An acceptable concept of morality?   108

IX ABSOLUTE SUBMISSION, UNDIVIDED
   SOVEREIGNTY   111

   1. The dangers of visible virtue   111
   2. Making it safe for morality   114
   3. Safety at what price?   118
   4. Citizenship without judgment, civil society without
      civilization   123

X SEDITION, SUBMISSION AND SCIENCE   127

    1. 'Heads of pretence to rebellion'   128
    2. Reason, eloquence, and persuasive civil science   133
    3. Civil science as exemplary science   137
    4. Hobbesian science and latter-day philosophy   140

Notes   145
Bibliography   155
Index   158

For my parents,
Adi and Dora Sorell

Preface

Hobbes's writings are dominated by a preoccupation with science: what it is, how it is organized and learned, and why creatures like us cannot do well without it. Accordingly, the early chapters of this book present a sketch of his philosophy of science. It differs in a number of ways from sketches made by other commentators, notably in emphasizing how science is supposed to improve the condition of Fallen Man. The sketch eventually serves as background for a discussion of Hobbes's first philosophy and mechanistic geometry, his theory of external bodies and the mind, and his moral and political philosophy. Chapters 5 to 10 deal with all of these topics in turn, but at greatest length with the moral and political philosophy, what Hobbes called his 'civil science'.

This is the best understood of his intellectual productions, and it is also the one whose theoretical apparatus, at least on the surface, is closest to that of work in Anglo-American philosophy today. Its contractarian approach, its use of the device of the state of nature, its amenability to interpretation in terms of game theory, its preoccupation with justice and the extent of liberty compatible with government – all of these things align Hobbes's civil science with moral and political theory as it is now being developed, at any rate in the English language. But the alignment is often not exact enough to permit systematic discussion of Hobbes and modern social contract theory at the same time. The reader will some-times have to look in the endnotes for connections with latter-day accounts. It is different with Hobbes's moral psychology. This does engage relatively recent work on self-interest and prudence quite directly, and some links, usually quite general ones, are made explicit in the body of Chapter 8. Overall, where simple juxtapositions of old and new would have depended on interpreting Hobbes in ways that I realized were strained, I decided to forgo them. His own views are interesting enough when presented in their own terms.

The moral and political philosophy of Hobbes that emerges from this book is unlike the moral and political philosophy sometimes attributed to him, in that it contains much more advocacy than explanation, much more moralizing than abstract decomposition of states into their working parts. Chapters 1 and 2 outline my approach to the civil science, and the outline is filled in toward the end of the book, finishing up in Chapter 10, where a connection is made between methodical persuasion and demonstration in civil philosophy. It is in this area that Hobbes's ideas about philosophy engage modern ones by standing in sharp opposition to them. At the very end of the book I indicate how certain features of his approach, namely its 'coerciveness', its revisionary strain, and its pretensions to conclusiveness, are all attractive despite being out of fashion.

In general, published research on Hobbes's thought is ageing and needs renewal, but some of it, especially on Hobbes's civil philosophy, is so valuable that it is unlikely to be superseded. The writers I have learnt most from are Frithiof Brandt and Michael Oakeshott. Brandt's book, now about 60 years old, is still the best guide to Hobbes's mechanics and optics. Oakeshott's essays are extremely suggestive pieces of political thought in their own right, not just excellent reviews of Hobbes's ideas about civil association. Still, there is a dearth of material on Hobbes's philosophy as a whole, and no excuse or apology is needed for adding to the small number of books that try to take the wider view. In adding this one, I have been helped in various ways by my wife, Alison Finlay, by Ted Honderich, Godfrey Vesey, Alan Malachowski, Stuart Brown, Gary Jenkins, and a seminar audience at Bradford University. Angela Sheffield produced the final typescript with great speed and accuracy.

Editions and Abbreviations

Until his death in February 1985, Howard Warrender was preparing a new edition of Hobbes's works for Oxford University Press. Too little of this had appeared for it to be used here. The standard edition is Sir William Molesworth's, and it falls into two parts: *The English Works of Thomas Hobbes*, published in eleven volumes in 1839, and the *Opera Latina* (five volumes), which appeared in 1845. With a few exceptions indicated below, all texts used are from the *English Works*, in the Scientia Verlaag Second Reprint. References are by volume and page, preceded by 'E' for *English Works*. Books of Hobbes's collected in the *English Works* are cited by abbreviated title, part (where necessary), chapter, and article or section (where possible). Thus '*De Corp.*, ch. 1, vii. E I 8' is short for '*De Corpore*, chapter 1, article vii, *English Works*, vol. 1, p. 8'. The following abbreviated titles are used.

LT   *Little Treatise* (1630?), Appendix I in F. Tönnies, ed., *The Elements of Law Natural and Politic* (London: Simpkin & Marshall, 1889). I use Frithiof Brandt's title in preference to Tönnies' more ponderous 'Short Tract on First Principles'. Page numbers at the end of 'LT' citations are those of Tönnies' edition.

EL   *The Elements of Law Natural and Politic* (1640), Tönnies, ed., op. cit. This is the correctly edited version of a manuscript work in two Parts published in London in 1650 without Hobbes's consent. 'EL' citations end with the Tönnies page number. In the unauthorised version each of the parts appeared as a separate work. The first part was entitled *Human Nature or the Fundamental Elements of Policy*; the second part, *De Corpore Politico*. It is as separate texts under these titles that Molesworth published the parts of the *Elements of Law* (E IV). Because some of Hobbes's critics refer to this pair of texts, it will sometimes be necessary for me to refer to them as well. '*HN*' stands for *Human Nature*; *De Corp. Pol.* for *De Corpore Politico*.

TW	*Thomas White's* De Mundo *Examined*, H. W. Jones, trans., (Bradford: University Press, 1976). This is a relatively recently discovered commentary Hobbes wrote in Latin at Paris in 1641 or 1642. Citations end with Jones's page numbers.
Third Objs.	*Third Set of Objections to Descartes's Meditations* (1641), in E. Haldane and G. Ross, trans., *The Philosophical Works of Descartes* (Cambridge: University Press, 1970), vol. 2, pp. 60–78. This is referred to in the familiar style 'HR' followed by a page number.
De Cive	*Elementorum Philosophiae, Sectio Tertia, De Cive* (1642). Following the convention, I use 'De Cive' to refer to Hobbes's English translation of his Latin work. The title he gave to the translation was *Philosophical Rudiments Concerning Government and Society*. The translation appeared in 1651.
MDO	*A Minute or First Draught of the Optiques* (1646).
L	*Leviathan, or the Matter, Form and Power of Commonwealth, Ecclesiastical and Civil* (1651).
L&N	*Of Liberty and Necessity* (1654).
De Corp.	*Elementorum Philosophiae, Sectio Prima de Corpore* (1655). I refer to the English translation, *Elements of Philosophy, the First Section concerning body* (1656).
LNC	*The Questions Concerning Liberty, Necessity and Chance, Clearly Stated and Debated between Dr Bramhall, Bishop of Derry, and Thomas Hobbes, of Malmesbury* (1656).
SL	*Six Lessons to the Professors of Mathematics . . . in the University of Oxford* (1656).
De Hom.	*De Homine, sive Elementorum Philosophiae Sectio Secunda* (1658). I refer to the English translation and abridgment, B. Gert, ed., C. T. Wood, T. Scott-Craig, B. Gert, trans., *On Man*, in *Man and Citizen* (New York: Humanities Press, 1972). Citations end with the Gert page number.
SPP	*Seven Philosophical Problems* (1662).
Cons. Rep.	*Considerations on the Reputation, Loyalty, Manners, and Religion, of Thomas Hobbes of Malmesbury* (1662).
B	*Behemoth, or the Long Parliament. Dialogue of the Civil Wars of England*, composed *circa* 1668; published posthumously, 1680.
DCL	*Dialogue Between a Philosopher and a Student of the Common Laws of England*, composed *circa* 1666; published posthumously, 1681.
DP	*Decameron Physioligicum or Ten Dialogues of Natural Philosophy* (1678).

I

The Science of Politics and the Unity of Science

Thomas Hobbes's philosophical ideas were formed by two great upheavals of the 17th century. One was local, political, dangerous, and as Hobbes believed, deeply irrational. This was the English Civil War. The other was largely Continental, benefited people in obvious ways, showed what reason could accomplish when properly guided and applied. This was the upheaval in scientific ideas that Hobbes thought had been started by Galileo. Mainly on the strength of writings occasioned by the first upheaval Hobbes claimed to have contributed something important to the second. His book *De Cive*, published in Paris close to the beginning of the Civil War, was supposed to have put morals and politics on a scientific footing for the first time. Questions of right and authority that Hobbes said England was 'boiling hot with' in the years before the Civil War, were treated according to a method comparable to that of geometry and pure mechanics.

1 A project within a project

De Cive was published in 1642. It was neither the first nor the last of Hobbes's treatises on civil government. He came at the subject again and again, first in a manuscript intended for private circulation, *The Elements of Law* (1640), next in *De Cive*, once more in his best-known book, *Leviathan* (1651). Then there were writings in which the principles of politics provided the main subtext. One was *A Dialogue Between a Philosopher and a Student of the Common Laws of England*, complete by 1666 but only published after Hobbes's death in 1681. Here he pursued the question of the relative authority of the statute and the common law in terms provided by his theory of the rights of sovereigns. And in *Behemoth*, his history of the English Civil War, he used the same theory to relate the 'causes, pretensions, order, and artifice' of the events of 1640 to 1660.

1

THE SCIENCE OF POLITICS AND THE UNITY OF SCIENCE

He did not write about morals and politics to the exclusion of all else. Far from it. He claimed that in his works as a whole he had laid the ground of two new sciences. One was civil science or the science of natural justice; the other was optics. But he did not think the two achievements were on a level. Optics he called the most 'curious' of the sciences, but the science of natural justice was 'the most profitable of all other' (*MDO*, Ep. Ded., E VII 471). It surpassed the other sciences in usefulness. For as he explains in *De Cive*,

> in matters wherein we speculate for the exercise of our wits, if any error escapes us, it is without hurt; neither is there any loss, but of time only. But in those things which every man ought to meditate for the steerage of his life, it necessarily happens that not only from errors, but even from ignorance itself, there arise offences, contentions, nay, even slaughter itself (Pref. to the Reader, E II ix).

A science of morals and politics, by remedying ignorance and correcting false opinions, might actually save lives.

De Cive's Preface to the Reader (E II xi–xii) gives a sampling of the false opinions that could lead to general slaughter. The belief that a tyrant might lawfully be put to death was one. Another was that the king was not superior to, but only functioned as administrator for, the multitude. A third was that it was for private citizens to decide which of a king's decrees were just. These and related beliefs Hobbes thought he could expose as false with a single argument from the nature of sovereignty, and in each of the political treatises there is a chapter in which he rebuts in turn some six or seven of the opinions most likely to cause bloodshed through civil war (*EL*, Pt. 2, ch. 8; *De Cive*, ch. 12, *L*, ch. 29).

In confronting what he took to be the most dangerous of the opinions leading to sedition, Hobbes tried to point out the injustice of acting on those opinions. He produced a moral argument, but one he took to break new ground in moral philosophy and also in rhetoric. Where traditional morals and rhetoric, notably Aristotle's, had assumed general agreement between people over what was good and evil, Hobbes thought he could prove that disagreement was the rule. And where traditional ethics and rhetoric had assumed that discussions of right conduct had to be imprecise, Hobbes demanded and purported to give exact definitions. The civic virtue of justice, which he alleged had always been misrepresented in traditional moral philosophy, he thought he had defined correctly for the first time. He went further to claim that he had found the basis for the distinction between virtue and vice itself (*EL*, Pt. 1, ch. 17, xiv. 94; *De Cive*, ch. 3 xxxi–xxxii, E II 47–49; *L*, ch. 15, E III 146–7). What made certain patterns of action virtuous and others vicious, was that certain patterns of action promoted civil order or peace, while others disturbed it. Justice, or the keeping of covenants one had entered into, was the pre-eminent moral virtue (cf. *De Hom.*, ch. 13, ix); practically all forms of peace-keeping behaviour were prefigured in keeping faith.

It was necessary to define justice properly and to ground the distinction between vice and virtue, if there was to be any effective art for dissuading people from sedition and persuading them to behave well. 'For it is to no purpose to be bidden in every thing to do right, before there be a certain rule and measure of right established' (*De Corp.*, ch. 1, vii, E I 9). In other words, a workable moral rhetoric had to await the development of a rigorous moral philosophy. That involved a major reform of traditional ethics. The need for such an overhaul explicitly motivates the first two of the political treatises. In both, Hobbes announces and then undertakes a programme of reform. One of his objects was to reduce the doctrine of virtue to a definite technique people could actually apply. Another was to derive the doctrine in such a way that its precepts would not seem disputable. 'To reduce this doctrine [of justice] to the rules and infallibility of reason' is how he describes his aim in *The Elements of Law* (Ep. Ded., xv). And in *De Cive* he said he would substitute for moral philosophy in its 'counterfeit and babbling form' an art 'derived from true principles by evident connection' (Pref. to the Reader, E II xi).

Ambitious as it was, the programme of reform Hobbes first announced in *The Elements of Law* did not look beyond the 'doctrine of policy and justice'. In *De Cive* the renovation of morals and politics is presented as a contribution to something bigger. It is described as a project within a project. *De Cive* was to be read as the third of a three-part exposition of the elements of philosophy as a whole. Hobbes lived to complete this exposition. His work on a unified science of body, man and citizen dominated most of a philosophical career begun in middle age. The result, the trilogy of *De Corpore*, *De Homine* and *De Cive*, was supposed to have arranged the elements of science in an order appropriate to 'teaching' or 'demonstrating' each of the special sciences (*De Corp.*, ch. 6, xvii, E I 87–88).

What is the relation between the project in morals and politics and the project he carried out in composing the trilogy? The question has been raised often, but it has not, I believe, received a satisfactory answer. Hobbes's work on the 'doctrine of justice and policy' is usually interpreted in the light of his exposition of a unified science. Its claim to have put politics on a scientific footing is standardly understood as a claim to have grafted politics on to the body of natural science sketched in *De Corpore* and *De Homine*. Up to a point the interpretation is correct. Hobbes *was* concerned to show that natural and civil philosophy were parts of a single subject. But he did not think his politics derived its

3

scientific status from the possibility of being located within a unified science. And although he acknowledged connections between natural philosophy and politics, it was not on account of these links that politics was supposed to be a science. He thought politics had an independent claim to be a science, indeed a better claim to be a science than physics. Or so I hope eventually to show, in opposition to some common interpretations.

2 Teaching philosophy from the elements

A division of the elements of philosophy into three 'sections' had occurred to Hobbes at some time before 1642, perhaps in the late 1630's.[1] But it was in the Preface to the Reader of *De Cive* (in the edition of 1647), that he first gave notice of a three-part exposition of the elements. The first 'section' was to have 'treated of *body* and its general properties; . . . the second of man and his special faculties and affections; . . . and the third, of *civil government* and the duties of subjects' (E II xx). Publication of the three sections did not go to plan. *De Cive*, or the 'Third Section,' was the first to appear. *De Corpore*, the 'First Section,' followed *De Cive* into print after an interval of thirteen years, in 1655, and the trilogy's second instalment, *De Homine*, came out three years after that. Parts of *De Homine* were ready for press before *De Corpore* was complete, and Hobbes took time off from work on the 'First Section' to compose *Leviathan* and translate *De Cive* from Latin into English. This disarray is not reflected in the body of the texts themselves, and read in the intended order they do seem to put over a unitary doctrine in keeping with Hobbes's original scheme.

De Corpore, the opening volume of the trilogy, served a double purpose. On the one hand it was intended to 'lay open the few and first Elements of Philosophy in general' (ch. 1, i. E I 2). On the other it was supposed to 'put into a clear method the true foundations of natural philosophy' (Ep. Ded., E I xi). There is a parallel between the task Hobbes set himself in natural philosophy and the programme of reform he undertook in morals and politics. He was writing at a time when, as he thought, the dominant ideas in natural philosophy in the English universities were derived from Aristotle's *Physics* and *Metaphysics*.[2] Outside the universities the only widely available scientific books in England were almanacs, manuals, and tables of experimental results. In *Leviathan* he somewhat patronizingly calls these collations of experimental findings 'natural *histories*' in contradistinction to books of natural philosophy (cf. *L*, ch. 9, E III 71).[3] And he has stronger words for the physics and metaphysics of the 'school divines' in Oxbridge. 'So far from the possibility of being understood,' he says of their 'supernatural philosophy,' and 'so repugnant to right reason, that whoever thinketh there is anything to be understood by it, must needs think it supernatural' (*L*, ch. 46, E III 671–2). The 'true foundations of natural philosophy' that he intended to set out in *De Corpore* were supposed to overthrow or exorcise the metaphysics and physics of Aristotle and the schoolmen. No less than traditional morals and politics, the old natural philosophy had once and for all to be abandoned.

But abandoned in favour of what? Not the new experimental science that had given rise to the manuals, almanacs and natural histories. He had only faint praise for 'chymists . . . and mechanics' (cf. *Cons. Rep.*, E IV 436–7) and artificers (cf. *L*, ch. 10, E III 75). For observation, instrument-making and experimentation provided only the raw material of natural philosophy. It was for natural science not just to collate facts but to disclose relations of dependence between facts (*L*, ch. 5, E III 35). Registers or tables that merely listed observations were no substitute for books in which general truths subsuming these observations were rigorously derived. What was wrong with 'natural histories' was not so much that they reported false or doubtful findings, but that they reported correct findings without their principles.

It was mainly in treatises from the Continent that he saw evidence of genuine demonstrations, and such books were his model for 'books of natural philosophy'. When he said in *De Corpore* that he would put into a clear method the foundations of natural philosophy, he meant that he would identify and arrange in proper order the elements of a *demonstrative* natural science. As for the 'few and first Elements' of philosophy in general, these would be the principles or starting points of a global demonstrative science in which the preferred natural philosophy and the preferred civil philosophy were combined.

Combined how exactly? It is often claimed that the unified science expounded in the trilogy is a continuous deduction. The principles of morals and politics, which are placed last in the order of demonstration, are supposed to be deduced from the truths of physics, the truths of physics from those of mechanics, and the truths of mechanics from those of geometry.[4] But Hobbes himself never puts it this way. It is true that he regarded natural philosophy as the 'first part' of philosophy (*De Corp.*, ch. 6, vii, E I 74) and geometry as the 'first part of natural philosophy' (*De Corp.* ch. 6, vi, E I 73). It is true, too, that he prescribed an order for passing from the first to the last part of natural philosophy: mechanics was to be studied after geometry, and after mechanics the two 'parts' of physics: first the doctrine of sense, next the doctrine of sensible qualities and changes (*De Corp.*, ch. 6, vi, E I 71–2).

But Hobbes does not say that the truths of mechanics are to be deduced *from* those of geometry, only that they are to be deduced *after* those of geometry. He does not say that physics is to be demonstrated from, only after mechanics (*De Corp.*, ch. 6, vi, xvii, E I 72, 87). In

5

THE SCIENCE OF POLITICS AND THE UNITY OF SCIENCE

fact, the truths of physics are in a special case. To the extent Hobbes thinks they are deducible at all, he thinks they are deducible with the aid of hypotheses (cf. *De Corp.*, ch. 30, xv, E I 351; *SPP*, Ep. Ded., E VII 3–4). And although the hypotheses of physics have to be *consistent* with the truths of mechanics and geometry (cf. *DP*, ch. 2, E VII 88), they are not truths of geometry and mechanics themselves. This means that even within natural philosophy Hobbes envisaged no simple deduction of one special science from another. When he claimed that geometry was the most basic natural science he did not mean that from its axioms the rest of the special sciences could be deduced. He seems to have held that geometry was basic in the weaker sense that it had to be understood before the rest of the natural sciences could be taught (cf. *De Corp.*, ch. 6, xvii, E I 87–88). In a similar way someone might now hold that linear algebra has to be understood before certain parts of economic theory can be understood: such a person would not be committed to holding that parts of economic theory are deducible from linear algebra.

'After *physics*,' Hobbes writes in *De Corpore*, 'we must come to *moral philosophy*; in which we are to consider the motions of the mind, namely, *appetite, aversion, love, benevolence, hope, fear, anger, emulation, envy* &c; what causes they have and of what they be causes' (ch. 6, vi, E I 72). The use of the term 'moral philosophy' for the theory dealing with the 'motions of the mind' is unfortunate: elsewhere Hobbes calls his natural law doctrine 'moral philosophy' (cf. e.g. *L*, ch. 15, E III 146). 'Ethics' is another label Hobbes sometimes uses (*De Corp.*, ch. 1, ix, E I 11), and it is preferable. The reason ethics comes after physics is that the motions of the mind 'have their causes in sense and imagination, which are the subject of physical contemplation' (*De Corp.*, ch. 6, vi, E I 73). The idea is that sense and imagination have to be understood before the workings of the passions can be understood, and sense and imagination being the topics of the 'first part' of physics, physics must inform ethics. As before, there is no evidence that Hobbes took ethics to be deducible from physics.

What about the connection between ethics and civil philosophy, i.e., between the doctrine of the motions of the mind – conative psychology if you like – and the doctrine of moral and civil duties? Hobbes takes the trouble to signal the relative independence of the two subjects in chapter 6, article 7 of *De Corpore*. Using 'moral philosophy' to refer to the study of the motions of the mind, he says that '*civil* and *moral philosophy* do not so adhere to one another, but that they may be severed' (E I 73). Although he believes that one has to understand the 'motions of the mind' if one is to see the point of one's moral and civil duties, he thinks that there are two ways of understanding the motions of the mind, and that either will serve as a starting point for civil philosophy. There

6

is a philosophical or scientific understanding of the motions of the mind, arrived at from a prior acquaintance with principles given in physics. There is also a pre-scientific understanding, available to anyone who bothers to introspect and observe within himself the passions that move him (E I 73).

Because the motions of the mind, the passions, are accessible to 'experience' and not just to ratiocination, the point and even the content of moral and civil duties can be grasped by them 'that have not learned the first part of philosophy namely, *geometry* and *physics*' (*De Corp.*, ch. 6, vi, E I 74). Outside *De Corpore* the message is the same. Explaining why the last part of the trilogy could be read in the absence of the parts meant to precede it, Hobbes wrote that the statement of his civil science, 'grounded on its own principles sufficiently known by experience . . . would not stand in need of the former sections' (*De Cive*, Pref. to the Reader, E II xx). And again in *Leviathan* he points out that 'sovereigns and their ministers . . . need not be charged with the sciences mathematical, as by Plato they are,' in order to learn from Hobbes how to govern (ch. 31, E III 357). The precepts of his civil science were supposed to be applicable by rulers and ruled alike, and neither rulers nor ruled needed any grounding in the first part of philosophy to understand and do their duty.

3 The autonomy of civil science

Hobbes's remarks suggest that civil philosophy is a part of science, and yet teachable and learnable in isolation from the rest of science. There is a good idea here, but it is obscured by Hobbes's ordering of the parts of science, and, as we shall see later, by his explanation of what the various topics of science have in common. The good idea is that while there can be something better than mere intuition or opinion about moral and political matters, while there can be such a thing as knowledge or science concerning the good and the just, it is not esoteric knowledge or science. It can be acquired by anyone with ordinary intellectual capacities, and it presupposes no special training. Plato had held that a genuine science of the good and of the just was possible, but that it was not accessible to everyone; Aristotle had held that practical wisdom could be acquired by most people but that there was no real (i.e. exact and systematic) science of the good and the just; Hobbes contrives to have it both ways. He holds that there can be a science of the good and the just, and that it can be made available to practically everyone, rulers and ruled alike.

It is to Hobbes's credit that this democratic conception of moral and political science is not extended to all kinds of science. Hobbes does not claim, as Descartes implausibly does in the *Discourse* and the preface to his *Principles*, that anyone with a clear head and the right method can work his way through metaphysics, mathematics and physics. The principles of what Hobbes calls the 'first part' of philosophy, i.e., geometry, mechanics and physics, are always supposed to be far more difficult than the principles of politics (cf. esp. *De Hom.*, Ep. Ded.), and Hobbes addresses parts of *De Corpore* only to people who are 'versed in the demonstrations of mathematicians' (Ep. Ded., E I vii; cf. E I xi–xii, ch. 4, xiii, E I 54; ch. 15, i, E I 203–4). The political treatises were naturally directed to a wider audience, dealing as they did with matters each person needed to meditate upon for 'the steerage of his life'.

How did he define the aims of the political treatises? In the Preface to the Reader of *De Cive* he says that he is setting out to demonstrate 'by most firm reasons' that there are 'no authentical doctrines concerning right and wrong, good and evil, besides the constituted laws in each realm and government' (E II xiii). He mentions no laws of any 'realm' in particular. He assumes that his readers will know what specific legal requirements apply to them; indeed, he makes it constitutive of something's counting as a civil law that its content be universally known (*L*, ch. 26, E III 259). He relies only on premisses about what all civil laws have in common, and assumptions about people subject to law. One premiss is that all civil laws restrict the liberty of people; another is that people naturally dislike that restraint. His task is to explain to people why they should obey the civil law, given that it is natural for them to dislike doing so.

He produces what in his terms is a moral argument, that is, an argument from 'the laws of nature'. These are precepts enjoining behaviour that is 'good' in a public and well-defined sense of that term. In *The Elements of Law, De Cive* and *Leviathan*, the statement of the laws of nature assumes the form of a deduction. The first law is supposed to be plausible in the light of both science and common sense about the behaviour that people would display if they were not under government. Considered as existing in pre-political groups or in the 'state of nature', people would be driven by their passions into violent and ultimately fatal competition for scarce goods. Reason would dictate to each person the desirability of ending the conflict if taking steps to do so was not itself too dangerous. Thus the first law of nature: that whoever can safely do so seek peace and keep it (cf. e.g. *L*, ch. 14, E III 117). The second law of nature calls for behaviour calculated to secure peace: the right of each person in the state of nature to do and take what he likes, is to be laid down by each in return for a similar laying down of right by each other person (*L*, ch. 14, E III 118). The medium of this laying down of right is a covenant of each person in the state of nature with every other. Each agrees by entering the covenant to vest responsibility for his security and well-being in a designated man or body of men, who thereby become the government and are empowered to declare and enforce laws. By entering the covenant people become subject to these laws and are bound to observe them by what binds them to keep the covenant, namely the third law of nature. This identifies justice with keeping covenants.

Hobbes's argument for obedience to the civil law is an argument from justice in the sense of 'justice' given by the third law. He invites his readers to think of a state as the outcome of a covenant among the ruled, vesting responsibility for the public safety in whomever is designated as head of state. The laws of the realm are to be seen as restricting the liberty of each citizen only to the extent that each person's security and well-being demand it. Obedience to the law is a means of avoiding the all-out war there would be if, by the dissolution of the state, nothing was enforceably prohibited and people were free to pursue their goals as ruthlessly as they liked. Avoidance of all-out war is a moral require-ment. It is enjoined by the first law of nature, and backed up, once the state is in existence, by the third law of nature. The state exists only as long as a certain kind of covenant is kept, and if one is party to the covenant one cannot stand by and let the state wither away, still less hasten its undoing, for it is morally required that one keep the peace. That means keeping the state going, and *that* means abiding by its laws.

In *Leviathan* Hobbes concedes that his deduction of the laws of nature – there are at least a further fifteen or sixteen such laws – is perhaps too subtle to be followed by everyone (ch. 15, E III 144), but he denies that there is anything deep or difficult about the laws themselves. All of them, he claims, are implicit in the maxim, 'Do not do that to another, which thou wouldst not have done to thyself'. And he thinks that as he states them the laws of nature only call for types of behaviour that his readers would anyway have regarded as virtuous. Equity, justice, a willingness to be accommodating – all of these things he assumed his readers would call 'good' in advance (*De Cive*, ch. 3, xxxii, E II 48). But he claimed that in his deduction he had managed to say in what the good of each of the virtues consisted: each was instrumental in getting a peace that the passionate part of human nature always threatened to disrupt. By relating the good of the virtues to the overriding good of peace, he thought he had for the first time defined the difference between vice and virtue: once the work of definition had been done the same piece of behaviour could not be called 'good' now and 'bad' later, or be called 'good' by one person and 'bad' by another at the same time (*De Cive*, ch. 3, xxxii, E II 48–9; *L*, ch. 15, E III 146; *De Hom.*, ch. 13, viii, 68).

Defining the virtues and exhibiting their relation to the agreed good of peace was essential to expounding an applicable doctrine of virtue. Any citizen who was contemplating a given course of action, and who wondered whether it was just, could implement a simple decision-procedure:

> For if a question be propounded, as *whether such an action be just or unjust*; if the *unjust* be resolved into *fact against law* and that notion *law* into the *command* of him or them that have *coercive power*; and that *power* be derived from the wills of men that constitute that power, to the end they may live in peace, they may at last come to this, that the appetites of men and the passions of their minds are such, that, unless they be restrained by some power, they will always be making war upon one another; which may be known to be so by any man's experience, that will but examine his own mind. And, therefore, from hence he may proceed, by compounding, to the determination of the justice or injustice of any propounded action (*De Corp.*, ch. 6, vii, E I 74).

The pattern of reasoning makes practical deliberation, at any rate on the part of subjects, algorithmic. Figuring out whether an action is just is no harder than finding out whether a law prohibits it.

The decision-procedure involves the resolution of terms into definitions or parts of definitions, and then the drawing of consequences. Hobbes sometimes describes this process as one of recollection or remembering, and identifies the drawing of 'true and evident conclusions of what is right and wrong, and what is good and hurtful to the being and well-being of mankind,' with wisdom (cf. *EL*, Pt. 2, ch. 8, xiii. 176). He thinks that practical wisdom can be reduced to a definite technique, and he supposes that the starting point of the reasoning that yields the 'true and evident conclusions of what is right and wrong' is knowledge of the meanings of terms (ibid., cf. *De Cive*, ch. 27, xxviii, E II 295f; ch. 28, iv, E II 302f; *L*, ch. 5, E III 35–6). It is a view that does not lump together wisdom with prudence or the accumulation of experience, and that rests a good deal on deduction from definitions and principles known by experience.

Hobbes offers subjects two different ways of discovering that justice requires action in conformity with laws. On the one hand there is the 'analytical' or 'resolutive' method just described: a contemplated course of action is considered together with the definition of 'injustice' as 'fact against law'. This tells someone that an undertaking has to be legal to be just. Further resolution tells the person why an action has to be legal in order to be just: because the laws are the commands of a sovereign who is empowered by the wills of the many to keep the many at peace. The second, 'synthetical' method starts from some general truths about people, goes on to deduce some truths about the way people would treat one another were they unconstrained by law, and then, eliciting from those truths agreement to the proposition that peace is good, it proceeds to the deduction of means of obtaining it and means of keeping it once the state has been set up. The synthetical approach is Hobbes's preferred method of teaching or demonstration (*De Corp.*, ch. 6, xii, 80–81). It is the one in force in all of the political treatises, but in particular in *De Cive* and the rest of the trilogy.

Neither method trades on specialized knowledge. It is true that when Hobbes follows the synthetical approach in *The Elements of Law* and *Leviathan*, he embeds the principles of human nature in a general exposition of a mechanistic psychology. But *De Cive*, which Hobbes often seems to single out as the authorized version of his civil science, contains nothing like an extended treatment of psychology, still less a psychology expounded in mechanistic terms. Indeed, Hobbes seems to cover in the opening sentence of the book what he devotes chapters and chapters to in *The Elements of Law* and *Leviathan*. He thinks that experience alone bears out the principles of human nature his doctrine requires, and he launches with practically no preliminaries into a description of the all-out conflict people would be in if they lived in a state of nature rather than under laws and government. It is a very self-contained demonstration of 'the absolute necessity of leagues and contracts' and of the 'rudiments both of moral and of civil prudence' (Ep. Ded., E II vii). The premises of the demonstration are not themselves demonstrated, and the whole doctrine is presented in terms intelligible to the lay observer of human behaviour. This much, taken together with his saying that the principles of his science only put people in mind of what they know anyway (cf. *EL*, Pt. 1, ch. 1, ii. 2), makes it a question how exactly his civil science is supposed to improve on moral and political common sense. How can it only tell us what we know already and improve enough on what we know already to count as science?

One way in which the doctrine is supposed to improve on what we know already is by imposing an order on it. From a mass of moral lore, common sense psychology, rudimentary information about law and the average citizen's knowledge of which people in the state hold offices of authority, Hobbes purports to sift out what is basic and what is not, what has to be known before other things are known. He identifies principles. He takes certain truths that he thinks candid people will agree to, and he says those are the starting points of systematic thinking about morals and politics. He does not expect the content of those truths to come as news to anyone, at least anyone who has not been confused by book learning, but he *does* expect the status of those truths *as* principles to be a substantive discovery. From the principles he thinks he is able to get to some other truths known in advance and also to some not known beforehand. Relations of dependence are thus revealed between truths that might otherwise seem to be on a level. Hobbes's claim to have invented a science of politics is in large part a claim to have imposed a deductive or demonstrative order on moral and political truths.[5]

But deductive or demonstrative order is not the whole story. The theory given in the political treatises does not improve on moral and civic common sense just by organizing what is true in that common sense. It also purports to correct a kind of distortion in the naive or natural view. For if Hobbes is right, the naive or natural perspective is neither impersonal enough nor sensitive enough to consequences. What is good tends to be identified by individuals with what is good for them, and not with what is beneficial to human beings. Again, the good tends to be identified with what will produce (immediate) pleasure: the possibility of something not giving pleasure, but nevertheless being worth pursuing because the consequences of doing so would be better than the consequences of not pursuing it, this possibility does not naturally come into practical deliberation. The same bias toward the self and the immediately gratifying is supposed to infect the ordinary understanding of political arrangements, magnifying into injustice what is actually a perfectly tolerable burden of government on the governed. Hobbes speaks of the 'notable multiplying glasses, that is their passions and self-love' through which men view the inconveniences of government (L, ch. 18, E III 170). Moral and civil science are supposed to correct that undue magnification of the inconveniences by showing what would happen if government were removed.

Hobbes's civil philosophy can claim to be a science because, above all, it points out, explains and has the resources to counteract, the distortion in the natural view of the good and the just. It is supposed to correct and not just systematize moral and civic common sense. It purports to differentiate somehow between the real and the apparent good, and between real and apparent injustice, and so it acquaints us with the kind of distinction, namely an appearance/reality distinction, that is characteristically introduced when an advance is made from common sense to science, or, within science, from a theory that is roughly true to one that is more nearly correct.

Hobbes, then, is not obliged to rest the scientific status of his civil philosophy on any content it shares with the natural sciences. In particular, he need not trade on any overlap between a mechanistic physics and ethics, though he thinks such an overlap exists. Instead, he can rest the scientific status of his civil philosophy on its demonstrative or deductive character, and on its power of transforming for the better a view of the good and the just it begins from. Making out the idea of a civil science in these terms is of course compatible with saying that there are connections between civil science and the other sciences. But it is one thing to say that there are connections between subjects with independent claims to be sciences, and another to say that a subject is a science only if it has the connections. This latter view is the one I am saying Hobbes does not need to take of his civil philosophy. Indeed, his thesis that civil philosophy is autonomous suggests he does not take that view.

Unfortunately, as the next chapter will show, Hobbes sometimes describes the subject matter of science, the methods of science and the organization of science in ways that obscure the sense of the autonomy thesis. The autonomy thesis *is* consistent, in the end, with Hobbes's other views about science, but the two chief parts of science – natural and civil – turn out to have less in common than Hobbes, and some of his interpreters, are at times inclined to suggest.

II

The Parts of Science and the Methods of Science

1 A strained parallel

'The subject of philosophy,' Hobbes writes, '. . . is every body of which we can conceive any generation, and which we may, by any consideration thereof, compare with other bodies, or which is capable of composition and resolution' (*De Corp.*, ch. 1, viii, E I 10). This much is supposed to follow from the definition of 'philosophy'. By definition, philosophy searches out 'the properties of bodies from their generations, or their generations from their properties' (*De Corp.*, ch. 1, viii, E I 10). Any body of which we may conceive a generation is open to philosophical or scientific investigation, but of the many sorts of bodies that can be studied,

> two chief kinds of bodies, and very different from one another, offer themselves to such as search after their generation and properties; one whereof being the work of nature, is called *natural body*, the other is called a *commonwealth*, and is made by the wills and agreements of men. And from these spring the two parts of philosophy called *natural* and *civil* (*De Corp.*, ch. 1, ix, E I 11).

Natural and civil philosophy are the two chief parts of philosophy (*De Corp.*, ch. 1, ix, E I 11), and there is supposed to be a parallel between them. Though the bodies each studies are 'very different from one another,' they are for all that bodies, and bodies that have discoverable causes or generations. No less than natural philosophy, Hobbes seems to be saying, civil philosophy is concerned with the generations and properties of bodies. But as will emerge, the parallel between the two chief parts of philosophy is strained, strained by Hobbes's description of the content of philosophy, and also by his belief in the autonomy of civil philosophy.

'Body', 'properties' and 'generation' are all technical terms. In Chapter

One of *De Corpore*, where Hobbes explains what he means by 'philosophy', and indicates which of the parts of philosophy are the chief parts, he defines 'property' and puts off elucidating 'body' until later in the book. By a 'property' he means some sensory appearance that makes us distinguish one body from another (*De Corp.*, ch. 1, iv, E I 5). He gives the example of a tree and a man. We do not mistake the one for the other because we can see the signs of animation in the man – his moving from one place to the other – which we do not observe in the tree. So animation is a property of the man. By 'body' Hobbes means anything that can be conceived as taking up space and as existing independently of, or outside the mind (cf. *De Corp.*, ch. 8, i, E I 102). A 'generation' is the whole progress of motions from an initial efficient cause – itself an episode of a body's changing place – to something's appearing to the senses in a certain way at a certain time (*DP*, ch. 1, E VII 78).

Reading Hobbes's definition of philosophy (cf. *De Corp.*, ch. 1, ii, E I 3), and his description of the two parts of philosophy in the light of his glosses on 'body' and related terms, it is easy to arrive at the following: that philosophy or science is always concerned to relate the sensory appearances of bodies to the motions responsible for their production, and that if there is to be such a thing as a civil science in the preferred sense of 'science', it must assign to the properties of bodies politic the kinds of causes science assigns to the properties of any body, namely motions. Civil philosophy, in short, seems to be constrained by Hobbes's view of science to be mechanistic.

If this really is what Hobbes is committed to, then it seems to conflict with his idea that civil philosophy can be learnt and applied by anyone, with no prior grounding in the first part of philosophy. Whatever else civil philosophy is supposed to do, it is supposed to engage questions of right and authority that ordinary men can ask, and that ordinary men *were* asking in pre-revolutionary England. But if civil philosophy only engages these questions when they are rephrased as ones about the causes of bodies politic, then ordinary men have to learn a new way of posing their questions before civil science can help them. They have to see the point of asking questions in that form, and they have to see that the content of the questions is not altered when the questions are given their preferred reformulation. But if all of these preliminaries have to be gone through before civil science can be picked up and applied, then it starts to look like a science for the initiated, precisely what it is *not* supposed to be if Hobbes's autonomy thesis is taken seriously.

The question to ask is whether civil philosophy does only engage issues of right and authority when the issues are cast beforehand in terms of bodies politic, their properties and generation. We already have reason to think the answer is 'No'. For in a passage quoted earlier Hobbes describes how anyone can decide whether a contemplated course of

15

action is just or not, and the decision-procedure trades only on the possession of resolutive-compositive method, knowledge of the law, and on what people can agree are the senses of 'just', 'command', 'law', and so on. Of course, Hobbes does not assume that the relevant senses of those terms are clear to people in advance: it is for civil philosophy to define the terms, and to put the definitions into the context of facts about human nature. But the relevant facts, and the senses of the terms, are not in the least arcane. Civil philosophy only imposes a pattern on the terms and facts, and gives people a method of combining the facts and the senses of the terms in a given piece of practical deliberation.

Someone who is able to apply Hobbes's decision-procedure and estab-lish whether an action is just or not, has acquired the substance of civil science. Or so Hobbes comes very close to saying (*De Corp.*, ch. 6, vii, E I 74). But the reasoning gone through in following the decision-procedure is not reasoning from the properties of bodies politic to their causes. Indeed, the general notions of body, body politic, property of a body politic and generation of a property do not seem to come into it at all. So it is a question whether these notions are crucial to civil science. I think the answer is 'No', but that this answer leaves a problem of interpretation. Hobbes seems to apply simultaneously two quite different conceptions of civil science, and it is not obvious how they go together.

On the one hand, civil science is supposed to tell people how they ought to conduct themselves. It should state, presumably in the form of precepts, the 'rules of civil life' or the 'duties which unite and keep men in peace' (*De Corp.*, ch. 1, vii, E I 8). More, civil science should give people a procedure for making sure that a given action is in accordance with the rules or duties; otherwise it invites the complaint Hobbes makes against the books of pre-scientific morals and politics. 'What is chiefly wanting in them,' he says, 'is a true and certain rule of our actions, by which we might know whether that we undertake be just or unjust' (*De Corp.*, ch. 1, viii, E I 9). Again, the content of the rules, and the procedure for applying them to specific actions, cannot be so difficult as to allow anyone the excuse of lack of knowledge or lack of cleverness for failing to implement them. In short, civil philosophy is conceived to be normative, universally accessible, and easy to apply.

A different conception of civil philosophy seems to be at work when it is described as a branch of the general theory of bodies. The question civil philosophy answers under this description is not the plain man's 'What should I do?' or 'May I do this?' but rather the sophisticated question of why a state is as it is. This is a sophisticated question because in order to pose it one needs to have a conception of a polity in the round. One needs to start with a view of civil society as a 'whole' and as having certain identified properties before one can ask about the provenance of the properties. Arriving at this synoptic initial conception

16

of the polity is itself a kind of intellectual feat, and perhaps it is only possible with the aid of theory. Its sophistication apart, the question of the causes of the properties of a body politic does not seem to elicit an answer in the form of precepts. A civil science that reconstructs the nature of a certain commonwealth from the causes of its properties, or from the causes of the properties all commonwealths have in common, is not on its face a normative or prescriptive theory at all. Indeed, if there is to be an exact parallel between the theory of natural bodies and the theory of bodies politic it *cannot* be normative. No theory in Hobbesian natural science tells us how things ought to be or what we ought to do, though such a theory may suggest that by applying certain motions to bodies we can produce a phenomenon we have decided is desirable independently of the theory.

Does Hobbes get these apparently different conceptions of civil science to mesh with one another? To some extent he does, but in a way that compromises the supposed parallel between the science of natural bodies and the science of bodies politic. What unifies the two conceptions of civil philosophy is that both *are* conceptions of a normative science. Hobbes thinks that when a polity is understood in the light of the causes of its properties it is understood to have a certain purpose, namely that of assuring the survival of its citizens (cf. *L*, ch. 17, E III 153; ch. 15, E III 144), and he thinks that the preservation of life is a good which all moral precepts or laws of nature promote (cf. *L*. ch. 14, E III 116–7). Since the purpose of a polity can be discovered in the course of inquiring into the causes of its properties, and since the purpose of the polity turns out to be morally good, discovering the causes of the polity can be a way of discovering why one should avoid doing what will dissolve the state, notably break the law if one is a citizen, or not carry out the duties of rulership if one is sovereign. Of course, and this is what keeps the decision-procedure approach to civil science distinct from the body-politic approach, it is not necessary to ask about the properties of the body politic and their causes in order to find out why one should not break the law. The starting point can be more homely. One can be put in mind of the need to be law-abiding by an interest in acting justly and by a plausible definition of 'justice'.

2 Bodies politic, natural bodies, and method

Even if it is granted that civil philosophy *need* not be learnt by reference to the properties of bodies politic and their causes, doesn't the fact that it *can* be learnt that way keep in force a parallel between natural and civil philosophy? It is sometimes claimed that the causal inquiry into the properties of bodies politic is a special case of a type of inquiry Hobbes thinks can be carried out with respect to bodies generally.[1] One starts

17

with a conception of a 'whole' body, either a natural body or an artificial body like a commonwealth; one then takes notice of its 'parts' or 'properties'; by the method of analysis or resolution one arrives at the causes of the properties; and from the causes of the properties one reconstructs or 'composes' in reasoning the 'whole' one began with, the whole thereupon becoming more intelligible than it was before resolution had taken place. Especially in the opening sections of Chapter 6 of *De Corpore*, Hobbes writes as if this sort of method of understanding were applicable throughout philosophy (E I 65–9). But it is in fact very far from clear that his own civil science (supposedly the *only* specimen of the subject there then was) unfolds according to this method. And there is some reason to think that, being a normative science, it *cannot* unfold that way.

For evidence of Hobbes's applying the method just described to bodies politic, commentators usually fasten on a passage from *De Cive*'s Preface to the Reader. 'Concerning my method,' Hobbes writes,

> I thought it not sufficient to use a plain and evident style in what I
> had to deliver, except I took my beginning from the very matter
> of civil government, and thence proceeded to its generation and form,
> and the first beginning of justice. For everything is best understood
> by its constitutive causes. For as in a watch, or some such small
> engine, the matter, figure and motion of the wheels cannot be
> known, except it be taken insunder and viewed in parts; so to make
> a more curious search into the rights of states and duties of subjects,
> it is necessary, I say, not to take them insunder, but yet that they
> be so considered as if they were dissolved; that is, that one rightly
> understand what the quality of human nature is, in what matters it
> is, and in what not, fit to make up a civil government, and how
> men must be agreed amongst themselves that intend to grow up into
> a well-grounded state (E II xiv).

He is comparing what has to be done to understand the working of a watch with what has to be done to 'make a more curious search into the rights of states and duties of subjects'. But in making the comparison, Hobbes in fact indicates differences between what has to be done in the two cases.

First, the watch has to be physically disassembled; the rights and duties are only to be operated upon in thought. Next, while the watch is supposed to be disassembled into its working parts, the rights and duties are to be considered as *dissolved*, i.e., as entirely absent. Hobbes is not setting out to consider the rights and duties by way of their component parts. He is not proposing to show how the rights of states divide up into those of judicature, punishment, levying taxes, making wars and so on. He is not proposing to show either, how there are certain corresponding duties on the part of subjects. Instead, he is going to imagine away the rights and duties altogether, and consider men as if they had no ties of justice to one another, no obligations from covenants. Notice, too, that in the passage Hobbes does not compare watches with *bodies politic*, but with the rights and duties already mentioned. If the passage did give evidence of his intending to apply a method of decomposing bodies, bodies politic *would* be compared with watches. But that is not what we find. Nor is his plan of abolishing in thought the rights of states and duties of subjects an application of the method of resolution.[2]

The reason it is hard to find evidence in the passage of Hobbes's assimilating the method of civil philosophy to a method of studying bodies in general, is that Hobbes is intent on no such assimilation in the passage. To see this it helps to read the passage in context. In the paragraph that precedes it, a paragraph that stretches over some five pages in the English Works, he is describing the kind of doctrine he is putting forward in *De Cive*. His main point is that the doctrine is supposed to refute a number of false opinions about the grounds for deposing kings and the grounds for obedience to a king's commands (cf. E II xi, xii). To refute these opinions, he develops a theory of the basis of kingly power and of civil obedience, and in order to detach the theory from any specific disputes about when kings may be deposed and disobeyed, he starts from the hypothetical situation – the state of nature – in which no rights of kings and no duties of subjects exist at all. This enables him to ask whether it would be necessary to invent such rights, and if so which.[3]

Now the stated purpose of *De Cive*, namely to dispel a lot of seditious hot air about the injustice of kingly powers, and the justice of civil disobedience, is also a purpose of the other political treatises. Hobbes bills the second part of *Leviathan* as a 'discussion of the rights and *just* power and authority of a sovereign' (*L*, Intro, E III x – my emphasis), and chapters 18, 26, and 29 of the Second Part take up and answer the same false opinions about kings and disobedience that Hobbes outlines at the beginning of *De Cive*. In The *Elements of Law*, chapters 5 and 8 of Part Two play the same role. It seems that in the political treatises generally, Hobbes is primarily occupied with showing which distribution of rights and duties between rulers and subjects is a just distribution.

He is only incidentally concerned to explain how bodies politic are functionally organized, i.e., to explain how the functioning of the whole commonwealth depends on the functioning of a lot of working parts. He is only incidentally concerned, that is, with the sort of explanatory task that would exploit the general method for decomposing wholes into parts. The differences he acknowledges between understanding watches and understanding rights and duties reflect this.

It must be said that Hobbes is not always very clear about which explanatory task is primary. He can sometimes be read as saying that commonwealths have a functional organization that is not obvious, and that an advance on naive political understanding is achieved when the polity is viewed on the model of a special self-moving machine or automaton (cf. *L*, Intro, E III ix–x). The functional organization of a commonwealth comes into focus, he suggests, when the commonwealth is seen as an automaton in the form of an artificial man. In a natural man various organic working parts contribute to prolonging the whole creature's life; it is similar with the working parts of a commonwealth: the continued artificial life of the state depends on the proper functioning of the state's counterparts of human limbs, nerves, and vital organs (*L*, Intro, E III ix–x).

Now the figure of the artificial man seems to cut out one sort of work for civil philosophy, namely that of spelling out in detail and non-metaphorically, what 'parts' and what organization of parts, is realized by any actual commonwealth. This sort of work is not incompatible with that of specifying a just distribution of rights and duties; indeed, it seems a natural preliminary to that sort of specification. The fact is, however, that in *Leviathan* Hobbes does not discuss rights and duties on the basis of an understanding of the parts of a body politic. The order of investigation is the reverse of this. Hobbes says as much at the beginning of chapter 22 of *Leviathan*: 'Having spoken of the generation, form and power of a commonwealth, I am in order to speak next of the parts thereof' (E III 210). By 'parts' of the commonwealth he meant, besides the departments of government, the corporate associations within the commonwealth. Families were 'parts' in this sense, as were groupings of merchants and universities. But their role in the state was to be understood in the light of the rights of sovereigns and duties of subjects, not the other way about.

Enough should now be before us to establish that the decomposition of commonwealths into their parts is not the central or the first task of civil philosophy. Accordingly, we should not expect a method of decomposing bodies politic to be the dominant method of civil philosophy. More generally, there is reason to doubt that civil philosophy is primarily a venture in taking apart and reconstructing a kind of body whose nature is not very clear to us. For one thing, the main question before Hobbes seems to be: 'Which rights of sovereigns and duties of subjects are rights and duties in keeping with the demands of justice?' It is only by way of this question that he comes to ask which functionally organized body would realize a proper distribution of rights and duties.

Second, Hobbes was not trying to take apart in thought any actually existing state or any actually obtaining distribution of rights and duties. The rights and duties he derived were ones he thought should have been acknowledged by kings and subjects but that had not yet been acknowledged (cf. *L*, ch. 20, E III 195). They were rights and duties that people *would* acknowledge, Hobbes claimed, once they realized what extra-political life had to be like, and once they started to see life in the state as the welcome alternative to a stateless existence. One purpose of the political treatises was to show that political life of any kind, even life under the imperfect arrangements of actual commonwealths, had to be better than none. But another purpose was to show which political arrangements were ideal. Given just how ugly human behaviour could be conceived to be if imagined free of all legal restraints, an ideal political organization would be such as to keep inhibitions on this behaviour permanently in place. Not just any distribution of rights and duties was as likely as any other to be proof against degeneration into anarchy. There had to be absolute sovereign power, whether vested in one man or a body of men, and there had to be total submission in any area where there were sovereign decrees.

Since the preferred concentration of power in the sovereign had yet to be embodied in an actual state, Hobbes's argument for absolutism was not an argument for preserving commonwealths as they were known to be from experience. This point is important for identifying the kind of method Hobbes follows in civil philosophy. Just as he does not begin by analysing or resolving any experienced political arrangements, so he does not end up rationally reconstructing them. Yet if there had been important affinities between the method practised on natural bodies and the one he used in civil philosophy, then starting and ending up with bodies as experienced is exactly what would be called for. Hobbes's concern was with commonwealths as they should have been, not with why they were as they were.

3 The methodological disunity of natural and civil science

Very little of what Hobbes actually does in civil philosophy conforms to the pattern of decomposing things in thought and putting them back together again. Instead, things as experienced are dissolved in thought, and something new is constituted out of the residue of dissolution, something *not* as yet experienced, namely an ideal distribution of rights and duties. There is a tension here. How can Hobbes follow one method in civil philosophy, a method of dissolution and innovation, and yet advertise another method as the method of philosophy in general? For the fact remains that in chapter 6 of *De Corpore* he seems to identify philosophical method with that of decomposition and reconstruction. Again, the opening chapter of *De Corpore* co-ordinates the two chief parts of philosophy by saying that both are concerned with the generation and properties of bodies. Taking the remarks in the two chapters together, it is reasonable to expect both chief 'parts' of philosophy to

21

study the generations and properties by the method sketched in chapter 6 of *De Corpore*.

In fact, however, chapter 6 of *De Corpore* draws all but one of its illustrations of how its method works from *natural* philosophy. In general, it is as if Hobbes's remarks are really about method not in both chief branches of philosophy, but only in one. This impression is reinforced by the parallelism between *De Corpore*'s chapter on method, and chapter 2 of *Decameron Physiologicum*, which claims to be about the method of natural philosophy alone (E VII 82). Was Hobbes trying to pass off the method of a part of philosophy for the method of all of philosophy? Or was he trying to *generalize* the method of natural philosophy into a method for civil philosophy, much as philosophers since Mill have tried to extend the methods of physics to those of the social sciences?[4]

I think he was trying to do neither of these things, and that there is a relatively simple explanation of what happens in *De Corpore*'s chapter on method. Recall that *De Corpore* opens the triology and is called upon to serve a dual purpose: to lay open the 'few and first Elements of Philosophy in general' and to 'put into a clear method the true foundations of natural philosophy.' Up to a point these are distinct roles and are represented by distinct chunks of text in *De Corpore*. Hobbes sets down 'such premisses as appertain to the nature of philosophy in general' (*De Corp.*, ch. 1, ix, E I 12) in Part One of *De Corpore*, and starts to 'discourse of bodies natural' from the beginning of Part Two onward. Chapter 6, on method, comes at the end of Part One, just where one would expect Hobbes to stop discussing philosophy in general and prepare the reader for the full-scale discussion of natural philosophy: hence the bias toward natural philosophy in his illustrations of method.

Hence, too, the bias toward the foundations of natural philosophy in his abstract description of method. Hobbes is working up to a treatment in Part Two of the very general concepts needed to apply geometry, mechanics and eventually physics, and so in the chapter on method he has something to say about how knowledge of these 'universals' is derived (E I 68–70), and also what knowledge is made possible once the 'universals' are grasped (E I 70ff). Civil philosophy is hardly touched upon. This is not because it lacks a method, but because its method is not the same as that of natural philosophy: Hobbes is too emphatic about the differences between the bodies studied by the two chief parts of philosophy to assimilate the method of understanding the one to the method of understanding the other. He says that the two chief types of body, artificial and natural, are 'very different from one another' (*De Corp.*, ch. 1, ix, E I 11), and this is not the sort of remark that would sit well with the unexplained deployment of a single method for both. When civil philosophy drops out of *De Corpore*'s chapter on method, that is because its method can be understood and applied independently of the knowledge of the foundations of natural philosophy.

Though chapter 6 of *De Corpore* does not make it very clear, Hobbes actually recognizes the methodological *distinctness* of civil and natural philosophy, in keeping with the autonomy thesis. This becomes evident when we take the detailed description of the method of natural philosophy with what has already emerged from *De Cive* about the procedure he follows in morals and politics.

The best source for Hobbes's account of the method of natural philosophy is chapter 2 of the dialogue, *Decameron Physiologicum*. This specifies the form of question that is typically asked in natural philosophy, and also the types of things that have to be known before an answer to such a question can be given:

> Your desire . . . is to know the causes of the effects or phenomena of nature; and you confess they are fancies, and consequently, that they are in yourself; so that the causes you seek for only are without you, and now you would know how those external bodies work upon you to produce those phenomena (E VII 82).

A question about an effect or phenomenon, which might naively be posed by asking why a certain thing appears as it does, is better put by asking what causes a certain 'fancy' or sensory representation in a perceiver.

Once the preferred form of question has been asked, the enquirer's work is cut out for him. He must first get clear on what is meant by 'cause' (E VII 82; cf. *De Corp.*, ch. 6, x, E I 77), and in particular 'efficient cause'. In order to do that, he must 'enquire diligently into the nature of motion. For the variety of fancies, or (which is the same thing) of the phenomena of nature, have all of them one universal efficient cause, which is motion' (E VII 83; *De Corp.*, ch. 6, v, E I 69–70). What the enquirer will find, when he considers the nature of motion, is that it is nothing but change of place (E VII 83–4; cf. *De Corp.*, ch. 6, v, E I 70). And after he has found out how 'place' is to be defined and also 'time', having in short understood the nature of motion from the definitions of terms in the definition of 'motion', the enquirer is to draw from 'these definitions, and from whatsoever truth else [he knows] by the light of nature, such general consequences as may serve for axioms, or principles of [his] ratiocination' (E VII 85). More, and crucially, the enquirer 'must consider also the several kinds and properties of motion' (E VII 88; cf. *De Corp.*, ch. 6, vi, E I 71), and also furnish himself with 'as many experiments (which they call phenomenon) as [he] can' (E VII 88).

With all of these preliminaries attended to, the enquirer is poised to hypothesize some type of motion as the cause of the fancy he is investigating. Working from that hypothesis about a type of motion, he must then demonstrate that an instance of that type of motion could have operated consistently with the existence of the phantasm he is studying, and consistently with every other known fact or experiment considered relevant (E VII 88). The enquirer is not constrained to demonstrate that an instance of the selected type of motion *had* to be at work to produce the relevant effect, only that it could have been at work (E VII 88). No more than this is expected, because in trying to assign causes to natural phenomena one is trying to assign causes to effects God produced, and 'there is no effect in nature which the Author of nature cannot bring to pass by more ways than one' (E VII 88).

Now there are three respects in which the method of civil philosophy, as described in *De Cive* and reflected in the content of the other political treatises, diverges from the method just outlined. First, and to touch upon what I have emphasized already, the method just described is all about reconstructing a sensory experience from its causes; the method of civil philosophy is not like this. Rather than being primarily concerned with saying why bodies politic are as they are or present the appearances they present, civil philosophy has a method appropriate to saying how they ought to be. Second, and relatedly, there is Hobbes's restriction of causes sought for in natural philosophy to efficient causes. He explicitly denies that final causes have any bearing on investigations in natural philosophy, and says that they only come into moral philosophy (*DP*, ch. 2, E VII 82). In civil philosophy, on the other hand, the proper distribution of rights and duties in the polity is wholly deduced from a final cause, namely the purpose that people would have if their belonging to a commonwealth came about by mutual agreement in the state of nature.

The third discrepancy between method in natural and in civil philosophy is a discrepancy in exactingness. Enquiry into natural effects is supposed to be informed by a knowledge of the 'types and degrees of motion' and by a knowledge of lots of experiments and phenomena relevant to the effects one is studying. In other words, acquaintance with mechanics is presupposed, and an enquirer is supposed to be well-versed in what Hobbes calls 'natural history'. Civil philosophy, on the other hand, is supposed to be acquirable by someone who has no specialized knowledge in advance. That is the message of Hobbes's autonomy thesis.

4 The order of the parts of science

The message of the autonomy thesis turns out to be muffled rather than contradicted by Hobbes's comments on the 'subject' and 'method' of philosophy, and it is the same with his comments about the 'order' of the parts of philosophy. Let me enlarge on this 'order' with a view to clearing up a last possible misunderstanding of the autonomy thesis.

The misunderstanding is invited by Hobbes's placing civil philosophy last in the order of demonstrating the special sciences or 'parts' of philosophy (cf. *De Corp.*, ch. 6. xvii, E I 87). Given his understanding of 'order of demonstration', this means that while the principles of politics are not supposed to be deducible from any of the prior sciences, the principles of politics should be more *intelligible* when considered in the light of the prior sciences than when they are considered in isolation. But the substance of the autonomy thesis is that the principles of politics are perfectly intelligible on their own. Can he have it both ways?

To sharpen the question, consider the view he takes of geometry. That, too, is one of the special sciences, and yet it is supposed to have principles that are independently teachable and learnable. But we *expect* Hobbes to say geometry is independently teachable and learnable because he holds that geometry is where philosophy or science begins. Civil philosophy is not first but last in the order of demonstrating philosophy; so shouldn't it be approached only by the scientifically initiated?

No. Hobbes's ordering of the parts of science (*De Corp.*, ch. 6, vi, E I 70–73) is determined by his ordering of the types and degrees of motion. Each science is concerned with a different type of motion, and the ordering of types is from more to less general. Geometry studies motion in general – motion in the abstract – in body in general (E I 71). The rest of the sciences deal with differentiated motions in differentiated bodies. Thus mechanics deals with motions in bodies considered only as numerically distinct from one another, and as having parts. It deals with the effects of motions of the parts of bodies on whole bodies, and also with the transmission of motion in collisions involving different numbers of bodies (E I 71–2). Physics deals with the sensory effects in animate bodies, of motions transmitted by inanimate bodies. It deals also with the after-effects of sensory episodes – retained images (memory images), and images compounded in the imagination (E I 71; ch. 25, vii, E I 396–7; cf. *L*, ch. 1, E III 6).

Ethics takes up further after-effects of sensory episodes, namely the appetites and passions and their effects in behaviour. In the light of the effects of the passions civil philosophy demonstrates the necessity of fulfilling one's moral and civil duties. Now the reason this part of science comes after the others is that it starts from considerations about the passions: the passions are highly differentiated types of motion, and as considered by civil philosophy they are motions in a highly specific type of body, i.e., rational, animated body or man. Given that the sciences follow the order of more to less general, it is no wonder that civil philosophy comes last in the order of demonstrating the sciences at large.

At this point it is worth asking whom the ordering of the special sciences is supposed to guide. The answer can be gathered from chapter 6, article 3 of *De Corpore*, where Hobbes distinguishes between two types of interest in science. Some people, he says, turn to science for answers to specific questions. Others 'search after science simply or indefinitely: that is, to know as much as they can, without propounding to themselves any limited question.' It is clear from the next article, article 4 (E I 68), that the full-scale ordering of the sciences is for those out to get as much knowledge as they can. But now consider someone who only wants to know what his civil duties are, and what his moral obligations are. Call him 'Everyman'. This sort of person need not have any initial interest in science in general. He wants to know how to conduct himself properly, and that is all. Hobbes alerts Everyman to some principles about the passions that have to be understood before his duties are understood, but Everyman is not required to know the passions under the descriptions that connect the theory of the passions with physics and mechanics, for Everyman can know the passions and some of their workings directly, by introspection.

For Everyman, Hobbes's preferred order of demonstrating the sciences is irrelevant, because it is an order that is appropriate for acquiring as much knowledge as possible, not just knowledge of one's duty. There is no tension, then, between Hobbes's placing his civil philosophy last in the order of demonstrating the sciences, and his saying that civil philosophy can be understood perfectly well independently of the prior sciences. Civil philosophy *can* be acquired with no preliminaries, but if it is being approached out of a wish to know as much as one can, then it is best approached last, by way of prior sciences that make it more intelligible.

5 The parts of science and the concept of science

Would it be correct to conclude that the two chief parts of science have nothing, or nothing important, in common? Not exactly. There *is* a connection of a kind between natural and civil philosophy, but it is important that it can only be described at a fairly high level of generality. What natural and civil science have in common is that they are both specimens of science.[5] They both result from the exercise of the same cognitive capacity, namely the capacity for reasoning. They both result from reasoning guided by method. And methodical reasoning in the two areas has the same general point or purpose, namely to find ways of improving human life, where that is understood as a matter of enlarging the number of effects producible by the human will.

It is this very general conception of science as the beneficial product of reason guided by method that unifies the 'parts' of science. Enlarging on this conception is no easy matter, for it is a strange conception, even when Hobbes's distance in time from us is taken into account. To begin with, it is a conception of science that co-exists with his general scepticism about human powers of prediction and retrodiction. Since God could have brought about any observed effect in more ways than one, any hypothesis about the way an observed effect *was* brought about is always uncertain. As for prediction, Hobbes declares that there is no scientific conclusion flatly to the effect that something *will* occur, only scientific conclusions that say something will occur *if* something else occurs first (cf. *L*, ch. 7, E III 52). Added to this scepticism about the predictive and retrodictive power of science is a certain vagueness about the connection between science and measurement. Though Hobbes learnt from the writings of Galileo some of the uses of Euclidean measurement by proportionality and though these techniques may be what he has in mind when he claims that geometry is responsible for the commodious arts of architecture, navigation and instrument making (cf. e.g. *EL*, Pt. 1, ch. 13, iii. 65; *De Cive*, Ep. Ded., E II iv; *De Corp.*, ch. 1, vii, E I 7), he never says enough about why geometry is responsible for the commodious arts to make it clear how the applied sciences depend on measurement.

He concentrates instead, as we shall see, on connections between science and apt naming, on connections between science and correct assertion, and on connections between science and valid syllogizing. It is to the powers of names that he traces the human capacity for thinking in general terms, and he thinks it is on account of a capacity for general thought and talk, and for assembling general propositions into chains of reasoning, that people can have scientific or causal knowledge. Motions may explain everything we observe happening in nature, but general names are what allow us to connect phenomena with hypotheses about types of motion. General propositions are also the medium of knowledge of the causes of war and peace. Without the use of linguistic devices people would have at most a miscellaneous, fragmented and narrow view of nature, and a flawed because overly subjective and short-sighted estimate of how to live in groups.

It is important that on Hobbes's assumptions the linguistic and intellectual capacities needed for science are largely acquired capacities. One implication of this is that people are not innately well adapted for finding out how nature works, for getting what they want, or for treating one another properly in society. As Hobbes's description of the method of natural philosophy has already indicated, getting into a position where one can so much as form *hypotheses* about natural phenomena involves a great deal of learning. As for knowledge of one's moral and civic duty, though that is relatively easy to acquire once spelt out, it is very difficult for creatures like us to put into practice, calling as it does for patterns of behaviour that go against our deeply anti-social inclinations. Yet, and this is what gives the difficulty of acquiring natural philosophy and the difficulty of applying moral and political knowledge a kind of poignancy, human beings cannot be sure of living long or well unless they acquire the one and apply the other. Relative to the demands of a hostile natural domain and a hostile social order, we are by nature both ignorant and impotent. These are the main costs to people of the Fall. Science, Hobbes thinks, puts people in a position to cut some of those costs. Or so the next chapter will suggest.

III

Knowledge and Power in Fallen Man

Human beings cannot live well without science, according to Hobbes, and yet science does not come naturally to human beings. Science is the kind of knowledge that makes men achieve their goals without the help of good luck (cf. *L*, ch. 5, E III 36), but it is a kind of knowledge that has to be acquired, and acquired by hard work. People are not born with science; they are not even born with the capacities it presupposes (*L*, ch. 5, E III 35). In order to acquire science they have to be able to name things, affirm propositions, and, above all, reason or draw consequences (*L*, ch. 5, E III 35; cf. *EL*, Pt. 1, ch. 6, iv. 26; *De Cive* ch. 17, xii, E II 268). But people come into the world knowing how to do none of these things. At most they are born able to form sensory representations of things and born able to learn from sense-experience (cf. *EL*, Pt. 1, ch. 1, viii. 2; ch. 6, i. 24; *L*, chs. 1, 2, E III 1–6; ch. 5, E III 35). With these capacities alone, however, they can only hope to blunder along or cope *ad hoc* in nature and society.

1 Ends, means and the limitations of experience

To do well human beings have to know what evils to avoid and what goods to pursue, and also *how* to pursue and avoid the relevant goods and evils: experience does not give us the right sort of guidance. True, it alerts us to sources of pleasure (*EL*, Pt. 1, ch. 7, iii. 29; *L*, ch. 6, E III 42; *De Corp.*, ch. 25, xii. E I 406f). But something pleasant is good only in relation to an occasion and the constitution of the one who experiences the pleasure (cf. *L*, ch. 6, E III 40–1). A person may find a thing pleasant on one occasion and call it 'good' then, only to change his mind later (*De Cive*, ch. 14, xvii, E II 196; *L*, ch. 15, E III 146). And the very thing one person calls 'good' on an occasion, another person may call 'bad' on the same occasion. Experience cannot be expected to generate consistent valuations over time or between people.

29

It tends to suggest not only fluctuating but also defeasible valuations. People can pursue what is pleasurable, avoid what is painful, and yet pursue and avoid the wrong things (*De Cive*, Pref. to the Reader, E II, xvi f). Something that seems to be worth avoiding because it is unpleasant may turn out to be worth suffering all things considered, and something that seems to be worth pursuing because it is gratifying, may not really be worth pursuing when all relevant considerations, including calculable consequences, are allowed to weigh. To give some illustrations important to Hobbes's civil philosophy, the felt unpleasantness of losing one's liberty under government does not by itself show that the loss of liberty is evil and to be avoided (*EL*, pt. 2, ch. 5, ii. 138f; *De Cive*, ch. 10, i–ii, E II 126–9). Symmetrically, the fact that it is exhilarating to people to compete with one another and highly gratifying to win, does not mean that competing and winning are good things. On the contrary, in view mainly of their consequences, they turn out to be bad things (*El*, Pt. 1, ch. 9, xxi. 47–8; ch. 14, iv–xii. 71–74; *De Cive*, ch. 1, vi–xiii, E II 8–12; *De Hom.*, ch. 12, i. 55f; *L*, ch. 13, E III 110–111).

Experience is not a trustworthy selector of ends because pleasure and pain are not sure indicators of what is to be pursued and avoided. But pleasure and pain are the only indicators people naturally have of what to pursue and avoid. So there is no assurance that people will pursue or avoid the right things by nature. There is no assurance either that they will get what they go after or avoid what they have found unpleasant. This is because, by nature, people have only experience to inform them about means-end relations, and the type of means-end relation revealed in experience is (as Hobbes conceives it) a loose relation of succession (cf. *EL*, Pt. 1, ch. 4, vi. 14–15). To learn about successions of types of events or about 'antecedents and consequents' is only to find that types of events or phenomena tend to be conjoined.[1] It is not to learn what *must* happen when a type of event occurs. It is not to learn what *always* happens when a type of event occurs. So while experience of successions is expectation-forming, the expectations can easily be disappointed (*EL*, Pt. 1, ch. 4, x–xi. 16–17; *L*, ch. 46, E III 664).

There is an upshot for practical deliberation – deliberation about means to ends. When informed only by experience, such deliberation is fallible. Courses of action it suggests succeed, if at all, by accident. When practical deliberation is founded on methodically worked-out relations of cause and effect, on the other hand, there can be nothing accidental about success. By contrast with relations of antecedence and consequence, genuine causal relations are such that certain accidents being present, such and such a change *must* come about (cf. *De Corp.*, ch. 9, E I 120f). So if one knows what the cause of a desirable type of effect is, and if one is able to arrange for the co-presence of the necessary or concurring accidents, then the desirable type of effect cannot but be made to occur.

Though Hobbes believes that experience compares unfavourably with reason as a source of ends and as a basis for deliberation about means, it is not his view that reason ought to operate in *place* of experience when someone makes and executes plans of action. This is not even a possibility on his assumptions, since the medium of reasoning is the significant proposition, and since there could be no significant propositions if terms did not signify items of experience or conceptions (cf. *EL*, Pt. 1, ch. 6, iv. 26). Instead of taking the place of experience, reason is supposed to transform, partly by introducing new ways of organizing, experience.

In its raw state experience is either a disorganized stream of representations or else a coherent sequence. If it is a coherent sequence, it is "regulated" by some design or plan, or by curiosity about an observed body's effects (*L*, ch. 3, E III 13). Regulated in either way, a train of experience is only ordered as past experience allows it to be. Going by its past associations of observed phenomena, the mind will focus on a means to some goal or purpose in hand, or will suggest properties it is accustomed to conjoin with other properties it is now curious about. Once there are words for the things the mind has conceptions of, words that can be used to signify the elements of experience, the possible ways of juxtaposing the words significantly, of analysing them and drawing consequences, introduce ways of ordering the elements that are *not* foreshadowed in previous experience.

New ways of regulating thought become possible because, for one thing, it is not necessary for a body spoken about to be present or remembered in order for a train of thought about the thing to be created. The train of thought can be generated instead by exploiting logical relations or analytic truths to get from one speech or thought to another. Reasoning can thus introduce new possibilities of combining things given separately in experience; it can also introduce ways of taking apart or separating things confounded in experience. And all of this, at the level of the elements of experience, has implications for the build-up of experience over time. If reasoning can extend the intellectual operations performable with individual conceptions, then it can extend the cognitive capacities of people who already enjoy the product of accumulated experience, i.e., prudence.

Just how much of a difference reason and its product, science, make when added to prudence, is supposed to be reflected in the difference between civilized life and the life of savages or primitives. At one time, according to Hobbes, all of humanity lived as in his day the Indians of America lived. They had a command of speech, and with that a limited ability to reason. But in the pre-scientific age, 'true, general and profitable speculations . . .

> were at first few in number; men lived upon gross experience; there was no method; that is to say, no sowing, nor planting of knowledge by itself, apart from the weeds, and common plants of error and conjecture. And the cause of it being the want of leisure from procuring the necessities of life, and defending themselves against their neighbours, it was impossible, till the erecting of great commonwealths, it should be otherwise. *Leisure* is the mother of *philosophy*; and Commonwealth is the mother of *peace* and *leisure* (*L*, ch. 46, E III 666).

When men lived only by experience they were unable to discover *how* to procure the necessities of life effectively. They always lived in fear of losing their possessions and even their lives. Once formed into common-wealths they were able to create conditions for science, and thereby for procuring the necessities of life efficiently. Had they kept up their pre-political existence, they would have prolonged the misery of incessant toil and insecurity from attack.

Hobbes is no admirer of the life of primitives. Though he admits that even savages can possess 'some good moral sentences' (*L*, ch. 46, E III 665), he does not think savages are likely to behave nobly toward one another. And though he acknowledges that the American Indians were able to measure and calculate a little, he doubts that primitives have the intellectual resources to live well. For lacking science, primitives are not only ignorant of what makes things happen round them; they are likely to clutch at fanciful, even debilitating explanations of phenomena, as when they think observed effects are brought about by invisible powers who also have the fate of men in their hands (cf. *L*, ch. 12, E III 95). Or, if they do not latch on to wild explanations, they may come up with no explanations at all. Either way primitives are condemned to suffer anxiety and fear.

As for their morality, that cannot be detached from their ability to cope in nature. If people do not know how to produce enough to feed and shelter themselves, and if any one person is likely to die if he does not help himself to what food and shelter exists, then since no-one can be blamed for trying to survive, since each has an inalienable liberty of preserving his life (*EL*, Pt. 1, ch. 14, vi. 71; *De Cive*, ch. 1, vii, E II 8; *L*, ch. 14, E III 116f), no-one can be blamed for dispossessing the next person of food and shelter if not doing so means death. A life-threatening scarcity of goods is more likely to prevail in a pre-scientific society than in a society that enjoys sciences of agriculture and architecture; where a society is defenceless against a scarcity of material goods, there too a lapse of general benevolence can be expected if anything goes wrong. It is a kind of natural good fortune if scienceless people, people who live by experience alone, do not suffer some bad turn of events that drives them into open fighting.

Hobbes thought that beneath the thin skin of civilized manners even the peoples of Europe were primitives. And just as the outwardly primitive improved their chances of being able to dispense good will and feed and clothe themselves when they formed commonwealths, so it only made sense for the civilized peoples of Europe to preserve theirs. Commonwealths made possible the division of labour that created time and energy for science, and science spared people the insecurity of living at the mercy of nature. But there was no preserving commonwealths unless members of them had the knowledge necessary to guard against their dissolution. What was supposed to complete the passage from primitiveness to civilization was not the creation of commonwealths but the acquisition of a science – civil science – for keeping commonwealths intact. Civil science was the useful science *par excellence*. Valuable as the commodities or benefits of natural philosophy and geometry were (*De Corp.*, ch. 1, vii, E I 8), human beings could be helped even more when science was taken into the sphere of morality and government. Unless they had a science of politics they risked losing all of the goods that had accrued from natural science. For the production and enjoyment of these goods would last only as long as there was civil order.

It was no good relying on experience to teach people how to behave peaceably and preserve this order, for on Hobbes's assumptions about experience, each individual's experiences would generate conflicting estimates of good, bad, right and wrong, and it was such conflicting valuations that started contention and eventually war (cf. *L*, ch. 15, E III 146). In order to agree about what was right and wrong people had to gain detachment from their own particular case, and even from the particular circumstances of their commonwealth. That meant using reasoning to uncover facts any political order would depend upon, facts about human nature and in particular the passions. Understanding how these worked was supposed to be preliminary to understanding the causes of the breakdown of order and of pre-political hostility. But it took reasoning to make accessible the connections between disorder and the passions: experience was not enough.[2]

2 Reason, science and human improvement

Does only good come of the acquisition of reason and science? Hobbes often writes as if human beings have everything to gain and nothing to lose by adding a skill of ratiocination to a native capacity for learning from experience. He tends to suggest that the effects of science are thoroughly beneficial. So does he overlook what Rousseau was later to make something of, the loss, through science, of human innocence and simplicity of life? He does not so much overlook the loss of human innocence as disagree with Rousseau about how it was lost. He does not suppose that innocence is lost every time a primitive people is civilized, or that the change that *does* occur when primitive people are civilized is the change for the worse Rousseau thinks it is.

Hobbes seems to assume as common ground between him and his readers the Biblical story of the Fall.[3] As he interprets the story (cf. e.g. *L*, ch. 20, E III 194), the loss of human innocence dates from the time Adam disobeyed God and ate from the tree of knowledge. What caused the disobedience, and so the loss of innocence, was human vainglory. Adam and Eve vaingloriously believed they could become judges of good and evil, and thereby raise themselves to the level of gods. How they thought they could become judges of good and evil was by eating from the tree of knowledge. But in their choice of end they aimed impossibly high, and they also misjudged the means. Eating from the tree of knowledge did open their eyes, but not in the desired way. Instead of beginning to judge as God did, Adam and Eve actually formed judgments impiously in conflict with God's. For example, when they became conscious for the first time of the nakedness God had thought best for them, they were ashamed – thought it bad – they were unclothed, and so, as Hobbes thinks, they rebuked or censured God (*L*, ch. 20, E III 194).

Adam and Eve lost their innocence when they tried to make themselves judges of good and evil, and part of their punishment was exile to an environment in which they would *have* to exercise their own judgment. In Paradise Adam enjoyed, or is thought by Hobbes to have enjoyed, the gift of immortality (cf. e.g. *L*, ch. 38, E III 438). Immortality in conditions of ready abundance. Everything he could properly want was there for the taking. Punished for eating from the tree of knowledge Adam lost his immortality. He lived, as Hobbes puts it, under a death-sentence (*L*, ch. 44, E III 624). Adam also lost the abundance of Eden. Banished to a place outside Paradise, he had for the first time to work for a living, and toil in a relatively inhospitable environment. *Genesis 3*, xxiii, says that God sent '[Adam] forth to till the ground from which he was taken.' And five verses earlier God is reported as saying of the ground that 'thorns also and thistles shall it bring forth to thee . . .'

Adam's descendants, the rest of humanity, inherit from him not only their mortality but also life outside Paradise. Thanks to Adam's transgression human beings in general live in a physical world it takes ingenuity and hard work to survive in. And thanks to human carnality, Adam's descendants have to eke out a living in the company of, and almost inevitably in competition with, a great many of their own species. These facts of life do not make it easy to do well. In order to flourish in a sometimes harsh physical environment people have to know which of the effects they observe in it are beneficial and which harmful; they have to know how to reproduce the beneficial ones and prevent, or reliably avoid, the harmful ones. And in order to flourish in a heavily populated environment, people have to know how to co-operate with one another. What is more, these problems have to be coped with simultaneously. As things naturally are, these problems overtax the creatures they face. For being descended from Adam, human beings inherit the cognitive and conative capacities of someone designed to live in Paradise, not in the harsh world outside.

If things had gone according to plan, Adam would not have needed to get causal knowledge of nature, because he would not have needed to get power over nature; he would not have had to cope, either, with the effects of overpopulation. Had they stayed in Eden Adam and Eve would not have reproduced their kind continually or perhaps at all (cf. *L*, ch. 38, E III 440). So they would not have been faced with a problem of co-operation. Used to a life without problems, Adam did not need, and consequently lacked the means, that is the science, to solve the problems. In *Leviathan* Hobbes takes the trouble to say that there is no evidence in Scripture of Adam's having had the vocabulary to do science (ch. 4, E III 19), and yet he says often that without this vocabulary and without science, we should be no better off than savages or beasts (cf. *De Hom.*, ch. 10, ii, iii. 38–40; *EL*, Pt. 1, ch. 5, iv. 19). The implication is that Adam in Eden lacked some of what people outside Eden need to survive and flourish.

In the habitat they have had to occupy since the Fall, people live at the mercy of the elements and of one another. They either adjust to that way of life (the primitives of America) or make scientific progress (the civilized peoples of Europe, Africa and Asia (*De Corp.*, ch. i, vii, E I 8)). Either way, they live under constraints that have been in force since the Fall. Even civilized peoples, who enjoy all of the fruits of science, do not enjoy a life that is perfectly satisfactory. Indeed, it is impossible for creatures like us ever to enjoy such a life. When Hobbes remarks that 'the state of man can never be without some incommodity or other' (*L*, ch. 18, E III 170), he means that however many desires people, even scientifically sophisticated people, have managed to satisfy, there will always be further unsatisfied desires to be fulfilled, and inconveniences to be overcome.

Since he does not promote science as a panacea, he is not guilty of the most extreme kind of science-worship. But isn't he guilty of science-worship all the same? More specifically, doesn't he overdraw the advantages of science by overdrawing the grimness of a life without science? It is hard to make this objection compelling. Hobbes does sometimes write, it is true, as if science alone made the difference between primitive-

35

ness and civilization (*De Corp.*, ch. 1, vii, E I 7–10; *De Cive*, Ep. Ded., E II iv; *EL*, Pt. 1, ch. 13, iii. 65), and as if primitiveness had to be bad, or at least a great deal worse than civilization. And while it is possible to have far-reaching second thoughts about all of this, as Rousseau had,[4] and turn Hobbes's valuations upside down, it is not possible to do this without making assumptions radically different from and no more plausible than Hobbes's own assumptions about human nature.

Hobbes believed that the way of life that came most naturally to people and that survived among the Indians of America, was a bad way of life because there was nothing to relieve its misery and hardship. Whether or not his Indian contemporaries really did toil incessantly and live in fear of being attacked by their neighbours is irrelevant: the thought behind Hobbes's low valuation of their way of life is the perfectly reasonable one that there ought to be more to living than the unceasing struggle to stay alive. Rousseau found this thought suspect because he saw that with ease and plenty people could begin to become mindlessly acquisitive, flabby and overly-dependent. Eventually they would fall into the lumpish immobility of domesticated, over-indulged animals.

Even if Rousseau is right and civilization does denature creatures who start out by being hardy, alert and active, it is not clear, as he seems to assume, that they will be self-sufficient enough or modest enough in their desires to keep from competing with one another.[5] It seems just as plausible to hold that some will want more territory or a larger harem than others, and that they will be prepared to fight for that advantage. Since it is not obvious that the hardy, self-reliant and regularly violent life is to be preferred to the admittedly more acquisitive, even decadent one that post-scientific civilization sometimes affords, it is not clear whether Hobbes's preference for civilization over the state of nature is more controversial than Rousseau's.[6] Hobbes's assumption that scarcity will drive men into conflict in the state of nature does not seem unreasonable, especially if men are assumed in advance to lack any technology worth the name. If it is granted that the primitive life can be as harsh as he says, then it is hard to deny that science can very well improve people's lot, first by suggesting to them efficient means of producing what they need to survive, second by showing them how to keep the peace when they live together at a level above subsistence.

Suppose, then, with Hobbes that science does improve people's lot: can't the improvement have harmful or at least undesirable side-effects? One version of this objection seems to have particular force against the background of the story of the Fall. This is the objection that the advance of the sciences can nourish human vainglory. If science has already given humanity power over a large range of natural effects, and if in the future it promises to give us still more, why can't human beings believe that with enough science they will be powerful enough to be god-like themselves? In other words, why can't we be seduced into thinking, as Adam and Eve were seduced into thinking, that an acquirable sort of knowledge can put us on a level with our Maker? Though Hobbes does not, to my knowledge, consider the question, it seems to me to be possible to gather a good answer from what he says in other connections.

The good answer is that science itself provides some insurance against the sort of pride just described. For the would-be subjects of the pride are themselves topics of science, and science reveals their limitations both as knowers and as agents. Science reveals, for example, that there are many effects in nature that are out of our sensory range, being either too small, too big or too distant to be registered by the senses, effects that can at best be conceived with the aid of techniques of reasoning (*De Corp.*, ch. 27, i, E I 446–447). In acquainting us with magnitudes and motions that are quite outside our sensory range and that even tax our conceptual powers, science makes us sensitive to the large gap between our cognitive and active powers and God's. What we find is possible only to take apart in thought, for example, God can take apart in practice (*De Corp.*, ch. 27, i, E I 446). Science also counteracts our pride in another way, by pointing out the smallness of the gap between our natural cognitive and active powers and those of the lower animals. Only reason, speech and a native interest in causes separate human beings from other animals, and where people differ from the animals they are not necessarily superior. The same acquired capacities that make it possible for us to do science make us liable to believe falsehoods and involve ourselves in absurdities (cf. *L*, ch. 5, E III 33). Capacities we have and e.g. bees lack, make discord likely for us but not for them (cf. *L*, ch. 17, E III 156). And so on.

3 The conditions of science

Science is supposed to improve the lot of human beings, but only within limits. It gives people power over nature they do not natively have, but not power over nature comparable with God's. It gives people resources to counteract some of the ill effects of competition in conditions of scarcity, but not the power to rid their lives of all incommodities. Still, the power science delivers is not negligible: what makes that power available to creatures with as modest a natural endowment as human beings? Hobbes's answer is all to do with additions to that endowment, i.e., with the acquisition of capacities for naming, affirming and reasoning.

In *The Elements of Law*, Hobbes considers a sampling of 'all those excellences, wherein we differ from such savage people as live in America,' and asks where the excellences come from. His answer is clear-cut. They are due, he says to 'those men who have taken in hand to consider nothing else but the comparison of magnitudes, times, and motions, and their proportions to one another' (Pt. 1, ch. 13, iii. 65). The writings of these men, the '*mathematici*' as he calls them, are exemplary works of science. Not only have the findings in their writings many beneficial applications; they are also presented in a way that pre-empts controversy. However sophisticated the conclusions, the *mathematici* always reach them in a way that makes them evident. How they proceed (cf. *EL*, Pt. 1, ch. 6, iv. 25–6; *De Corp.*, ch. 6, xvi–xvii, E I 86–8) is by joining names of things we all have conceptions of into truths, joining truths into syllogisms, and syllogisms into demonstrations.

Although the imposition of names is the first step in the preferred method of science, Hobbes has very little to say about how the names are imposed or how they can be ordered into affirmations. Such comments as he does make suggest that the imposition of a name is accomplished at will and privately. A single speaker simply takes a sensible mark and, in affixing it to an object, makes it into a reminder for himself of a conception raised by the object (cf. *EL*, Pt. 1, ch. 5, ii, 17–18, *L*, ch. 4, E III 18–20; *De Corp.*, ch. 2, iv, E I 16). So taken, a name is a mark that means something only to the one who imposes it on a thing. For a name to convey the imposer's conception of a thing to someone else, it must occur within the context of a speech (*L*, ch. 4, E III 18–20; *De Corp.*, ch. 2, iii, E I 15). It is a notably psychologistic sketch of name-imposition and the merest gesture toward the way in which naming contributes to communication, but it is important that Hobbes intends no more than a sketch or a gesture. There is no evidence that he was concerned to elaborate a free-standing theory of reference, let alone a full-blown philosophy of language. Instead, he presented such bits of doctrine concerning linguistic devices as would enable him to show that science was possible for people despite the limitations of experience.[7]

One limitation of experience, at least as Hobbes conceives experience, is that items of experience are short-lived. Properties of things registered now can be forgotten later. And items that survive for a time are liable to be lost track of in a constantly flowing stream of consciousness or unordered train of thought. He has to explain how we are able to store some of what we register, and also how we are able to convey to others some of what we store. Both abilities are required if anyone is to be able to go in for reasoning of any complexity, and if the conclusions of the reasoning are to be of use to anyone other than the reasoner himself. Or in other words, both abilities are required if there is to be shared science of any complexity. To explain these abilities Hobbes invokes an unanalyzed power of written or spoken things, once 'imposed' on non-linguistic items, to call to mind conceptions of those items. A written or spoken thing with this power is a name that functions as a *mark*. And a name that is also able, in the context of a speech, to convey a speaker's or writer's conception of a thing to someone else, is a *sign* (cf. *De Corp.*, ch. 2, iii, E I 15).

Not just any names that function as marks or signs have a scientific use. An item of science is a true proposition reached as the conclusion of a piece of syllogistic reasoning, and Hobbes says that only universal affirmative propositions can serve as the premises or conclusions of scientific syllogisms (*De Corp.*, ch. 4, vii, E I 49). A universal proposition is one 'whose subject is affected with the sign of a universal name' (*De Corp.*, ch. 3, v, E I 34), i.e., a proposition of the form 'All *F*'s are *G*' or 'Every *F* is *G*', where '*F*' and '*G*' are what Hobbes calls 'universal names', names of each of a plurality of things, like 'horse', 'man' or 'tree'. Since only universal names are allowed to figure in the grammatical subject position of a proposition of science, since any such proposition is true (indeed, eternally true), and since predicates of all true propositions have to have extensions at least as wide as those of subject terms (*De Corp.*, ch. 3, vii, E I 35), the predicates must also be universal names.

Universal names, then, are *the* items of scientific vocabulary. The proper name, and with it the singular proposition, do not properly occur in a scientific syllogism at all (cf. *De Corp.*, ch. 4, iv, vii, E I 46, 48). In *Leviathan* Hobbes says that a universal name is 'imposed on many things for their similitude in some quality or other accident' (ch. 4, E III 21). This much is neutral between the use of universal names within science and outside it. Suppose each of several creatures I see has four legs, and suppose that I impose 'horse' on each for the property of having four legs. Then though 'horse' has been imposed on many things for their 'similitude in some accident', 'horse' may be imposed by someone else on the very same things for their similitude in respect of some other quality or accident. Under these conditions 'horse' is equivocal in conversation (cf. *EL*, Pt. 1, ch. 5, vi. 20). It can also be equivocal when a single speaker imposes it for one similitude on one occasion and for another on another. In science equivocation is avoided (cf. e.g. *L*, ch. 4, E III 23): universal names in use are always defined. So it is really only universal names imposed for a *fixed* similitude in some quality or accident that are items of scientific vocabulary.

'And of names universal, some are of more, and some of less extent' (*L*, ch. 4, E III 21). By the 'extent' of a universal name he means the plurality of things to which a universal name applies severally. Different universal names that belong to the same category or 'predicament', e.g. 'man', 'body', and 'living creature' have extents that contain one another or that overlap (*L*, ch. 4, E III 21), and because certain affirmations built out of such universal names can be re-expressed as assertions about how the extents are related, it is possible, by means of universal propositions, to bring relations between the extents or pluralities into a train of reasoning. Extralinguistically, or in experience, we never have access to a plurality of things at a single time, let alone relations between pluralities. All our prelinguistic or extralinguistic conceptions are particular and of one thing at a time (*De Corp.*, ch. 5, viii, E I 60). Consequently, while experience can disclose facts concerning as many of a plurality of *F*'s as have been observed or remembered, it cannot convert that long conjunction of known facts concerning *F*'s into known facts about all *F*'s, even if the observed *F*'s are all the *F*'s there are. Experience, as Hobbes puts it early in *The Elements of Law*, 'concludeth nothing universally'.

With the availability of defined universal names this shortcoming of experience is overcome. Once a universal name '*F*' has been 'aptly' imposed, i.e., imposed for a similitude in an accident *G* that all *F*'s have, then accidents of *F*'s conditional on being *G* can be put into 'universal rules' or exceptionless truths concerning the *F*'s. Hobbes gives the example of someone who has the use of the word 'triangle' and who observes that the three angles of a particular triangle are equal to two right angles. He

> that hath the use of words, when he observes, that such equality was
> consequent, not to the length of the sides, nor to any other
> particular thing in his triangle; but only to this, that the sides were
> straight and the angles three; and that this was all, for which he named
> it a triangle, will boldly conclude universally, that such equality of
> angles is in all triangles whatsoever . . . (*L*, ch. 4, E III 22).

On the other hand, someone who lacks the use of words – Hobbes has just been considering the case of someone who is born and remains perfectly deaf and dumb (ibid.) – though he may find of a particular triangle that its three angles are equal to two right angles, cannot 'without a new labour' know the same of any other triangle.

Only the linguistically competent man, and one possessed of universal names, is a potential scientist. Though he, too, can only have in mind one triangle at a time, he can know that whenever the word 'triangle' applies, it applies to a thing with three angles and three straight sides, and he can know that if a thing has three angles and three straight sides, then its three angles will be equal to two right angles. This discharges him, as Hobbes says, of his 'mental reckoning, of time and place; and delivers [him] from all labour of the mind, saving the first, and makes that which was found true *here* and *now*, to be true in *all times* and *places*' (*L*, ch. 4, E III 22). Two things make it possible for such general conclusions to be reached. One is a power of universal names, i.e., their power of designating each of many things at a single time. The other is what Quine calls 'semantic ascent'. For it is only when the linguistically competent enquirer realizes that it is on account of a certain property

40

that the word 'triangle' is applied to a given triangle, that he can arrive at the universal rule about triangles and angles. He must be able to make expressions and their semantic properties into objects of thought in order to think about all or every one of a kind of object.

Once universal rules or propositions have been established by an enquirer, material is available for establishing more – syllogistically. Hobbes indicates how universal names are to be combined into truths, and how universal propositions are to be combined into syllogisms, in *De Corpore* (chs. 4, 5, E I 44–64). It is to the churning out of consequences from syllogisms that science is supposed to be geared. Starting from a class of aptly imposed, well-defined universal names with overlapping extents, one proceeds to make universal propositions and then to register their consequences. That is what one calls 'science' (*L*, ch. 5, E III 35).

4 Logic-book science?

Passages equating science with syllogistic reasoning from definitions, or agreed significations of general words, are to be found in *The Elements of Law* (Pt. 2, ch. 8, iii. 176–7), *De Cive* (ch. 27, xxviii, E II 295–6; ch. 28, iv, E II 303–4), *Leviathan* (op. cit.), and *De Corpore* (ch. 6, xvi, E I 86). What these passages seem to describe is a kind of logic-book science, at first sight too formal, with first principles too concerned with the elucidation of meanings, to give power over observed effects. Hobbes usually writes as if definitions are supposed to generate, either directly or indirectly, all the conclusions of science, and he also writes as if the conclusions of science enable people to intervene in the course of nature and produce beneficial effects. But it is not immediately clear how by knowing definitions, which only explicate the senses of words by paraphrase or example (*De Corp.*, ch. 6, xiv, E I 83–4), or how by knowing the consequences of definitions, people become equipped to intervene and alter the properties of things they observe.

Indeed, given what Hobbes typically says about definitions, it is hard to see how they *could* aid intervention. For he typically says that if definitions give any information at all, it is semantical, and that getting it is strictly preliminary to the acquisition of causal knowledge or science (*De Corp.*, ch. 3, ix, E I 37; *SL*, Less. 2, E VII 225–6). And his standard example of a definition used in a scientific demonstration – 'Man is a body, animated, rational'– seems to back up his point. As it stands the definition tells one nothing one would need to know to change men. So is there a tension between his apparent commitment to logic-book science and his apparent identification of science with knowledge suitable for altering the properties of things?

There is no real tension. Hobbes thinks that to intervene in nature

41

one needs knowledge of definitions and their consequences *as well* as non-definitional, experimental knowledge. One needs to work also with the merely probable, with hypotheses. In making use of experiments and hypotheses one departs twice over from logic-book science. First, hypotheses are non-evident propositions (cf. *EL*, Pt. 1, ch. 6, vi. 26), whereas definitions and their deductive consequences are all evident. Second, experiments are findings reported by singular propositions, not the universal ones to which Hobbes confines logic-book science. In order to obtain knowledge of the causes of the phenomena of nature, and hence in order to know what it takes to alter such phenomena, one needs a kind of science that, unlike logic-book or purely deductive science, is *hypothetico*-deductive (cf. *De Corp.*, ch. 25, i, E I 388; *DP*, ch. 2, E VII 88).

Logic-book science, then, was not the only kind of science Hobbes recognized. From quite early on in his philosophical development, though not from the beginning, he believed that there were two kinds of science, alike in being demonstrative, but with different types of proposition at the premiss-end of the demonstrations.[8] If logic-book science tends to be the more prominent in his writings that is because outside *De Corpore*, Hobbes wrote about science with a view to expounding civil science, and he held, no doubt strangely, that moral and political philosophy were purely deductive. But both types of science, deductive and hypothetico-deductive, were catered for. Whether Hobbes had a coherent concept of demonstrative science to subsume the two types of science is another matter, as we shall see presently.

IV

Two Problems with Demonstrative Science

1 'Demonstration'

'Demonstration' is Hobbes's term for a syllogistic arrangement of truths (*De Corp.*, ch. 6, xvi, E I 86), and also for the activity of communicating in syllogisms, an activity he sometimes calls 'teaching' (*De Corp.*, ch. 6, xi, E I 80). Demonstrating or teaching is 'leading the mind of him we teach, to the knowledge of our inventions, in the track by which we attained the same with our own mind' (ibid.). Or, in other words, it is the orderly re-enactment for the benefit of others of the process by which the truth of a given matter was found out. In *Leviathan* Hobbes says that it is a sure sign of someone's having acquired the science of a given subject that 'he can teach the same; that is to say, demonstrateth the truth thereof perspicuously to another' (ch. 5, E III 37).

Nothing less than perspicuous demonstration is supposed to put it beyond doubt that a given claim or theory really belongs or amounts to science. When someone 'pretendeth to the science of any thing' and 'only some particular events answer to his pretence', then he is not necessarily a scientist. His pretence to science is not even borne out conclusively when events 'upon many occasions prove so as he says they must' (E III 37). To qualify as a scientist someone must not only turn out to be right some or most of the time: the basis for his being right has to come out in demonstrations of his claims.

But if perspicuous demonstration is the mark of science, what is the mark of perspicuous demonstration? More generally, how is the apparently rigorous demonstration of a false claim or theory to be told apart from the teaching of a truth? The question is tersely answered in *The Elements of Law*. 'The infallible sign of teaching exactly, and without error, is this: that no man hath ever taught the contrary . . .' (Pt. 1, ch. 13, iii. 65). Or, as he goes on to put it, 'the sign of [teaching] is no controversy' (ibid., 66). This much tells us what the effects of demon-

43

stration or teaching are, when the demonstration or teaching is perspicuous, but it does not tell us what makes for perspicuous demonstration. What is it about the content and format of such demonstration that keeps controversy from breaking out? Hobbes points to the practice of successful teachers. They 'proceed from most low and humble principles, evident even to the meanest capacity; going on slowly, and with most scrupulous ratiocination (viz.) from the imposition of names they infer the truth of their first proposition; and from two of the first, a third, and from any two of the three a fourth, and so on' (*EL*, Pt. 1, ch. 13, iii. 66).

Practitioners of this method are called 'the *mathematici*', and 'of the two sorts of men commonly called learned', they alone really are learned. The other sort

> are they that take up maxims from their education, and from
> authority of men, or of authors, and take the habitual discourse of
> the tongue for ratiocination; and these are called the *dogmatici* (*EL*,
> Pt. 1, ch. 13, iv. 67).

These men are the breeders of controversy, breeders of controversy precisely because they take their opinions undigested from authorities, and act as mouthpieces for views they have not worked out from 'low, humble and evident' principles. He seems to be referring to the same class of men at the beginning of *De Corpore*, when he speaks of the people 'who, from opinions, though not vulgar, yet full of uncertainty and carelessly received, do nothing but dispute and wrangle, like men that are not well in their wits' (*De Corp.*, ch. 1, i, E I 2). And in the same vein there is the remark in *Leviathan* that 'he that takes up conclusions on the trust of authors, and doth not fetch them from the first item in every reckoning, which are the significations of names settled by definitions, loses his labour, and does not know anything, but merely believeth' (ch. 5, E III 32).

He blames the *dogmatici* for the backward state of moral and civil philosophy before *De Cive*, and he traces the then modest development of natural philosophy, to a misconception that had for a long time prevailed about how far the methods of the *mathematici* could be applied. The misconception went back to the Latins and Greeks (cf. *De Corp.*, ch. 6, xvi, E I 86). They had been wrong to think that demonstration or ratiocination was only applicable to geometrical figures, as if it were the figures that made the conclusions of geometrical demonstration evident. What in fact made the geometrical conclusions of the ancients so compelling (by contrast with the 'controversy and clamour' of 'their doctrines concerning all other things'), was not the use of figures, but the use of 'true principles' as the starting points of geometrical ratiocination. Were other doctrines to start from similar principles, they too

44

would enjoy conclusiveness and truth. Or, as it is put in *De Corpore*, 'there is no reason but that if true definitions were premissed in all sorts of doctrines, the demonstrations also would be true' (ibid., E I 87).

The idea that 'all sorts of doctrine' might be true, i.e., that doctrine on all sorts of topics might be true, if it were to begin from true definitions, has an epistemological counterpart: demonstrative *knowledge* of all sorts of truth might be acquired, were the knowledge to be the result of reasoning from definitions known to be true. Hobbes's account of demonstrative science places a heavy burden on definitions. Perhaps it is too heavy a burden. It may be that by making the theoretical use he does of definitions, he is committed to an implausible, conventionalist theory of science. This is the first of two problems to be discussed in the present chapter. The second is created by the tension between Hobbes's claim to be laying new foundations for the demonstrative sciences, and his apparent deployment of the 'old logic' for the purpose.

2 Science, truth and convention

Conventionalism is a doctrine about truth, typically mathematical truth. It says that when a proposition is true, the definitions of its terms make it so, and that the definitions hold when, as a rule, users of the relevant language understand by the *definiendum* just what they understand by the *definiens*, and apply the two interchangeably. Hobbes often writes as if he were a conventionalist with respect to the truth of all of the propositions of science.[1] In *The Elements of Law*, for example, he contrasts experience-knowledge with science. Experience, he says, is the source of only one kind of knowledge. The other kind

> is the remembrance of the names or appellations of things, and how every thing is called, which is, in matters of common conversation, a remembrance of pacts and covenants of men made amongst themselves, concerning how to be understood of one another. And this kind of knowledge is generally called science, and the conclusions thereof truth (Pt. 2, ch. 8, xii. 176).

This sounds conventionalist. In *De Cive* he distinguishes in a complementary way between questions of faith and questions of science, 'whose truth is sought out by natural reason, and syllogisms, drawn from covenants of men, and definitions, that is to say, significations received by use and common consent of words' (ch. 17, xxviii, E II 295). He is not just saying that the way to *find out* the truth of scientific questions is to go back to definitions and reason from them. For he goes on to speak of particular truths themselves depending on the 'consents' of men (E II 296). Once again his remarks are conventionalist-sounding.

The passages just cited were written before Hobbes had begun to distinguish explicitly between purely deductive and hypothetico-deductive science. How do things stand in later writings? How do they stand in particular in *De Corpore*, where not only the distinction between kinds of science, but also an account of hypothetico-deductive physics, is given? At first sight at least, some of the things he says in *De Corpore* seem to be of a piece with claims in the earlier writings. In chapter 5, he discusses ways in which propositions can fail to be true by being incoherent copulations of subject and predicate. Incoherence is supposed to be avoided if subject and predicate are each names of the same category of thing. Thus, coherent propositions are supposed to be formed if subject and predicate are both names of bodies, names of accidents, names of phantasms, or names of names (ch. 5, iii, E I 58). But coherence is only necessary, not sufficient for truth; so faced with propositions in which e.g. names of bodies are copulated with names of bodies, it can still be 'doubtful whether such propositions are true'. The method Hobbes suggests for clearing up such doubt seems to make him a conventionalist. If we wonder whether propositions we know to be coherent are true, he says,

> we ought then in the first place to find out the definition of both those names, and again of such names as are in the former definition, and so proceed by continual resolution till we come to a simple name, that is, to the most general or most universal name of that kind; and if after all this, the truth or falsity thereof not be evident, we must search it out by philosophy, and ratiocination, beginning from definitions (ch. 5, x, E I 61–2).

Hobbes does not say that at some stage what the proposition says must be compared with how the named things stand in reality: he seems to hold, as a conventionalist would, that the truth of a proposition is intralinguistically determined.

But Hobbes is not speaking in the quoted passage of any and all propositions of science. In Chapter Five of *De Corpore* he is describing a method for finding out the truth of coherent propositions *that occur in syllogisms*, and he has said earlier, in Chapter Four, that in the scientific syllogisms he is concerned with, 'all the propositions are both universal and affirmative' (ch. 4, vii, E I 49). The passage just quoted at length continues by saying that the reason the method of resolving into definitions determines truth, is that the method is being applied to universal propositions, and universal propositions, when true, are either 'definitions or parts of definitions'. Examples of the universal propositions Hobbes has in mind are 'Every man is a living creature' and 'Every man is a body'. No doubt he is wrong to hold that every universal proposition, when true, is either a definition or a part of one: 'Every creature with a heart is a creature with a kidney' would be a counter-example.

No doubt he is rash to make the corresponding claim that the truth of universal propositions can be determined in every case by resolving their terms into their definitions. But these objections are beside the present point, which is, that conventionalist as he may be about true universal and affirmative propositions, he is not a conventionalist about the truth of all scientific propositions. Definitions alone are not supposed to make singular propositions true, and many of these have a use in science as the starting points of analysis in physics (cf. ibid., ch. 25, i, E I 388).[2]

Granted that Hobbes is not a conventionalist with respect to all of the propositions of science, is he not a conventionalist with respect to too many? We have already seen that he does not hold all of the propositions of physics to be of a kind made true by convention. What of the truths of geometry and mechanics? To judge by the opening of Part Four of *De Corpore*, these *are* supposed to be true in virtue of 'cohering' with definitions, and the definitions are supposed to be true in virtue of 'agreement' and 'consent' between speakers who use the relevant *definienda* (*De Corp.*, ch. 25, i, E I 388). Unless Hobbes means something special by 'consent', it looks as if he is saying that Euclid's theorems and Galileo's Law of Fall are true ultimately by human stipulation and convention. Their truth is inferred, and the reason the inferences work is that people agree that it is permissible to pass to those truths from certain definitions. The reason the definitions are true is that people lay down and abide by the rule that such and such a term will have such and such a sense.

If this *is* what Hobbes is saying, then he is hard pressed to explain how e.g. the accelerations of descending bodies are accurately predicted by the Law of Fall. For even if human agreement alone determines whether the Law is properly derived, human stipulation does not bring it about that the distances from rest of falling objects are as the squares of the elapsed times. On the one hand Hobbes needs an account that does not make it mysterious that some of the propositions of pure mechanics are satisfied independently of our will. On the other hand, he wants an account that will explain why no-one can rationally doubt or dispute the truth of propositions of geometry and mechanics when they are demonstrated in the abstract. In practice, Hobbes seems to be sensitive to the second of these desiderata but not the first. For he sometimes seems to explain *why* there is no doubting a demonstrated truth of geometry or pure mechanics by saying that to doubt it is to go back on a prior decision about what meanings to assign to certain terms. As if *no more* than a decision between giver and receiver of a definition mattered to the truth of a demonstrated conclusion in geometry and pure mechanics.

But when Hobbes speaks of agreement and consent in connection with geometry and mechanics, *does* he mean that it is for people to decide which definitions hold, and therefore which demonstrated conclusions are true? As I understand it, 'consent' in the relevant sense occurs between people when they attach the same conceptions, in the same order, to a given speech. A special case of consent is where a hearer of a proposition speech is caused by the speech to have the same conceptions as the maker of the speech (cf. *EL*, Pt. 1, ch. 13, ii, 64–5). And a special case of this sort of consent is where a definition is given by one person to another, for a definition is a propositional speech.

When it comes to Hobbes's account of the truth of definitions and the drawing of conclusions in abstract demonstrations, the same notion of consent seems to be at work. The truth of a definition is secured when the *definiens* raises the same conception as the *definiendum* not only in the mind of the giver of the definition but in the mind of the receiver. If the *definiens* and *definiendum* raised ideas that seemed different from one another to the receiver, then the definition would be false. For it is a condition of the truth of a definition that its predicate (the *definiens*) signify the same thing as the subject (the *definiendum*) signifies (cf. *De Corp.*, ch. 6, xiv, E I 83), and 'signifies' means 'signifies to the hearer' (cf. *EL*, Pt. 1, ch. 13, x. 69; *L*, ch. 31, E III 350). As for a conclusion reached by evident steps from definitions in abstract demonstrations, it is true if the hearer of a demonstration cannot but conceive its subject and predicate to apply to the same thing, given how the hearer follows the demonstrator in conceiving the application of names in the premises (cf. *De Corp.*, ch. 3, xviii. E I 42).

Now nothing about this sort of consent between receiver and giver of a demonstration brings in the choices or decisions of parties to the demonstration. Someone who is being given a demonstration does not *decide* to go along with the demonstrator and attach the same senses to terms. The demonstrator's definitions either raise the relevant conceptions or they do not. As for the demonstrator, *he* does not decide what senses will be attached to terms he starts his demonstrations from. For he is ruled by the order of conceptions he had in the process of discovering the truth he is about to demonstrate (*De Corp.*, ch. 6, xii, E I 80–1), and that in turn is fixed by an order of analysis or decomposition (cf. *De Corp.*, ch. 6, iv, E I 68–9), which itself depends on how the natures of things under investigation are put together (cf. *De Corp.*, ch. 6, ii, E I 67).

In the case of the demonstrations of geometry and mechanics, the conceptions that the definitions capture are ones that dawn on the investigator when he takes the analysis of certain natural appearances to the limit, and encounters the "universal things" there have to be for the natural appearances to exist at all. For us to be affected with experiences or conceptions of objects having certain properties, there must be, according to Hobbes, bodies in motion that generate the appearances, either our own bodies or external ones (cf. *De Corp.*, ch. 9, vi, E I 123; ix, E I 126). Now however unfaithful the content of experiences or conceptions may be to the relevant bodies, the bodies cannot play their role in generating the appearances and lack some size or other, some shape or other, some motion or other. Shape, size and motion, then, are among the universal things. The definitions of geometry distinguish, and even at times explain, the generation of different kinds of shape or figure (cf. *De Corp.*, ch. 6, v, E I 69–70; ch. 8, xii, E I 111; *SL*, Ep. Ded., E VII 184–5). The definitions of mechanics convey conceptions of things with different sizes and shapes taking over different portions of space (cf. *De Corp.*, ch. 6, vi, E I 71–2).

Since the definitions of geometry and mechanics are concerned with things there must be, or rather with properties or accidents bodies cannot conceivably lack if they are to produce experiences, namely, size, shape and motion in the abstract, it is not surprising that calculations of size, shape and motion in the abstract, such as Hobbes thinks lie behind the Law of Fall, turn out to have application to bodies. Hobbes does *not* have a theory of these definitions that makes their application to things in nature an accident. But, by the same token, the truth of conclusions in geometry and mechanics cannot be owed just to people's agreeing in how they use words. In the case of universal things definitions must actually put over conceptions of the nature of body, conceptions that have a basis in reality. Similarly with parts of definitions or explications. For example, the connection between being a body and having a magnitude does not consist merely in our all being willing to ascribe magnitude to whatever we call 'body': the absence of the connection in nature is inconceivable (cf. *De Corp.*, ch. 8, xx, E I 116).

If the connection between being a body and having a magnitude is written into nature, if it does not consist just in our always applying the name 'has magnitude' where we apply 'body', how is it with other definitional connections? Is there, corresponding to 'Man is rational, animated body' some connection in nature? Or is Hobbes prepared to relax his conventionalist-sounding talk about definitions only in the case of names of universal things?

It seems he does only selectively objectify definitional connections. How he comes to do so in the case of 'body' and 'has magnitude' is by asking what change in a way of conceiving a thing would have to take place for it to be called now by the positive name 'body' and later by its contradictory 'not-body'. Underlying such a shift, he thinks, there would have to be a conception of a thing's losing its magnitude. He grants that such a conception can be 'feigned' by the imagination (*De Corp.*, ch. 8, xx, E I 116). But he denies that there could be any explanation of how what is feigned could actually happen in nature. In the case of a switch from calling something 'man' to calling it 'not-man', on the other hand, the underlying conception would be of a thing's losing its animateness or rationality, both perfectly intelligible developments. In this case Hobbes's conclusion would seem to be that 'man' is applied to a thing for mere appearances it presents, whereas 'body' is applied for a property or properties a thing must have, or cannot conceivably lack.

3 Old logic, new science

Hobbes doubts the objectivity of the properties for which species- and genus-names are given. He doubts that there are any such things as species or genera in the abstract. He makes the point more than once in *De Corpore* that 'species' and 'genus' are names of names, not names of things (cf. *De Corp.*, ch. 2, x, E I 21; ch. 5, v, E I 59). He has a complementary point of view on definitions and demonstrations in science: these do not recover objective relations of inclusion between species and genera. Nor do copulations of subjects and predicates in propositions signify the inherence of an attribute in a thing. Nor, again, does a syllogism recover the 'reason of a connection' between a subject and an attribute. It ties these points together to say that Hobbes rejects the old Aristotelian interpretations of terms, propositions and scientific syllogisms. How can he reject those interpretations and yet find a use for the apparatus of the 'old' logic in his philosophy of science?

In this connection it is worth noting the discrepancy between Hobbes's views and those of his contemporaries. In Part Two of his *Discourse on Method* Descartes writes that 'among the different branches of Philosophy, I had in my younger days to a certain extent studied Logic.' But 'I observed in respect to Logic that the syllogisms and the greater part of the other teaching served better in explaining to others those things that one knows . . . than in learning what is new.' Hobbes can agree with this much, for it is in the method of teaching, not in the method of discovery or invention, that he thinks syllogisms and their theory are useful. But Descartes goes on,

> And although in reality Logic contains many precepts which are very true and very good, there are at the same time mingled with them so many others which are hurtful or superfluous, that it is almost as difficult to separate the two as to draw a Diana or a Minerva out of a block of marble that is not yet roughly hewn.[3]

Comments like these keep Descartes well apart from Hobbes. For Hobbes thinks that the study of the true natural philosophy has to start with the study of logic, and by organizing *De Corpore* accordingly, he invites not only Descartes's objections, but the complaint Bacon makes in *Novum Organum* against Aristotle himself, 'who made his natural philosophy a mere bondservant to his logic, thereby rendering it contentious and well-nigh useless.'

Two of Hobbes's reasons for employing syllogisms are roughly the same as Aristotle's: he thinks that there are certain questions that are characteristic of scientific enquiry, and that answers to these questions can be organized as pieces of deductive reasoning. He thinks also, as we have seen, that unless the answers are presented as such pieces of reasoning, it is open to doubt whether the answers amount to scientific ones. But he differs from Aristotle in his choice of the questions distinctive of scientific enquiry.

Aristotle holds that there are only four sorts of question: whether a claimed connection holds between thing and attribute; why it holds; whether a thing exists; what the nature of a thing is.[4] Hobbes supposes that when a definite question is posed in philosophy the sort of thing one wants to know is

> what is the cause of *light*, of *heat*, of *gravity*, of a *figure* propounded, and the like; or in what *subject* any propounded *accident* is inherent; or what may conduce most to the *generation* of some propounded *effect* from many *accidents*; or in what manner particular causes ought to be compounded for the production of some certain effect (*De Corp.*, ch. 6, iii, E I 68).

One general respect in which these questions are unlike Aristotle's is that they are not framed within Aristotle's 'categories'.

Even where Hobbes's vocabulary seems reminiscent of Aristotle's, as when he gives as a typical question, 'In what subject any propounded accident is inherent', the content of the question is quite unAristotelian. This emerges when Hobbes illustrates that form of question by asking in what subject 'that splendour and apparent magnitude of the sun is' (*De Corp.*, ch. 6, ix, E I 76). Aristotle writes in the *Posterior Analytics* as if there could be no question about the identity of the subject of an accident or attribute, only a question about why or whether a subject and accident were connected. So in the example before us there could be the question whether the sun had that splendour or that magnitude, or why it had either, but not whether it was the sun or something else that had the magnitude or the splendour. The latter sort of question arises naturally for Hobbes because he thinks of effects or accidents as appearances produced in the mind by the operation of bodies on the senses, and he identifies the subjects of accidents with causal sources of the appearances, not, as Aristotle does, with 'substances' or the logical subjects of predications of quantity or quality.

There can be no doubt that Hobbes wants to replace Aristotle's category of primary substance – the individual member of a natural kind – with the category of *body*. Indeed, it is the sole category of existent in the strict sense, the sole sort of thing with an existence 'without the mind', that Hobbes recognizes. He admits that we can give names to phantasms, accidents, and names as well as to bodies (*De Corp.*, ch. 5, ii, E I 57–8), and so he acknowledges that we can be committed to 'things' besides bodies, but these are not 'things' in the strict sense (*De Corp.*, ch. 2, vi, E I 17): only bodies are. Accordingly, the only attributes that can be 'commensurate and universal' in something like Aristotle's sense, the only attributes that must belong to a given thing, and that are fit material for demonstrative knowledge, are properties inseparable from being a body. One such property is real extension or magnitude (*De Corp.*, ch. 8, xx, E I 116); another is motion.[5] The reinterpretation of Aristotle's categories does not stop at the category of substance. *Definition, property, genus,* and *accident* are all explicated anew, the first three as things sayable of names rather than of substances (*De Corp.*, ch. 2, x, E I 21), the last as a perishable manner of conception of a body (*De Corp.*, ch. 8, xx, E I 117).

If Hobbes's reinterpretation of the category of substance explains why his choice of universal things is different from Aristotle's, his reinterpretations of the categories in general go far to explain why his view of syllogistic explanation as a whole is unAristotelian. To see this, it helps to start with what is common ground. Both sorts of syllogisms, Aristotle's and Hobbes's alike, present their conclusions as causally dependent on more basic truths. But in Hobbes the truths under explanation are assumed to be truths relative to our ways of conceiving natural objects and our ways of naming them. In general, neither the content of our conceptions, nor our naming conventions, are supposed to be reliable indicators of what things exist in nature, what they are objectively like, or what their natures are. Names are not imposed on things from the natures of things (*De Corp.*, ch. 2, iv, E I 16). We do not give names to things on the basis of a prior knowledge of their natures, but on the basis of how we natively conceive things. Natively, we conceive things by perceiving them as particulars with determinate qualitative features; it takes reasoning to resolve the native conceptions into what is universal. There is no safe inference from the content of our native, unresolved conceptions, to the existence of external things with the corresponding qualities. Hobbes puts the point emphatically in *The Elements of Law*. ' . . . [W]hatsoever accidents or qualities our senses make us think there be in the world, they are not there, but are seemings and apparitions only' (Pt. 1, ch. 2, x. 7). And something like this formulation, from Hobbes's first full-length philosophical book, survives in the relatively late *Seven Philosophical Problems*: '. . . [T]hose things which the learned call the accidents of bodies, are indeed nothing else but the diversity of fancy, and are inherent in the sentient, and not in the objects, except motion and quantity' (ch. 4, E VII 28).

Now Aristotle agrees that facts under syllogistic explanation are discovered perceptually, but he does not seem to acknowledge that the facts discovered are facts described from within a perceptual and linguistic scheme that can diverge significantly from the scheme of nature. He takes it that the classes of predicate really do correspond to classes of thing in reality. He takes it, too, that properties of things we perceive actually enter the senses, so that sense content is objectively like the things the senses are trained upon.

In general, there is no room in his account for a big difference between how the world is natively sensed, conceptualized and described, and the world as it independently is. Accordingly, the explanation of observed facts is never a matter of passing from the *merely* apparent to its real basis. Aristotle's *explananda* are not subjective observings or seemings but objective facts observed. His causes are drawn from the same objective domain as the things for which causes are to be found. It is an objective domain which Aristotle supposed was subject to orderly change, and that is reflected in Aristotelian forms of explanation. As Kuhn puts it,

> When considering the science of physics, Aristotelians ordinarily
> made use of only two causes, formal and final, and these regularly
> merged into one. Violent changes, those that disrupted the natural
> order of the cosmos, were of course attributed to efficient causes,
> to pushes and pulls, but changes of this sort were not thought capable
> of further explanation and thus lay outside physics. That subject
> dealt only with the restoration and maintenance of natural order, and
> these depended on formal causes alone.[6]

Formal causes were forms 'in' objects that made the objects the types of objects they were, and that determined the kinds of changes they could naturally undergo. Hobbes's reinterpretation of the category of substance reduces the number of forms natural objects can have to the one form inseparable from being a body, namely magnitude. Final causes are outlawed (*De Corp.*, ch. 10, vii, E I 131). And while material causes remain (ibid., ch. 10, iv, E I 122), these take second place to efficient causes – motions (ibid., ch. 6, v, E I 70; *DP* ch. 2, E VII 73).

This reduction of the kinds of causal explanation to explanation by efficient cause alone, is appropriate given Hobbes's subjectivist interpretation of *explananda* in natural science. When things under explanation are seemings or apparitions within the mind, the question of the cause of their existence is not easily interpreted as a request for a statement of a final or formal cause. One wants to know what external thing produced this mental thing, not what purpose the mental thing serves, not what 'in' the mental thing makes it the kind of thing it is. And as for the correspondence of the content of apparitions or phenomena to things without the mind, this can no longer be assumed to consist in an objective resemblance between what is sensed and a thing's properties. Instead, sense content has to be traced to such properties as we can know, independently of phantasms, bodies have, namely magnitude and motion.

There is a second and more general reason why Hobbes would have had second thoughts about Aristotle's causes. This has to do with Hobbes's understanding of the human condition before philosophy improves it, the condition of Fallen Man. Before the Fall there was no need for philosophy, no need that is, for a method of reasoning by which Adam could get the better of 'effects' for his benefit. Eden supplied all of Adam's needs and presented no unavoidable dangers. In particular, conditions for uncertain survival had yet to obtain. Adam did not have to arrange to go on living; he did not even have to arrange to go on living well. When he disobeyed the order not to eat from the tree of knowledge and was sent out of Eden, he could no longer count on a co-operative environment. It was at this point that Adam took on one of the characteristics that, according to Hobbes, has been inseparable from human nature ever since. The characteristic is anxiety.

Anxiety is what disposes men to seek out causes (cf. *L.* ch. 11. E III 92). Finding causes relieves the characteristically human fear that something bad will happen if events are allowed to take their course. Not just any understanding of causes fits this picture of seekers after causes. If enquiry is prompted by fear of what will happen next in a hostile natural order, then the causes sought will typically be those that 'make men better able to order the present to their best advantage' (ibid.). Formal and final causes do not fill the bill. They are better suited to gratifying the disinterested curiosity of a creature like Adam before the Fall, someone who does not have to worry about survival, someone who can contemplate nature and try to find an order and organization in it. In the less than ideal conditions that actually govern human life, the interest in discerning an order is likely to be overwhelmed by the need to make desirable effects happen. This means forsaking a contemplative stance, and forsaking a search for the kinds of causes that a contemplator would try to discover. Instead of letting formal and final causes dawn on them in the course of their sense-experience of the world, men are constrained to work out what they can do to produce observed effects. This is a matter of finding efficient causes. Here is where methods of measurement or numbering will be indispensable, and also where a merely qualitative description of the phenomena will not serve.

V

First Principles, First Causes and the Sciences of Motion

When he attacked the old natural philosophy Hobbes complained mainly of its failure to give genuine explanations of natural effects. It left people ignorant of the 'subordinate and secondary causes of natural events' because its explanatory concepts and categories were not cut out for the relevant questions about causes. People who wished to know the causes of heat or gravity or various 'propounded appearances' were asking after efficient causes, not formal and final ones, motions rather than forms or essences. And phenomena or appearances were in question. The old natural philosophy could not fasten in the right way on the appearances of things to sense, because it did not recognize appearances as things in the mind categorically distinct from bodies. So Hobbes's objections go on. We have had an indication of the explanatory categories he rejects. In this chapter we shall see what he puts in their place.

1 The disclosure of universal things

In the preface of *De Cive*, Hobbes wrote that had he been able to expound the 'first elements' of philosophy in the proper order, he would have devoted the first section to 'body and its general properties'.

> Wherefore the first section would have contained the *first philosophy*, and certain elements of physic; in it we would have considered the reasons of *time, place, cause, power, relation, proportion, quantity, figure*, and *motion* (E II xx).

This is an early description of work Hobbes had in progress, and so it is understandably sketchy. It does not make clear which topics belong to first philosophy and which to 'physic'. It does not say whether the list contains everything belonging to first philosophy, and it does practically nothing to unify the various areas of first philosophical investigation.

55

A fuller description of the nature and scope of first philosophy can be pieced together from passages in *Leviathan* and *De Corpore*. First *Leviathan*:

> There is a certain *philosophia prima*, on which all other philosophy ought to depend; and consisteth principally, in the right limiting of the significations of such appellations, or names, as are of all others, the most universal; which limitations serve to avoid ambiguity and equivocation in reasoning, and are commonly called definitions; such as are the definitions of body, time, place, matter, form, essence, subject, substance, accident, power, act, finite, infinite, quantity, quality, motion, action, passion, and divers others, necessary to the explaining of a man's conceptions concerning the nature and generation of bodies (*L*, ch. 46, E III 671).

This time we are given more than a list of metaphysical topics. We are told that the business of first philosophy is to define the most universal names. And the definitions are said to be necessary to explain 'a man's conceptions concerning the nature and generation of bodies'. Not the scientist's or the philosopher's conceptions only, but 'a man's' – any man's. Though all other philosophy ought to depend on *philosophia prima*, Hobbes seems to be saying that even pre-philosophical understanding can be brought under its definitions of universal names.

In chapter 6 of *De Corpore* we are told why pre-philosophical understanding is subsumable by first philosophy. The reason is that the universal names first philosophy deals with signify the most universal conceptions or ideas people can have, and these 'universals' are latent or 'contained' in untutored conceptions of particular phenomena (*De Corp.*, ch. 6, iv, E I 69). By analytical reflection on our ordinary conceptions of particular phenomena we can come to recognize the universal ideas that organize our understanding of particulars.

> For example, if there be propounded a conception or *idea* of some singular thing, as of a *square*, this square is to be resolved into a *plain, terminated with a certain number of equal and straight lines and right angles.* For by this resolution we have these things universal or agreeable to all matter, namely *line, plain,* (which contains *superfices) terminated, angle, straightness, rectitude,* and *equality*; and if we can find out the causes of these, we may compound them altogether into the cause of a square. Again, if any man propound to himself the conception of *gold*, he may, by resolving, come to the ideas of *solid, visible, heavy,* . . . and many other more universal than gold itself; and these he may resolve again, till he come to such things as are most universal (E I 69).

By disclosing to themselves the universals 'contained in the nature of singular things', people find out the causes of singular things, that is the causes of 'those accidents by which one thing is distinguished from another' (E I 68). In other words, analytic reflection can take an enquirer beyond observed differentiating properties to ones that are more basic. He can find out not only that a square is a plane figure, whose four, straight, equal sides meet at right angles, but also the causes of a figure with those properties, i.e., the motions that generate such a figure in a geometrical construction. As Hobbes says, analysis can disclose universal things, and also, where they are conceivable, the causes of universal things.

First philosophy, then, is a special sort of summary of the universals that are brought to light when analytical reflection is taken to its limit. It is a summary of the first principles of things, but one which does more than register them in a single analyst's memory. It is a summary suitable for teaching first principles and their consequences to someone else, and it is the starting point for a demonstration of all the subordinate truths of natural philosophy. First philosophy is where enduring science or philosophy begins. Anyone who can reason methodically can penetrate by analysis to the universal in the particular, and so to the causes of observed phenomena, but unless he assembles his findings, organizes them syllogistically, and so presents them for consumption by the uninstructed, he will be 'a philosopher alone by himself' (*De Corp.*, ch. 6, xi, E I 80), and his results will last no longer than he does (*De Corp.*, ch. 2, xiv, E I 14).

It is notable that Hobbes's first philosophy reveals no 'first cause' in the capital-letter sense of that phrase. He does not recognize, as Aristotle and for that matter Descartes did, the possibility of a 'first science' dealing with a higher or divine substance. It is true that Hobbes finds a use in first philosophy for a name that *if* it designated anything would designate an immutable and insensible (but not divine) substance, namely body in general or *materia prima* (*De Corp.*, ch. 8, xxiii–xxiv, E I 118). But he denies that the name does designate anything. It signifies something, namely the conception of a body that can be formed when all of its determinate accidents are imagined away or left out of account. But there is no such *thing* as body in general and therefore, presumably, no observed effects traceable to such a thing. The closest Hobbes comes to acknowledging the effects of an insensible or higher substance is where he describes the effects of simple motion on a concrete body abstractly conceived. These effects are the things studied by geometry (cf. *De Corp.*, ch. 6, vi, E I 71). And the types of motion needed to generate the most basic of these effects – the straight line and the circle – are the first causes to be stated in philosophy. There are no prior, statable causes.

How is all of this to be squared with the claim, encountered a little earlier on in a passage quoted from *Leviathan*, that all of philosophy

57

ought to depend on first philosophy? It sounds like the claim that first philosophy ought to state *the* cause of *all* of the effects studied by the rest of philosophy, as in Descartes's first philosophy. In Descartes, God is the first cause of everything, mathematical facts included, and it has to be known that God exists and that other things exist only with His co-operation, before there can be knowledge (*scientia*) or anything else.[1] God's existence is not the only thing about His nature we need to know, according to Descartes; we need to know all at once about all of His properties before we can go any further.

Now Hobbes believes that there is a first mover, and he seems to believe that the first mover is God (cf. e.g. *L*, ch. 8, E III 92, 95–6; *Third Objs.*, HR II 67), but he denies that anything more can be known concerning God, since the only knowledge that is available to us comes from sense and reasoning, and God's nature is beyond the scope of both. He never mentions the concept of a First Mover as one of the topics of first philosophy. More important, however, and again by contrast with Descartes, he never claims that first philosophy discloses the ultimate explanation of all of the effects treated by the rest of the sciences. It only makes explicit a preferred *form* or *framework* of explanation, namely mechanistic explanation.

The framework is indicated by a certain choice of explanatory vocabulary and by the definitions of the relevant terms. When Hobbes says in *Leviathan* that all of philosophy ought to depend on first philosophy, the context shows he means that philosophy or explanation should not proceed until the terms to be used in explanation evoke the same clear ideas in everyone who gives or receives the explanations. And that defining terms so as to evoke clear ideas is strictly *preliminary* to explanation proper, comes over plainly in a passage from the *Six Lessons*:

> [H]e that telleth you in what sense you are to take the appellations of those things which he nameth in his discourse, teacheth you but his language, that afterwards he may teach you his art. But teaching of language is not mathematic, nor logic, nor physic, nor any other science; and therefore to call a definition . . . mathematical, or physical, is a mark of ignorance, in a professor inexcusable. All doctrine begins at the understanding of words, and proceeds by reasoning till it conclude in science. He that will learn geometry must understand the terms before he begin, which that he may do, the master demonstrateth nothing, but useth his natural prudence only, as all men do when they endeavour to make their meaning clearly known. For words understood are but the seed, and no part of the harvest of philosophy, . . . so that all definitions proceed from common understanding; of which, if any man rightly write, he may properly call his writing *philosophia prima*, that is, the seeds, or the

grounds of philosophy. And this is the method I have used, defining place, magnitude, and the other most general appellations in the part which I entitle *philosophia prima* (Less. 2, E VII 225–6).

As if first philosophy constitutes no more than a kind of lexicon of the general terms to be used in the sciences proper.

2 Motion and the 'several parts of science'

What determines the stock of terms to be defined? Hobbes usually gives open-ended lists of the relevant universal names, without saying what ties them together. But in a pair of sentences not yet quoted from the passage in which he distinguishes the seeds from the harvest of philosophy, he gestures at something which unifies the *definienda* of first philosophy:

> For words understood are but the seed, and no part of the harvest
> of philosophy. And this seed was it, which Aristotle went about
> to sow in his twelve books of metaphysics, and in his eight books
> concerning the hearing of natural philosophy. And in these books
> he defineth time, place, substance or essence, quantity, relation &c
> that from thence might be taken the definitions of the most general
> words for principles in the several parts of science (*SL*, Less., 2, E
> VII 226).

Described like that, Aristotle's procedure is also Hobbes's. Hobbes, too, is out to extract principles in the several parts of (natural) science from the definitions of the most general words.

The definitions could not play that role if they were not informed by a conception of the content of the special sciences, and a conception of the way the special sciences hang together. Chapter Six of *De Corpore* is devoted in part to the organization of the branches of natural philosophy (cf. E I 70–3). It says that natural philosophy as a whole divides into four parts. Two parts are theory of motion, two parts are physics. This set-up does not come out of nowhere. It is derived from a thesis about what explanations in the natural sciences have in common. It is this thesis that determines both his choice of terms in first philosophy, and their style of definition.

The thesis is stated at many places, but probably its most illuminating context is to be found at the beginning of Chapter Six of *De Corpore*. Here Hobbes puts forward what should by now be a familiar idea: that particular phenomena are to be understood in terms of universal things – accidents common to all bodies – and the causes of universal things. It is his thesis about the causes of universal things that is at the bottom of his first philosophy:

> But the causes of universal things (of those, at least, that have any
> cause) are manifest of themselves; or (as they say commonly) known
> to nature, so that they have all but one universal cause, which is
> motion (E I 69).

Call this 'Hobbes's Thesis'. It says that the most general features of
objects that we can discover, have a single general type of explanation,
an explanation in terms of motion. And by 'motion' he means simply
change of place or locomotion.

Hobbes's Thesis is not just a claim about the causes of universal things,
but also – because universal things explain everything less universal – a
claim about the explanation of all phenomena. Hobbes makes the scope
of the thesis explicit when he says that

> all appearance of things to sense is determined, and made to be of
> such quality and quantity by compounded motions, every one of
> which has a certain degree of velocity and a certain and a determined
> way (ibid., ch. 6, vi, E I 73).

This cuts out his work in first philosophy. All the definitions he gives
either contribute to explicating what motion in general is – what it is for
a body to change place – or else they help to provide the materials for
identifying the various kinds of locomotion.

Now for some details. There is only one continuous and systematic
exposition of Hobbes's first philosophy, and that occurs in Part Two of
De Corpore. It does not take up all of Part Two. Hobbes says in the
Epistle Dedicatory of the *Six Lessons* that 'from the seventh chapter of
my book *De Corpore*, to the thirteenth, I have rectified and explained
the principles of science' (E VII 185), and this leaves out the final chapter
of Part Two. Again, at the end of Part Two itself, Hobbes seems to
suggest that the three concluding chapters of the Part – on quantity,
proportion, angle and figure – belong to geometry rather than to first
philosophy (*De Corp.*, ch. 14, xxi, E I 202). That leaves five chapters.

In the first (Chapter Seven), Hobbes defines 'space' and 'time' (E I
93–95), purports to explain how times and places are individuated (E I
96), and also indicates properties of places and times that can enter into
reasoning: their numbers, their parts, and their arrangement into wholes.
In Chapter Eight, with 'time' and 'place' defined, Hobbes thinks he has
resources for defining 'body' (E 102) and its most general accidents.
Magnitude or real space-occupation is discussed; so are the spatial
relations of continuity and contiguity. Against this background he
defines 'motion' (E I 109), and in terms of 'motion' the ideas of length,
depth and breadth. After the three spatial dimensions are explicated he
defines quantitative identity and difference for motions and bodies (E I
112–13). Finally, he discusses the conditions of qualitative difference

between bodies over time. It is clear that Chapter Eight is the centrepiece of Hobbes's exposition. In the next chapter he considers the conditions under which qualitative change is caused, the discussion culminating in a would-be demonstration of what I have been calling 'Hobbes's Thesis': that all mutation is motion (E I 126). Chapter Ten is a reinterpretation, in terms of locomotion, of the role of potentialities and their actualization in change. Chapter Eleven is an attempt to assimilate conditions of identity and difference for sorted bodies over time, to the general account of qualitative difference given in Chapter Eight.

By what criteria are these five chapters to be judged adequate or inadequate? Plainly we are within our rights to exploit the conditions of adequacy on definitions that Hobbes himself imposes (*De Corp.*, ch. 6, xv, E I 84). It will turn out that these conditions are not always satisfied by Hobbes's explications of universal names. Then there is the acceptability of Hobbes's Thesis to consider. Can the idea of motion have the explanatory power that Hobbes thinks it has? If not, then a first philosophy centred on the definition of motion will simply not yield the principles of the special natural sciences. It is hard to show conclusively that Hobbes's first philosophy is deficient because Hobbes's Thesis is. One would have to examine in detail the many explanations in physics he thinks can be couched in terms of locomotion (cf. e.g. *SPP*, *DP*, E VII 1–177). I shall not attempt that examination. Instead, I shall briefly return (section 4 below) to the division of the natural sciences that Hobbes's Thesis seems to inspire, and in particular to the place that geometry is supposed to occupy in that scheme. If Hobbes's Thesis is right, then geometry, like any of the special natural sciences, must be a science of motion. Hobbes can even be read as saying that it is the pre-eminent science of motion. His working out of this claim invites objections he never properly answers. This starts a doubt about the cogency of Hobbes's Thesis as a principle for organizing the special sciences of nature.

3 Universal things adequately defined?

First, though, for the question of whether the definitions of the first philosophy meet Hobbes's own conditions of adequacy. In Chapter Six of *De Corpore* we are told that definitions must take away equivocation and make redundant 'all the distinctions (how many soever) that can be used about the name defined' (*De Corp.*, ch. 6, xv, E I 84). Definitions must do those things by paring away all unwanted connotation from terms under explication. They must exhibit 'clear' as well as 'universal' notions of whatever they define (*De Corp.*, ch. 6, xvi, E I 86). They must, where possible, mention the causes of the things defined (*De*

Corp., ch. 6, xiii, E I 82). And they must be evident in themselves, and not in virtue of some other proposition (*De Corp.*, ch. 6, xv, E I 84).

Nearly all of these requirements seem to be violated by one or another definition put forward in Part Two of *De Corpore*. For example, Hobbes makes use of some *ad hoc* distinctions to keep the sense of 'magnitude' apart from what he defines as 'space' (*De Corp.*, ch. 8, v, E I 105), and he invokes more distinctions to keep apart the conception of a thing's magnitude from the conception of a thing's location (E I 105). Again, having defined 'time' as the phantasm of a body in continual motion, he feels obliged to offer an argument in its defence (*De Corp.*, ch. 7, iii, E I 94), contrary to the requirement of self-evidence. When he refines the definition of 'time', stating that 'TIME *is the phantasm of before and after in motion*', it is hard not to suspect circularity: the definition seems to say that time is the phantasm of the succession of time in motion.

Deeper difficulties present themselves when two crucial definitions – the definitions of 'space' and 'body' – are tested against the requirement that definitions exhibit 'clear' as well as 'universal' notions of things under definition. The definition of 'body', like the definitions of 'time' and 'place' that precede it, is given in the context of a thought experiment concerning the annihilation of the external world. We are to imagine that all material objects have passed out of existence and that the only traces they have left are the images they produced in us when they did exist, images stored in memory. Hobbes claims that the content of any such image, when considered in the right way, will produce 'a conception of what we call space' (*De Corp.*, ch. 7, ii, E I 93).

Suppose I picture to myself a memorable object from the now depleted external world, Nelson's Column, say. Then, in order to get a conception of space, I am to ignore the fact that what my memory is of, is a column, an artifact, a landmark, a stone pedestal surmounted by a sculpture. I am to ignore everything that determines it to be such-and-such an object, and consider Nelson's Column as something that once had 'a being without the mind'. That done I will have a clear and universal idea of space, namely as of a phantasm or appearance of something as existing without the mind. And armed with a conception of space, I am supposed to be poised to conceive what body is. To conceive of body is to conceive space at the same time as one allows the hypothesis of the annihilated world to lapse. It is to conceive space at the same time as I 'suppose one of those [annihilated] things to be placed again in the world or recreated' (*De Corp.*, ch. 8, i, E I 102). When I picture the re-creation of one of the annihilated things, according to Hobbes, I conjure up more than an image of something that takes up part of space: I also conceive something with no dependence on my thought (*De Corp.*, ch. 8, 1, E I 102), or something with 'a being in itself, without the help of the senses' (*DP*, ch. 1, E VII 81). From what I conceive come the materials for the definition of 'body' as anything which 'having no dependence on our thought, is coincident or co-extended with some part of space' (*De Corp.*, ch. 8, i, E I 102).

Hobbes defines 'body' and 'space' by giving instructions for conjuring up the ideas of body and space in the abstract, and he thinks it is possible to form those ideas on the basis of information supplied by the senses and stored by memory (cf. *De Corp.*, ch. 7, i. E I 92). He also assumes a capacity for attending selectively to various 'parts' of the content of a sensory image. Since he is not giving an account of how the relevant universal ideas are acquired, only how they are brought to consciousness after being acquired, it is not clear that his account invites exactly the objections that have been urged against abstractionism by writers in sympathy with Wittgenstein.[2] But related objections do apply.

One problem is that the capacity for selective attention can operate only on materials the senses provide, and it is hard to see how the senses alone can give us the idea of 'being without the mind' and of 'having no dependence on thought'.[3] Another problem is that the capacity for selective attention to something in the mind's eye seems merely to be a capacity for attending to something in more or less detail. But to conceive a body as independent of thought is not to conceive an object in less detail than when one thinks of it as a London landmark. It is to conceive the object by way of a general property, and so a non-determinate property, but not 'non-determinate' in one sense of 'undetailed'. Hobbes does seem to run together non-determinate conceptions with undetailed ones. In an aside in Chapter One of *De Corpore* he says that the same idea for which a body is called 'body' by the linguistically competent, can be had by someone who lacks language but sees a body from far off (*De Corp.*, ch. 1, iii, E I 4).

4 Geometry and motion

Hobbes's conditions of adequacy for definitions are not always met by his own definitions. But it is clear that his first philosophy cannot be judged by those conditions of adequacy alone. Part Two of *De Corpore* does purport to exemplify the art of definition-making, but this is incidental to its main object, which is to supply to the special sciences principles, or the makings of principles, in keeping with Hobbes's Thesis. This suggests a second way of assessing the first philosophy. We may ask not only whether the definitions are evident, clear, non-circular and the rest, but also whether the special sciences can be brought under the thesis about locomotion that the definitions help to articulate.

The thesis says that all appearance of quantity and quality is due to motion, and 'appearance of quantity' includes geometrical features bodies present to the senses – the ways they are extended in space. Can geometrical definitions show, or help to show, that these geometrical properties are the outcome of motion? Hobbes thinks that unless geometrical definitions identify the motions that generate figures, geometry is no science. But, as one of his critics implied, if the definitions do make reference to motion, then it is not clear that they are geometrical. Something strange happens when Hobbes tries to bring motion into the principles of geometry. He holds that geometry runs 'quite through the whole body of natural philosophy' (*SL*, Less. 1, E VII 196); he also holds that 'nature worketh by motion' (*L*, ch. 46, E III 669). And to bring the two theses together he seems to hold that geometrical entities themselves result from the working of motion.

In Part Two of *De Corpore* Hobbes defines several geometrical ideas by reference to motion. His definition of 'line', for example, runs as follows:

> [W]hen any body is moved, the magnitude of it be not at all considered, the way it makes is called a *line*, or one simple dimension; and the space through which it passeth, is called *length* (*De Corp.*, ch. 8, xii, E I 111).

Or, in other words, line is the path described in space by a moving body, when the body is considered as a plane figure. The definition attracted criticism in a book intended to expose Hobbes's mathematical incompetence, *Elenchus Geometriae Hobbianae*, written shortly after the appearance of *De Corpore* by the then Oxford professor of geometry, John Wallis. In the *Six Lessons of Geometry*, the rejoinder to Wallis, Hobbes reports Wallis's objection to his definition of a line:

> Again, you [Wallis] object and ask, 'What need is there of motion, or of body moved, to make a man understand what is a line? Are not lines in a body at rest as well as in a body moved? And is not the distance of two resting points length, as well as the measure of the passage? Is not length one and a simple dimension, and one and a simple dimension line? Why then is not line and length all one?' (*SL*, Less. 2, E VII 214–15).

In reply, Hobbes first cites a precedent in Euclid's geometry of solids for bringing motion into a geometrical definition, the definition of 'sphere' (E VII 215). But he goes on to say that the definition can be defended without calling in the authority of Euclid. 'To me,' Hobbes says,

> however it may be to others, it was fit to define a line by motion. For the generation of a line is the motion that describes it. And having defined philosophy in the beginning, to be the knowledge of

64

the properties from the generation, it was fit to define it by its generation (E VII 215).

This is a question-begging defence of the definition of a line, for the definition of philosophy itself is never defended. In fact, Hobbes concedes in the opening chapter of *De Corpore* that 'there may be many who will not like this my definition of philosophy' (ch. 1, x, E I 12), and one ground for misgiving may be what it licenses, or what it may require, in the way of geometrical definition.

Hobbes does not rest his case for definitions by motion on his conception of philosophy alone. The further considerations have to do with alleged defects in definitions from Book One of Euclid's *Elements*, defects which are supposed to make Euclid's demonstrations suspect. Commenting on Euclid's definition of a circle as a plane figure contained by a circumference that can be joined by equal straight lines to a point within the circumference, Hobbes writes,

> This [definition] is true. But if a man had never seen the generation
> of a circle by the motion of a compass or other equivalent means,
> it would have been hard to persuade him that there was any such
> figure possible (*SL*, Less. 1, E VII 205).

His own definition of a circle – 'the figure made by the circumduction of a straight line in a plane' (*De Corp.*, ch. 6, xiii, E I 82) is not open to this objection. It tells someone how to make the figure, and so leaves no room for doubt about whether circles are possible figures. The only difficulty is that of believing in the doubt Hobbes's definition is meant to pre-empt.

Put briefly, Hobbes view is that some geometrical ideas can be acquired by considering bodies in motion in the abstract, i.e. by disregarding much of what is determinately true of them. Thus ideas in plane geometry can be acquired by considering the paths and positions of solid bodies when only two of their three dimensions are taken into account. And the meanings of 'point' and 'line' are accessible when only one dimension is taken into account. It is also Hobbes's view that unless geometry is taken to be about bodies in motion the constructive postulates of Euclidean plane geometry – such as that from any point to any point a straight line may be drawn – are 'impossible to be performed' (Ibid., E VII 211). He claims that by supplying what he calls the 'principles of motion' of geometry, he is helping to make the demonstrations of geometry secure against pyrrhonism (*SL*, Ep Ded., E VII 184; Less. 5, E VII 317–18). Indeed, he goes so far as to proclaim that 'I am the first that hath made the grounds of geometry firm and coherent' (*SL*, Less. 3, E VII 242).

But if answering scepticism about geometry is one of Hobbes's intentions in outlining the principles of geometry, it is one he keeps under wraps in *De Corpore*. He seems to announce anti-sceptical leanings in the *Six Lessons* as an afterthought, to take the sting out of Wallis's attack on his mathematics. In any case, it is clear that his defence against pyrrhonism is question-begging. This is so even in *De Corpore*, where Hobbes's recourse to the hypothesis of the annihilated universe might be thought to meet at least scepticism about the existence of an external world on its own ground. In fact, however, the hypothesis does not free Hobbes of commitment to the existence of an external world: it only allows him to assume that objects do not exist outside the mind *at the same time* as it is going through pieces of geometrical construction and reasoning. The medium of the construction and reasoning is assumed to consist of traces in the mind of ideas produced in the past by material things (cf. *De Corp.*, ch. 7, i, E I 92), and scepticism about the existence of the material world plainly puts into question the assumption that there *once* were external bodies, as much as the assumption that there are *co-present* bodies satisfying the content of our current experiences.

His assimilation of geometry to the sciences of motion is hard to justify, but it is not difficult to explain. It helps Hobbes to keep the relation between geometry and physics neat. Here is how he describes the relation in Chapter 6, article 6 of *De Corpore*:

> [P]hysics cannot be understood except we know first what motions are in the smallest parts of bodies; nor such motions of parts, till we know what it is that makes another body move; nor this, till we know what simple motion will effect (E I 73).

If, as Hobbes holds, geometry just is the science of 'what simple motion will effect', if geometry tells us what effect a body produces when we pay attention to its motion alone, then the dependence of physics on geometry is easily made out. But since there is no good reason to accept that geometry is the science of simple motion, what becomes of the unity of 'the first part of science'? Surely there is something in Hobbes's thought that physics studies motion and that it depends on geometry. Must he rely on a controversial theory of geometry to explain how geometry and physics go together?

Perhaps not. Various passages in Part Two of *De Corpore* and in the *Six Lessons* contain the makings of a better account. In the chapter on Quantity in *De Corpore*, he makes much of the fact that in order to calculate the measurable properties of bodies, including the measurable properties that are straightforwardly functions of their measurable motion, like the forces they exert, it is necessary to have a method for 'exposing' or sensibly representing what will enter into the calculations: times, spaces traversed, direction of motion, the position of a body at a time, and the like. Hobbes's preferred method of representation makes geometrical figures – lines, superfices, solids and the rest – stand for the things to be measured, and the method takes over from geometry not only its axioms and theorems but also techniques for operating on geometrical figures, techniques like superposition and section (ch. 12, iii. E I 140). Hobbes could have argued for the indispensability of geometry in the physicist's study of motion by arguing from the fruitfulness of that method of exposition and calculation.

This more plausible way of harmonizing geometry with the physicist's study of motion is consistent with Hobbes's idea that physics cannot do without geometry. But it does not require geometry to be understood as a science of motion. And it relaxes the commitment to the idea that knowledge of the nature of motion opens the 'gate of natural philosophy universal' (cf. *De Corp.*, Ep. Ded., E I viii). It allows Hobbes to hold instead that knowledge of the nature of quantity is the key. And in the opening pages of the *Six Lessons* (E VII 192–6) he does come close to acknowledging that quantity rather than motion is the formative universal idea in natural philosophy. He says that 'quantity can be considered in all the operations of nature' and that because geometry is the science of determining all kinds of quantity, including the quantity of motion, it runs through the whole of natural philosophy.

VI

Motion, Phantasms and the Objects of Sense

In geometry, officially the first part of science, Hobbes's principles are mechanical ones. Principles in other parts of science, not only in physics, but also in 'ethics' or moral psychology, are mechanical principles as well. Physics studies the motions that cause sensation; ethics studies some of the motions sensation in turn gives rise to. Physics is the explanation of sensible appearances and sensation in terms of the motions of the parts of bodies; ethics catalogues such 'motions of the mind' as appetite, aversion, love, benevolence and hope. Like sensation itself, these mental powers are only nominally motions of the *mind*: their principles reveal them to be effects of motions in the parts of a body. Mental effects are mechanical ones, no less than effects in the rest of nature.

Many effects, one model of explanation. Is mechanics equal to the burden imposed upon it? We have already considered some reasonable doubts of Wallis's concerning Hobbes's mechanistic reinterpretation of definitions in geometry. Other critics, Descartes for one, flatly denied that mechanics could recover the nature of mental phenomena, mind and motion being 'of two entirely different natures'.[1] We shall see later on that something like Descartes's objection is right. Not only is it doubtful that the whole variety of mental operations can consist in the variety of motions; it is not even clear that the variety of specifically sensory operations can consist in the effects of motion in the various sense-organs. Hobbes's theory of sensation does make an advance on the neo-Aristotelian accounts it is meant to supersede, and it is perhaps the most successful of his various attempts to apply principles of motion. But, as will become clear, the account suffers from Hobbes's liking for sweeping reduction.

1 The explanation of appearance

The theory of sensation is not only a part, but the first part of Hobbes's physics. The reason is that the data up for explanation in physics are phenomena or appearances, and these appearances could not exist if there were no process of sensation to produce them. We latch on to bodies in nature – things in the strict sense (cf. *De Corp.*, ch. 2, vi, E I 17) – by having sensory experiences or ideas or phantasms of things. And it is by reasoning from descriptions of the experiences or phantasms that we come to the 'principles' of the things themselves – the principles of nature.

Sense being what provides the data of physics, how does it work? Hobbes's answer is that it works by reaction, reaction to motion propagated through the parts of the sense-organs. He thinks of sense-organs in a rather inclusive way. In the case of vision, for example, the sense-organ is not just the eye, but the eye taken together with the nervous and arterial systems to which it is connected. In fact, any part of the body is part of the sense-organ appropriate to vision if damage to that part would prevent visual experience (*De Corp.*, ch. 25, iv, E I 392). Thus the heart and brain are parts of the sense-organ appropriate to sight. Indeed, 'we speak more correctly, when we say a living creature seeth, than when we say the eye seeth' (*De Corp.*, ch. 25, iii, E I 391).

The process that culminates in sense-experience affects the whole living creature, but it starts with pressure on some external and sensitive part of the living creature. This is the 'uttermost part' of the sense-organ. When 'it is pressed

> it no sooner yields, but the part next within it is pressed also; and, in this manner, the pressure or motion is propagated through all the parts of the organ to the innermost (*De Corp.*, ch. 25, ii, E I 390).

'Press' and 'pressure' are terms from the theory of pure mechanics. Hobbes defines them in Part Three of *De Corpore*. One body presses another when 'with its endeavour' the first body displaces the other or displaces a part of the other (*De Corp.*, ch. 15, ii, E I 211). In the case of sensation, the pressure on the outermost part of the sense-organ is worked either by the body sensed, the so-called 'object' of sense, or by some part of a medium, like air, which is itself set in motion by the object of sense. Throughout the process sensitive parts of bodies are set in motion by contact with immediately adjoining moving parts. Sensation does not result simply from this communication of pressure, but from the *resistance* of pressed to pressing bodies. Each action of pressure inwards is met with resistance or endeavour outwards by the parts of the sense-organ, so that there is a chain of reactions to a chain of pressures in the parts of the organ. From the last in this chain of reactions, however short-lived it may be, 'a phantasm or idea hath its being' (ch. 25, ii, E I 391).

This much of the theory of sense is supposed to explain not only how the individual phantasms come into existence, but also some features of their content. For instance, since the idea or phantasm results from the last of a chain of reactions or small motions *outwards* in the parts of the sense-organ, to have a phantasm of a thing is to have an experience as of something outside the organ of sense (*De Corp.*, ch. 25, ii, E I 391). Besides accounting for what Berkeley was later to call 'outness', the theory as so far outlined offers to make partial sense of the fact that 'things when they are the same seem not to be the same but changed' (cf. *De Corp.*, ch. 6, vi, E I 72). Hobbes gives the example of things that appear to sight to be of different sizes at different times. This is the effect of variations in the angle at which motion from the innermost part of the organ of sight is propagated outwards (*De Corp.*, ch. 25, xi, E I 405). Another phenomenon is variation in the number of stars visible in the heavens. This is the effect not of the generation or destruction of stars, but of the state of the medium through which the motion of the stars is propagated. Cold air facilitates, and hot air hinders, stellar action on the eyes; so more stars appear on cold, calm nights than on warm, windy ones (cf. *De Corp.*, ch. 25, xi, E I 406).

We have not yet seen, even in outline, the whole of Hobbes's theory of sense. He goes on to discuss, among other things, how phantasms can be recalled to mind, how they can be conjoined and told apart, what makes possible selective attention to the content of a phantasm, and the principles by which a succession of phantasms organizes itself into mental discourse. We shall come to the rest of the theory later. In the meantime it is worth pausing to note the dependence of what has already emerged on principles of motion worked out in the abstract in Hobbes's discussion of motion, cause and effect. In *De Corpore* Hobbes himself calls attention to the ways in which his theory of sensation exploits abstract results about motion. Three principles, from a running list of seventeen given in Part Three of *De Corpore*, are singled out for attention in the chapter on sense. The first is that 'all mutation is motion . . . in the internal parts of the thing that is altered' (*De Corp.*, ch. 25, ii, E I 389–90). The second is that 'no motion is generated but by a body contiguous and moved' (E I 390). The third is that 'all resistance is endeavour opposite to another endeavour, that is to say, reaction' (E I 391).

Hobbes thinks it is obvious from introspection that 'our phantasms or ideas are not always the same; but that new ones appear to us and old ones vanish' (*De Corp.*, ch. 25, i, 389). He thinks it is equally obvious that our ideas change because we apply our organs of sense at different times to different objects (E I 390). From these considerations

he thinks it follows that change in ideas is some change or other in the
sentient or the thing that has the ideas (E I 390). What *kind* of change
in the sentient he thinks can be inferred from a general principle relating
sensible (including introspectible) change, to change in the position of the
internal parts of a thing that undergoes the change. Thus his invocation of
the first of the three principles just cited. Observation informs us that
when sensible things change, a change takes place in the sentient; first
philosophy tells us that change *in* a thing, including a sentient thing, is
a matter of a shift of the relative position of the parts of the thing.

What is the argument for this dictum of first philosophy? The one
Hobbes gives is strikingly brief. 'That all mutation or alteration is
motion . . . in the internal parts of the thing that is altered

> hath been proved . . . from this, that whilst even the least parts of
> any body remain in the same situation with respect to one another,
> it cannot be said that any alteration, unless perhaps that the whole
> body together hath been moved, hath happened to it, but that it
> appeareth and is the same it appeared and was before. Sense,
> therefore, in the sentient, can be nothing else but motion in some
> of the internal parts of the sentient (*De Corp.*, ch. 25, ii, 389–90).

This is no *proof* that mutation is motion in the internal parts of the body.
Hobbes needs to argue that it is logically necessary and sufficient for
large-scale change that there be a change in the relative positions of a
body's particles. Necessity and sufficiency seems to be put over by
Hobbes's saying that mutation is, rather than that mutation involves,
disarrangement of the internal parts. He does not argue for the necessity
and sufficiency claim. He asserts the weaker proposition that an undis-
turbed arrangement of a body's parts is sufficient for its appearing to be
the same or unchanged over time. Besides being open to counter-exam-
ples he gives in other connections, and being weaker than the necessity
and sufficiency claim he needs, the proposition he asserts speaks of a
body's appearing to be unchanged when what is at stake is real, not
apparent, sameness or change.

Do comparable difficulties attend the other principles of motion
Hobbes's theory of sensation borrows from his mechanics and first
philosophy? Is there, for example, a genuine proof in Hobbes's first
philosophy of the principle that 'no motion is generated but by a body
contiguous and moved'? Hobbes leans on this principle when he says
that the 'immediate cause' of a sensation or motion within the sentient
has to be pressure from a surrounding medium or an object of sense, on
an organ of sense (*De Corp.*, ch. 25, ii, E I 390). Is there an argument
for the principle? At one place in chapter 8 of *De Corpore* (xix, E I 115),
there is something like an indirect argument. Hobbes is trying to defend

71

the thesis that a body at rest will always be at rest if there is no other local body in motion to displace it. He invites us to suppose

> that some finite body exist and be at rest, and that all space besides be empty; if now this body begin to be moved, it will certainly be moved some way; seeing therefore there was nothing in that body which did not dispose it to rest, the reason why it is moved this way is in something out of it; and in like manner, if it had been moved in any other way, the reason of the motion that way had also been something out of it; but seeing it was supposed that nothing is out of it, the reason of its motion one way would be the same with the reason of its motion every other way, wherefore it would be moved alike all ways at once; which is impossible.

The argument purports to eliminate the possibility of a self-moving body by considerations about movement in a direction. If a body at rest gets moving, it gets moving in a particular direction; but it might have moved in any number of other directions; so there must be, on the stated assumptions, something within the object capable of making it move in any number of directions. If this inner potential for movement in any number of directions were ever actualized, Hobbes reasons, the body would be made to move in all directions at once. That being absurd, it must be made to move in a certain direction by something outside it (moving in that direction), a different direction of impact for each direction of movement from rest.

But the absurdity Hobbes reduces his initial assumptions to is contrived. It does not follow from there being a single explanation of a body's moving in any direction, that a body, when it moves, moves in all directions at once. Take Hobbes's theory. That says there is a single explanation of moving in a direction, namely contact with a local moving body. But contact with a local moving body will not get another body to move in all directions at once. Similarly, on the view Hobbes is attacking, it is possible to posit in the body at rest a capacity for self-movement in a direction, and a lot of sub-capacities for self-movement in particular directions. This is a complicated and *ad hoc* form of explanation of bodily motion in a given direction; it is not logically incoherent, as Hobbes's argument is supposed to show.

Two of the principles of motion Hobbes brings into his theory of sensation are not really proved in advance in his first philosophy: does this finding demolish the account of sensation? The part of the theory we have been examining so far is supposed to be demonstrable from first principles that are themselves independently demonstrated. So this part of the theory must be defective when judged by the requirements of the method of demonstration or synthesis in philosophy. But perhaps those requirements are at fault. It is not clear why the principles under discussion have to be demonstrated before being made to do explanatory work. Perhaps the explanatory work they do is demonstration enough of their truth. The flaws in Hobbes's abstract demonstrations of the principles are only decisive if there is rigid adherence to the synthetic method. Perhaps Hobbes should have presented his account of sensation as one that was simultaneously analytic and synthetic, so that its principles are judged as much by the explanations they deliver as by proofs that prefix them. This was the approach Descartes favoured. Close to the end of the *Discourse on Method* he writes,

> If some of the matters of which I spoke in the beginning of the *Dioptrics* and *Meteors* should at first sight give offence because I call them hypotheses and do not appear to care about their proof, let them have the patience to read these in entirety, and I hope that they will find themselves satisfied. For it appears to me that the reasonings are so mutually interwoven, that as the later ones are demonstrated by the earlier, which are their causes, the earlier are reciprocally demonstrated by the later which are their effects. And it must not be imagined that in this I commit the fallacy which the logicians name arguing in a circle, for, since experience renders the greater part of these effects very certain, the causes from which I deduce them do not so much serve to prove their existence as to explain them; on the other hand, the causes are explained by the effects.[2]

Had Hobbes relaxed the analysis/synthesis distinction in the theory of sense he would have been in good company.

2 Sentient and insentient bodies

The exposition of Hobbes's theory of sense may now be resumed. In this section we can start to appraise the theory's success in accounting for sensory phenomena, and worry less about whether its principles are antiseptically demonstrated in the first philosophy or in the pure mechanics Hobbes outlines in Part Three of *De Corpore*. We have it so far that sensation is a reaction in the innermost part of a sense-organ to motion communicated by pressure from a local external medium or local object of sense. This much is more or less contained in Hobbes's definition of sense as 'a phantasm, made by the reaction and endeavour outwards in the organ of sense, caused by an endeavour inwards from the object, remaining for some time more or less' (*De Corp.*, ch. 25, ii, E I 391).

In chapter 25 of *De Corpore*, Hobbes moves from the definition of sense to a discussion of various types of cognitive operation with phantasms, but he pauses to disclaim something his definition seems to imply.

The definition does not imply, he says, that 'every thing that reacteth should have sense' (*De Corp.*, ch. 25, v, E I 393). He is right: formally speaking, his definition of sense does not have that implication. On the other hand, it does confine sense to a reaction in a sensitive or animate part of a body (the sense-organ) and it is not clear Hobbes has resources for distinguishing animate bodies or parts of bodies from others. Accordingly, it is not clear why any body should not be the site of sensation, provided that some reaction takes place in its internal parts. For example, if resistance to motion in the human body produces a phantasm, why should not a phantasm be produced by resistance to motion in the parts of a stone? Hobbes must either state conditions that configurations of matter have to meet to count as sense-organs, taking care not to restrict sense-organs to creatures with a human physiology, or a physiology too much like the human one; or else he must leave open exactly how a sensory apparatus has to be materially realized, and countenance the possibility of a stone with sensations. More briefly, he has to distinguish between the internal movable parts of a thing, and the internal sensitive parts of a thing, precisely the sort of distinction that is out of place in a theory that tries to reduce sensitivity to a special sort of movability on contact.

Hobbes takes seriously the possibility that there might be something like sensation even in brute matter. He concedes that 'by reaction of bodies inanimate a phantasm might be made' (*De Corp.*, ch. 25, v, E I 393), but he denies that this would be enough for out and out sentience. The reason is that sentience is not just a capacity for having phantasms, but a capacity for keeping them before the mind, comparing and distinguishing them (E I 393). This complicated capacity, roughly the combination of powers of memory and reflection, is unavailable, Hobbes says, to any body without sense-organs capable of retaining motion, like those in living creatures (E I 393). So a stone, lacking such sense-organs, would lack sense even if it had phantasms. Hobbes does not say why an inanimate body must lack a capacity for retaining motion in reaction, and he sometimes writes as if, on the contrary, at least one configuration of matter, namely a body of water, can retain the motion caused by e.g. the stroke of something being thrown into it, or the motion of the wind (*EL*, Pt. 1, ch. 3, i. 8). So in the end, the possibility that all bodies are 'endued with sense' is not ruled out. This is an embarrassing result, but it is hard to see how Hobbes's theory can be amended so as not to permit some sort of panpsychism.[3]

If he is to arrive at a concept of animate matter or of the living body that is an advance on a pre-scientific one, he must somehow get underneath the appearances our own and other people's living bodies present to us. He must at the same time come up with hypotheses from which it follows, or with which it is consistent, that living bodies are able to sense and remember, dream, deliberate and act. But given Hobbes's first philosophy, the hypotheses can only draw upon concepts for the sizes, parts, positions, numbers and motions of otherwise undif-ferentiated bodies. These concepts are not cut out for making a sharp distinction between animate and inanimate matter. And far from seeming to subsume the range of mental capacities they are supposed to explain, hypotheses couched in the preferred terms appear to change the subject. Yet in what other terms could the hypotheses be framed? Hobbes thinks that talk of 'incorporeal spirits' is at worst self-contradictory (*L*, ch. 34, E III 381), and at best an awkward expression of piety (*L*, ch. 46, E III 672). He holds that in scripture 'soul' 'signifieth always, either the life, or the living creature; and the body and soul jointly, the *body alive*' (*L*, ch. 44, E III 615). But he insists that 'life itself is but motion' (*L*, ch. 6, E II 51) or 'but a motion of limbs' (*L*, Intro, E III ix) or at any rate the effect of motion originating in the heart and kept going in the circulatory system (*De Corp.*, ch. 25, xii, E I 406–7): the thought that vital, let alone mental processes, might be irreducible, seems never to occur to him, with the result, as we have seen, that the boundary between the animate and the inanimate, and between bodies with minds and bodies without, is hard to discern.

The blurring of the boundary adversely affects the 'second' part of Hobbes's physics. After offering a general account of sense or sentience, he turns in the last Part of *De Corpore* to an account of the 'objects' of sense. He wants to show that the sensible qualities, by which we register differences between external bodies, are not qualities intrinsic to the bodies, but effects of their interactions with our sense-organs. The properties external bodies have to possess intrinsically in order to appear as they do, turn out not to be exactly the properties we experience them as having. Certain of their apparent properties are merely apparent, contributed to our phantasms not by what they are like, but by the way we are physiologically constituted to respond to the motions they impart. That the sensible qualities are somehow subjective is one of the main claims of Hobbes's physics, and in a sense the claim is right. There *is* an important subjective/objective distinction to be drawn in this area, but, as we shall see, not the one Hobbes calls attention to. His distinction, between phantasms in the sentient and accidents of bodies, is no less unstable than his distinction between matter that is animate and matter that is not.

3 Objects of sense

By an 'object' of sense Hobbes means an external body that both registers in experience as being the subject of certain qualities (cf. e.g. *De Corp.*, ch. 25, x, E I 404), and that sets off the process culminating in an 'act of sense' (*De Corp.*, ch. 25, ii, E I 390). The object of sense is very definitely not an idea or image, though an idea or image may be the medium of registering the object of sense.[4]

The most detailed survey in Hobbes's writings of the different types of objects of sense is given in *De Corpore*. Hobbes says there that the greatest of sensible objects is the world itself, as surveyed from some point within the world (ch. 26, i, E I 410–11). But concerning this object few intelligible questions can be raised and none conclusively answered. We can only ask whether it is of finite or infinite magnitude, whether it is empty or full, and how long it has lasted. The first and third matters are for lawfully appointed churchmen to discuss: they really belong to the doctrine of God's worship, not to philosophy or science. As for the second question, that *can* be pursued scientifically, but only to a probable conclusion. Hobbes thinks that probably the world is full, and that there is no vacuum (ch. 26, ii–iv, E I 414–426). His consideration of this question is not entirely disinterested. The mediumistic theory of sensation he puts forward presupposes that there is no vacuum and that small motions or endeavours on the part of any body always meet resistance by adjoining bodies. But though this is presupposed, it is only presupposed as hypothesis. He never claims to have proved that the world is full, only that it is legitimate to assume it is. This big assumption leads to another. There are invisible bodies, such as the ether and 'the small atoms disseminated through the whole space between the earth and the stars' to fill apparent spaces between the visible bodies.

At this point, however, questions that can be intelligibly pursued about the world give out, and Hobbes's attention turns in *De Corpore* to the sensible objects that make up the world. He begins with the stars, and offers some further hypotheses concerning the order, motion and relative positions of the planets (ch. 26, v, E I 426–7). From these he infers explanations of, among other things, the passage of the seasons, the succession of day of night, 'the monthly simple motion of the moon', and tidal activity (ch. 26, vi–xi, E I 426–44). The additional hypotheses are openly borrowed from Copernicus and Galileo, and so are the explanations founded on the hypotheses. Hobbes starts to theorize in his own right when he passes from Sidereal Philosophy in chapter 27 of *De Corpore*, to objects that remain when the planets are left out of account. These he calls 'intersidereal bodies'.

Foremost among intersidereal bodies is 'the most fluid aether'. This is the body widely distributed in the area between the earth and the stars. Hobbes proposes to regard it as if it were first matter and to suppose that its parts 'have no motion at all but what they receive from bodies which float in them' (*De Corp.*, ch. 27, i, E I 448). The intersidereal bodies that co-exist with the aether are such as have some degree of cohesion, i.e., hardness (cf. *De Corp.*, ch. 22, ii), and that differ from one another in degree of density or consistency, motion and figure. Hobbes makes no suppositions in advance about the different types of motion and figure the hard intersidereal bodies have (*De Corp.*, ch. 27, i, E I 448), and he postulates nothing specific about their different degrees of consistency. Instead, he is content to form hypotheses *ad hoc* and suit them to whatever phenomena are under investigation. But about the magnitudes of hard intersidereal bodies he does make one point, namely that it is possible for many of these bodies to be 'unspeakably little' or minute, since God's infinite power includes a power infinitely to diminish matter (E I 446).

Armed with these very general assumptions about the types of object of sense there are, Hobbes is in a position to explain the phantasms that proceed from them, sense by sense. In *De Corpore* he begins with the phantasm proper to vision, namely light. This treatment of light and illumination is only one of many in Hobbes's writings. He had considered illumination perhaps as early as 1630, in the so-called *Little Treatise*, and he returned to the topic in a number of optical works in the 1640s, altering his view significantly several times. His optical theory, which he claimed was his most valuable contribution to science outside morals and politics, was precisely a theory of the 'act of illumination' plus a theory of the 'act of sense' involved in vision. His physics was optical theory with accretions of astronomy, physiology and pure mechanics.

From the beginning, his optical theory was mechanical. In the *Little Treatise* sense is motion in the animal spirits (sect. 3); illumination is the striking of the eyes by substantial species of light, conceived as particles, emanating from a light source. The details change in the later optical treatises, but not the mechanical character of the theory. Illumination is still a matter of impact, but not impact caused by the emanation of particles. Instead, it is impact of the medium on the retina caused by the motion of a light source transmitted through the medium. Hobbes put forward two hypotheses about how the light source disturbed the medium so as to make it eventually 'press' the retina. When the optical theory was at an intermediate stage of development, he pictured the light source as dilating and contracting continually. Later on he framed the hypothesis of the 'simple circular motion'. It is in force in the mature optical theory, stated in *De Homine*, and also in the slightly earlier *De Corpore*. In this version of the theory the ultimate source of light is the sun. Its circular movement thrusts away the surrounding fluid aether at a tangent (cf. *De Corp.*, ch. 21, ix, E I 328–9), and the motion is propagated rectilinearly until the surface of the eye is pressed. The pressing prompts the endeavour outward from the innermost organ of sense, the heart. And the endeavour outward is 'the thing which is called light, and the phantasm of the lucid body' (*De Corp.*, ch. 27, ii, E I 448).

Colour results from the propagation of light through intersideral bodies that, differing in density, produce refraction. Refraction occurs when solid rays of light travelling from a rarer to a denser medium meet the denser medium at an oblique angle. The parts of the solid rays that meet the denser medium first are slowed down and deflected to the perpendicular. Colour results from refraction. Thus, when weak sunlight 'passeth through a more resisting diaphanous body, [such] as glass, the beams, which fall upon it transversely, make redness, and when the same . . . light is stronger, . . . the transverse beams make yellowness' (*De Corp.*, ch. 27, xiii, E I 461). And so on through the prismatic spectrum.

Whenever light is propagated through a medium, heat is a by-product at the place where the medium adjoins the skin surfaces. By a process of what Hobbes calls 'fermentation' similar to that by which clouds draw up water particles, the parts of the air surrounding the skin are continually displaced by the circular motion that starts off illumination (*De Corp.*, ch. 27, iii, E I 49). Into the gaps created by the displacement of the air go the bodily fluids closest to the pores of the skin. And into the gaps created by the displacement of the fluids go other fluids, including blood, from the internal parts of the body (E I 449–50). This creates the swelling and flushing that is characteristic of growing hot, and these are all the phenomena that a physical explanation of heat ought to encompass. The actual sensation of heat each person knows independently of physics, from experience (E I 448–9).

It is unnecessary to review in detail the remaining sensory phenomena Hobbes explains. Sound and odour, like colour and light, are brought under mediumistic theories (cf. *De Corp.*, ch. 29, i, xiii, E I 486ff, 502ff). Tastes and textures are each accounted for by the direct impact of objects of sense on cuticles and membranes that if pressed, press the *pia mater* in the brain (*De Corp.*, ch. 29, xvii–xviii, E I 506–7). Mediumistic or not, the theories of the different senses and the phantasms proper to them all contribute to a physics or explanation of phantasms that is highly unified. Whatever appearances bodies present, they all result from the motion of local matter.

Phantasms or phenomena can be divided roughly into two classes. There are phantasms we can conjure up of body in the abstract, from which e.g. the ideas of space and time are derived. Then there are phantasms of bodies as distinguished from one another in respect of colour, sound, odour and the rest (*De Corp.*, ch. 26, i, E I 411). The classification of bodies by species and genus depends on bodies being registered as qualitatively similar or distinct (*De Corp.*, ch. 11, i, E I 133; cf. ch. 8, xx, E I 116). But since qualities are no more than the results of impacts on the sense organs of intersideral bodies, and since these bodies differ from one another only in respect of degree of coherence, speed, shape, position. and magnitude, these quantitative differences must explain the qualitative differences between bodies as observed. In other words, the variety of observed phenomena must be traceable to the different speeds, sizes, positions, shapes and consistencies of bodies that are otherwise undifferentiated.

One consequence of all of this is readily stated: what external bodies seem to be like in experience, and what they must be like to produce our experiences of them, are two different things. When we have a sensory representation of an external body as having a certain colour, or such and such odour, as making a given sound, all of those aspects of the representation are pure appearance. For instance, if the sun at evening registers as a bright, red disc receding into the horizon, the brightness and redness are, according to Hobbes's physics, subjectively contributed, contributed by the beholder, not the sun. 'For light and colour, being phantasms of the sentient, cannot be accidents of the objects' (*De Corp.*, ch. 25, x, E I 404). It is the same for other sensible qualities. Sound is the phantasm made by hearing, odour the phantasm made by smelling, savour by taste (E I 405). They are effects in the sentient as subject of a sensory episode, not properties of the object.

But this is as far as Hobbes goes in applying a subjective/objective distinction in the area of things sensed. Colour, sound, odour, savour and hardness are all phantasms or things in the mind, and so are subjective. Other properties – all quantitative and all disclosed by reason as necessary for the production of phantasms – are objective. A different sort of subjective/objective distinction is sometimes drawn *within* the class of sensible qualities. This is the familiar distinction between primary and secondary qualities. But it is not clear that this distinction is drawn by Hobbes at all, let alone drawn to make a point about subjectivity and objectivity.[5] It is true that at one place in *De Corpore* he treats figure and magnitude as common to all bodies, and distinguishes these from all other properties 'which are not common to all bodies, but peculiar to some only' (ch. 8, iii, E I 104). But he does not confine the other properties to the usual specimens of the secondary qualities. He includes among them such accidents as motion or rest and hardness, which are commonly reckoned primary. I am aware of no other place where he comes any closer to acknowledging the primary/secondary quality distinction, and I know of no passage at all where he says that phantasms of shape and hardness have a basis in external bodies that phantasms of colour, odour, savour and sound lack. He does not even make the point that because apparent magnitude, shape and motion are phantasms of sight *and* touch, they are more likely to have counterparts without the mind than phantasms proper to only one sense.

79

His view seems to be that *all* of the sensible qualities are subjective in the sense that 'the subject of inherence is not the object, but the sentient' (*EL*, Pt. 1, ch. 2, iv. 4), and he seems to recognize no other standard of subjectivity by which e.g. the phantasm of colour would count as more subjective than the phantasm of shape. As he puts it in *The Elements of Law*, '*Whatsoever* accidents or qualities our senses make us think there be in the world, they are not there, but are seemings and apparitions only. The things that really are in the world without us, are those motions by which these seemings are caused' (*EL*, Pt. 1, ch. 2, x, 7 – my emphasis). It is a view he adopts in opposition to the scholastic doctrine that sensible species or forms have to be transferred from objects to the senses if we are to perceive them as coloured, shaped, noisy and so on. He thinks that the hypothesis of species and forms passing between objects and perceivers is hard to make sense of, and that it makes the causation involved in perception an unduly special case of what is involved in causal interactions at large. In holding that motions alone account for the sensible qualities, he is able to give a unitary account of causal processes. The interactions of external bodies with our sense organs is only a special case of causal interactions between bodies, and no more properties have to be attributed to external bodies to explain how they affect us with sensations, than have to be attributed to explain how they can alter the accidents of other external bodies.

According to *The Elements of Law* it is unnecessary to ascribe to external bodies any more than a variety of motions; according to *De Corpore*, it is unnecessary to ascribe to them more than a variety of motions, densities, sizes and shapes abstractly conceived. Either way the point is the same. From a standpoint on the properties of external bodies that is detached from a standpoint as subjects of phantasms, i.e., from a standpoint in reasoning rather than in sense-experience, the properties bodies have to have to account for how they appear are not sensible qualities at all, but such properties as are understood through a theory of mechanics. If the sensible qualities *seem* to inhere in external bodies, that is a by-product of our trying to understand what they are like independently of sense, on the basis of sense-experience.

Hobbes might have exploited the distinction between a sense-based understanding of bodies and a reason-based understanding of the causes of sense-experience, in arriving at an account of the subjectivity of the sensible qualities. He might have held that because abstract mechanical properties were conceivable abstractly, without too many assumptions about existence, and yet could explain the qualities of external bodies as sensed, they contributed to a more objective understanding of external bodies than one which postulated sensible qualities actually *in* the external bodies. Instead, Hobbes's distinction between the properties bodies objectively have and the properties subjectively contributed in our experience of them, is fixed by reference to the *site* of the sensible qualities. Certain properties are subjective because *in* us, others objective because outside the mind. Not only is this distinction cruder than Hobbes's apparatus allows, it is only as stable as the not very firm distinction he draws between sentient or animate bodies and insentient or inanimate ones. Since, as we have seen, he is unable to exclude the possibility that 'by the reaction of bodies inanimate a phantasm might be made', there is nothing to ensure that accidents created by interactions between external bodies are not phantasms in *them*, just as colours, sounds and the rest are phantasms in us.

VII

Sense, Thought and Motivation

1 Phantasms and the succession of phantasms

Hobbes's theory of the mind makes no firm distinction between sense and intellect. This emerges in chapter 25 of *De Corpore*, where Hobbes raises, only to dismiss, the possibility that all bodies might be sentient. He thinks the possibility is left open by theories that fail to acknowledge the complexity of the capacity for sensation, in particular the way the capacity involves memory or the retention of phantasms. To be endowed with sense, he believes, is not merely to be the momentary site of phantasms; it is to be able to recall ideas to mind, and to be able to compare and distinguish them. Indeed, judgment, which is the capacity to keep track of differences between objects presented to the senses (*De Corp.*, ch. 25, viii, E I 399; *L*, ch. 8, E III 57), is not really a capacity distinct from sense (*De Corp.*, ch. 25, viii, E I 399).

The various capacities sense involves seem to be gathered by Hobbes from what he takes to be the standard and proper use of the term 'sense' (*De Corp.*, ch. 25, v, E I 393). At any rate, he promises a theory in keeping with the term's usual connotation. 'Sense', he thinks, is typically used to mean a power of comparing and distinguishing ideas. So it is natural for him to ask what mechanism underlies this capacity of comparing and distinguishing. The mechanism must be such as to produce, in succession, many distinct phantasms. But there could not be a succession of distinct phantasms, Hobbes reasons, if the sense-organs were not continually being applied to external objects, and if the external objects were not individually in motion. In a world in which external objects were at rest, there could not be sense in Hobbes's sense (*DP*, ch. 2, E VII 83). Again, there could not be a continual succession of distinct phantasms if there were not a variety of external bodies imparting their motion to the sense-organs. We should be as good as senseless if all the objects the sense-organs could be applied to were exactly similar, or if there were only a single object of sense that never changed (*De Corp.*, ch. 25, v, E I 394).

Though there must be a continual succession of motions if we are to enjoy 'sense' in the usual signification of the term, if we are to have material for comparison and contrast, it need not happen that every reaction in us to external motion is a sensory reaction. Only the strongest of the endeavours outward from the innermost parts of the sense-organs will constitute a sensory reaction, and there can only be one sensory reaction at a time. Moreover, a given sensory reaction at a time can be an experience *of* no more than one object at a time (*De Corp.*, ch. 25, vi, E I 395), if the various sense-organs are applied at a single time to a single object. The reason is that the occupation of several senses by a single object drowns out motions from other objects (E I 395). The senses are literally *pre*occupied. By this pair of one-at-a-time principles Hobbes seems to be trying to reconcile the finding that sense involves continual reaction to unremitting motion, with the fact that the stream of consciousness is not a blur. Disturbances at the sensory surfaces get translated, by neurophysiological means if Hobbes is right, into an orderly passage of phantasms, different objects holding the sentient creature's attention in direct proportion to the vigorousness of motion they impart to the sense-organs.

He is thus able to make sense of a series or succession of discrete phantasms, and of a phantasm's presenting a single object of attention for a given length of time. But as he is out to show how things can be compared and contrasted, he must also account for phantasms being alike or different in content, and this means showing how phantasms can present objects as qualitatively similar or distinct. The account seems to run as follows. A phantasm of a given object assembles as many distinct types of feature as there are 'proper phantasms' of the various sense-organs applied to the object. In *The Elements of Law* Hobbes speaks of a conception of an object as 'composed of' colour, figure, sound, smell and so on (Pt. 1, ch. 2, iii. 3). The colour content is contributed by stimulation starting at the eye, information about figure and texture by stimulation of the eye and the organs of touch in combination, sound by stimulation beginning at the ear, etc. A broadly similar account is given in *De Corpore* (ch. 25, x, E I 402f). It says where the qualitative content of an individual phantasm comes from, and also the various respects in which the content of one phantasm can be like that of another. There can be similarity in colour, figure, shape, and so on. Hobbes is also able to explain how diverse qualitative content is harnessed together in a single phantasm: the sense-organs channel the various sorts of stimulation into a single entry point in the brain (*De Corp.*, ch. 25, x, E I 403), and thereafter the stimulation coalesces in an idea.

Hobbes denies that there is one faculty for sensing things, or having phantasms, and another by which differences in phantasms are registered for future reference (*De Corp.*, ch. 25, viii, E I 399). As far as I can tell he takes a similar line with the perception of similarity. To be subject to and retain phantasms is at the same time to register and keep track of difference and similarity over time. Or to put it another way, a capacity for sense involves a capacity for memory. But it is not made clear how exactly we are able to remember things, and memory is never clearly distinguished from other psychological capacities. It is not good enough for Hobbes to say that memory is the faculty by which sensory reaction is prolonged beyond the time at which an external body is actually working on the senses. For under this description there is nothing objectively to distinguish memory from imagination (E I 398). The only difference is a subjective one – a difference between what it is like to remember and what it is like to imagine. In remembering it is as if we take in the features of an object from a distance, and so in not much detail (E I 399); in imagining it can be as if the object of sense is vividly present.

The distinction between memory and imagination gets blurred in Hobbes's account; so does the distinction between imagination and dreaming (*EL*, Pt. 1, ch. 3, viii. 12; *L*, ch. 2, E III 6f; *De Corp.*, ch. 25, ix, E I 399f). The reason is that Hobbes tries to mark differences between these psychological capacities with the same apparatus he has applied in the account of sense proper. To explain the variety of sense-experience he appeals to the variety of the sense-organs, the different ways in which the sense-organs are linked up with the nervous and arterial systems, differences in the objects of sense, and differences in the motions they impart to the sense-organs. But when it comes to accommodating the variety of ways in which sense-information can be operated upon after transactions between the sense-organ and external objects are completed, he no longer has available to him a wide enough array of distinct causes for the distinct operations. He must make the retention of motion in the sentient suffice as a basis for memory, imagination and many other apparently quite distinct mental capacities. Unsurprisingly, this basis proves too slight for explaining the range of effects proper to individual capacities. By memory, for example, we are not only supposed to be able to compare and distinguish the individuals we observe; we are also supposed to be able to hit upon regularities involving them so as to be able to form expectations (*EL*, Pt. 1, ch. 4, vii. 15). Can all of this be managed by short-lived reflection on qualitative similarity and difference in objects we have fleeting contact with? Can even qualitative comparison and discernment be accomplished by memory if it is no more than a device for storing and scanning the colours, shapes, smells, etc. of unsorted bodies? Hobbes offers a sophisticated reconstruction of the mechanisms that make it possible for us to be affected with phantasms, but he lacks the resources for a substantial account of the various operations — memory is only one — that cognition involves.

Thinking, for example, he seems to identify with the succession of phantasms or images in the mind (*De Corp.*, ch. 25, i, E I 399; *L*, ch. 3, E III 11f; *EL*, Pt. 1, ch. 4, i, 13). The order in the succession of phantasms may simply recapitulate the temporal order in which features of objects were taken in by the senses, or it may be an order geared to noticed qualitative resemblance or feigned qualitative resemblance (*De Corp.*, ch. 5, i, E I 56). It may be an order determined by the passage in the mind from a conception of a given end to a conception of a possible means to that end, or, more generally, it may be a passage from a phantasm of a type of event to a phantasm of another which is customarily associated with it (*EL*, Pt. 1, ch. 4, vii. 15; *L*, ch. 3, E III 12f). Finally, in the limiting case, phantasms follow one another with no coherence at all: one's mind simply wanders. In the various writings in which he considers thinking, from the early *Elements of Law* to *Leviathan* and *De Corpore*, Hobbes usually starts with this list of regulated and unregulated 'mental discourses', without pausing to defend the implicit claim that thinking comes down to a procession of phantasms or images.

The problem with the implicit claim is that it makes the medium of thinking and the organization of thinking too simple a by-product of sense. It is plausible to hold that we think in or with *concepts* of things. Now to have some concepts may simply be a matter of being able to make the discriminations of colour, smell, texture and so forth, that Hobbes thinks our phantasms naturally encode. But further discriminations may depend on non-sensory capacities, like the capacity to reason and speak a language, and it may be in virtue of being able to make these further discriminations that we qualify as full-fledged thinkers. It is hard to be sure whether Hobbes misses this point. He sometimes writes as if people are able to make very sophisticated discriminations – categorical discriminations – in the absence of linguistic ability. His treatment of an example in chapter 1 of *De Corpore* suggests that if someone visually registers what are in fact signs of a body's being animate, then the body is thereby distinguished by a perceiver 'from a tree, a column and other fixed bodies' (E I 5–6). It seems implausible that visual stimulation by an inanimate body could by itself suffice for my distinguishing the animate from the inanimate. Yet the example is given to back up the point that we are able to think and reason to some extent without language, and presumably without concepts distinct from sense experience. Elsewhere in *De Corpore* he seems to suggest that the recognition of generic and specific differences is mainly a function of sense-information (ch. 11, ii, E I 133). Yet in *The Elements of Law* he writes that for lack of numeral words a beast cannot keep track of how many young she has in her charge, and that 'neither would a man, without repeating orally or mentally the words of number, know how many pieces of money or other things lie before him' (Pt. 1, ch. 5, iv. 19). Here the idea is that the ability to reckon in units, and so the capacity for computing quantities, is essentially linguistic. Hobbes makes a related point in *De Corpore* when he says that in comparing a thing with itself over time and making judgments of numerical identity or difference, what it makes sense to say (and, presumably, think) will depend on the name we use to assign the thing to a sort (ch. 11, vii, E I 137).

Sometimes, then, he does seem to acknowledge that certain concepts and thoughts are not available to us on the basis of sensory ideas alone. Some concepts and thoughts presuppose a linguistic in addition to a sensory capacity. But in general, he seems to hold that language is not needed to create conditions for thought. He says that what language or speech does is to put thought or mental discourse into a form in which it can readily be recalled by the thinker and made evident to someone else (cf. e.g. *L*, ch. 4, E III 19). And his remarks about the parts of speech – names – are in line with this. The first use of a name is as a sensible 'mark' for a conception or thought, something which jars the memory and calls to mind a thing previously conceived. This is a name's primary function: it 'serves also *by accident* to signify to others what we remember ourselves' (*De Corp.*, ch. 2, iii, E I 14 – my emphasis). But the general line invites powerful objections. To begin with, it is not obvious that a name can privately be set up as a mark and have a settled reference or meaning. This point, familiar from Wittgenstein, goes with another: that the use of a name as an expression suitable for communication, what Hobbes calls a 'sign', cannot be secondary to its use as a mark, but must, on the contrary, be basic. For an expression to have a use for a speaker it must first have a use for speakers. Hobbes offers no defence of his individualist as against communitarian leanings, but this is understandable. His individualism in semantics is an outcome of his explaining language and thought in the light of an individualist theory of sense.

Hobbes's theory of sense is not only the source of a questionable individualism in his view of language: it also encourages him to take for granted a simple connection between our having the range of concepts we have and our having the sense-experiences we have. I complained earlier that Hobbes tends to regard too many concepts as straightforward by-products of our sense-experience. This oversimplification is characteristic of an empiricist theory of thought. The surprising thing is that an empiricist theory should be Hobbes's. For he is plainly *not* one to think that all of our knowledge or much of science results from sensory ideas. Perhaps the best expression of his anti-empiricist attitude is to be found in chapter 15 of *De Corpore*, where he runs through a number of abstract principles about magnitude and motion. Commenting on the principle of the instantaneous propagation through infinite distance of very small motions (ch. 15, vii, E I 216–17), he notes that the very small motions propagated will eventually become indiscernible. It is no objection to the principle, he says, that the very small motion will get weaker and weaker, 'till at last it can no longer be perceived by sense; for motion may be insensible; and I do not here examine things by sense and experience, but by reason'. Elsewhere, in *Leviathan*, he says in so many words that experience is not to be accounted any part of philosophy or science (ch. 46, E III 664). Yet apparently he thinks that experience suffices for all types of thought other than the philosophical or scientific type. He was not an empiricist with respect to all types of thought, only with respect to too many.

2 Sense, appetite and passion

I have been suggesting that some of the difficulties in Hobbes's account of thought, and in his remarks about names and language, accrue from his theory of sense and sense-experience. The upshot is not that he has a bad theory of sense, but that the theory of sense is a bad basis for explaining the extent of our native capacity for cognition and the sources of linguistic ability. In this section we shall again see Hobbes's theory of sense under strain as the basis of his theory of motivation. He thinks that the whole range of our voluntary behaviour, what he calls 'animal motion', is due to the variety and succession of the passions people can be subject to at different times. But the variety of the passions is more a nominal than a real variety. Objectively viewed, the forces that move us to act are all variations of the forces of appetite and aversion, and appetite and aversion are no more than internal motions that arise in the course of sense-experience.

When a body registers in a sensory representation, when for example a person sees something, the thing imparts motion to the innermost part of the organ of sight. One effect of the motion is to set up an outward reaction which produces visual experience. But there can be a further after-effect. The 'motion and agitation of the brain which we call conception' can be 'continued to the heart, and there be called passion' (*EL*, Pt. 1, ch. 8, i. 31). The heart governs 'vital motion' in the body, i.e., the circulation of the blood. In general, when motion derived from an act of sense encourages vital motion, the sentient creature experiences pleasure at the sight, smell or taste of the object of sense, and is disposed to move his body in such a way as to prolong and intensify the pleasure (*De Corp.*, ch. 25, xii, E I 407).

If the object of sense is at a distance from the sentient creature, the creature will typically move toward it (*De Corp.*, ch. 25, xii, E I 407).

The approach toward the object, when it occurs, is the result of a complicated physiological process. The animal spirits impulse into the nerves and retract again, causing muscular swelling and relaxation and eventually full-scale bodily movements (E I 408). The 'first beginnings' of this process, the small movements in the body below the threshold of consciousness that start the process off, Hobbes calls 'appetite' (E I 407). There is a parallel account of aversion (E I 407).

When the after-effect of an act of sense is hindrance of the vital motion, the sentient creature experiences pain or displeasure at the sight, sound or smell of the object of sense, and is disposed to move his body so as to counteract the hindrance. Typically this is a matter of moving away from the object of sense. Aversion consists of the small internal movements that initiate the evasive action.

In the most basic case appetites and aversion are triggered immediately by the act of sense, the mere sight and sound of a thing being enough to prompt approach or retreat. Some things, however, present neutral appearances: it takes a 'trial of their effects' to establish them as objects of appetite or aversion for a given individual (L, ch. 6, E III 40). As a creature grows up it displays an increasingly elaborate pattern of selective response to the things it senses around it (De Corp., ch. 25, xii, E I 407–8). At first it neither actively pursues nor avoids many different things, but as its experience accumulates and as its control over its bodily movements develops, it comes to 'know readily what is to be pursued and avoided' (E I 408). It learns not only to steer clear of remembered sources of displeasure, but also to approach cautiously things whose effects it is unsure of (L, ch. 6, E III 40).

A more or less elaborate experience of various sources of pleasure and pain gives rise in an individual to a more or less elaborate system of valuation. The individual takes as good what it has learned to pursue, and regards as bad what it has learned to avoid. But in developing its system of valuation a creature is not discovering an objective distinction in nature between things that are good and things that are bad. Nothing is good or bad independently of its effects on creatures, and the effects may vary from creature to creature. So at most things are good or bad *to* individuals (L, ch. 6, E III 41), not good or bad 'simply and absolutely'.

The pattern of pleasure and pain in one creature's experience determines the things that are for him good and evil in life. Hobbes denies that in the sphere of good things in life there is any one that is highest and whose pursuit and attainment constitutes happiness (L, ch. 11, E III 85). Instead, there are many different goods for many different individuals. Becoming happy in life is not a matter of being successful in the pursuit of one favoured good, but of being continually successful in the pursuit of many (L, ch. 6, E III 51). So while human action in general is directed at the attainment of happiness and the avoidance of unhappiness, the system in human motivation will not be a system in the types of good pursued, but in the types of passion very diverse goods can inspire in different men. It is types of attitude pro and con things that men have in common, not objects of those attitudes (cf. *L*, Intro, E III xi). Accordingly, when he expounds his theory of motivation, Hobbes usually classifies passions, not their objects.

Though we have many names for the passions, and also passions for which we lack names, Hobbes claims that diversity in types of passions is largely superficial. There are only a few simple types and the rest can be reconstructed from these. He does not carry out the reconstruction at every place where he discusses voluntary or animal motion. In *De Corpore*, which contains perhaps his fullest account of the physical basis of motivation, he does not go far beyond asserting that 'all the passions, called passions of the mind, consist of appetite and aversion, except pure pleasure and pain . . .' (*De Corp.*, ch. 25, xiii, E I 409). In *De Homine* he does better, prefacing a treatment of the main types of passion in chapter 12, with a fairly detailed treatment of pleasure and pain and some of their causes in chapter 11. *The Elements of Law* is another source for an account of the passions (Pt. 1, chs. 7–10). But for the theory at its most elaborate we have to turn to chapter 6 of *Leviathan*. There Hobbes first offers a long chain of definitions of the 'simple passions' of appetite, desire, aversion, hate, joy and grief, and then proceeds to make out many further types as special cases of the simple types.

'Desire' and 'appetite' are taken for near synonyms, signifying the motion of approach toward a pleasing thing. Desire and love 'are the same thing; save that by desire we always signify the absence of the object; love most commonly the presence of the same' (*L*, ch. 6, E III 40). Joy is pleasure that results from the foresight or expectation of an object of pleasure, rather than from its presence (E III 43). On the other side is grief, or pain in anticipation. And aversion stands to hate in the same relation as desire to love (E III 40). These are the simple passions. The rest of the passions get their names from the 'diversification' of names of the simple passions.

> As first, when they one succeed another, they are diversely called from the opinion men have of the likelihood of attaining what they desire. Secondly, from the object loved or hated. Thirdly, from the consideration of many of them together. Fourthly, from the alteration or succession itself (E III 43).

Hobbes goes on to instance the four types. 'Hope' is a name of something included under 'appetite'. It is the name of an appetite, when the appetite co-exists with an opinion of getting the thing. So hope is one of the passions that gets its name from an estimate of the probability of satisfying the appetite. 'Kindness' is a name of a passion of the second type. It designates love, but love with a special kind of object, namely love of persons for society; 'lust' is also love of persons, but it is love of persons for gratifying one's senses (E III 44). Then there are passions which combine two of the simpler passions. Emulation is a case in point. It is part grief at a competitor's success in attaining goods, and part desire to husband one's resources for the sake of similar success for oneself (E III 47). Finally, there are appetites that get their names from their place in a succession of appetites and aversions. A succession of appetites and aversions is what Hobbes thinks a given stretch of practical deliberation consists in (E III 48), and a given appetite is called the will if it is the last in a series of appetites and aversions before the performance of the action.

The identification of will with the last appetite in a succession of appetites and aversions is a key to Hobbes's famous denial of freedom of the will. We shall come to that shortly. First we have to decide whether his attempt to trace all of the passions to a few simple ones, is a success or failure. Since his project is ostensibly that of analysing the names of some passions into names of motions whose causes are specified in a wider theory of sense, and in a still wider mechanical theory of nature, it seems inappropriate to assess his list of glosses on the passion words as if it amounted to an extended piece of descriptive semantics. He does not seem to be recovering the ordinary senses of the terms 'hope', 'kindness', 'lust' and the rest. What he is trying to do instead, is show that a relatively simple theory of cognition and conation is in fact adequate to account for the whole variety of the passions. It is clear that this is how he sees his task in *The Elements of Law*, where a catalogue of the passions similar to *Leviathan*'s is given:

> Having . . . presupposed that motion and agitation in the brain
> which we call conception, to be continued to the heart and there
> to be called passion; I have thereby obliged myself, as far forth as I
> can, to search out and determine, from what conception proceedeth
> every one of those passions, which we commonly take notice of (Pt.
> 1, ch. 8, i. 31).

He is setting out to show that the conceptions we can have are various enough to generate the variety we prescientifically recognize in the passions. Since the variety we prescientifically recognize is indicated in the range of names we have for the passions, he sets up the catalogue in *Leviathan* as if it were a register of the different words for the passions. But there is no evidence I can find that the purpose of the catalogue alters in *Leviathan*. I take it Hobbes is still trying to show that there is enough diversity of agitation in the brain – diversity of conception – to set up a diversity of the passions.

3 Difficulties with the reconstruction of the passions

If empirical rather than semantical reconstruction is what Hobbes is attempting, then it should not matter that some of his glosses on the passion words look revisionary. So we need not task Hobbes for e.g. glossing 'anger' as 'sudden courage' (L, ch. 6, E III 43). We can ask instead whether the causes of the simple appetites and their possibilities of combination, account for the variety of passions we experience. We can ask whether Hobbes succeeds in showing that all of the passions except pure pleasure and pain consist of appetite and aversion.

Unfortunately, the answer seems to be 'No'. The catalogue of the passions does not seem to work as a venture in empirical reconstruction. Partly this is because it is unclear exactly what sort of empirical reconstruction is being attempted. When he deals with the passions that underlie the basic types of behaviour – approach and retreat from the objects of sense – he seems to be trying to show what physiological processes appetite and aversion consist in. But the purely physiological account gives out soon after it has begun. Desire and aversion are dealt with, but love, hate, joy and grief are not treated at all. If a physiological account had been aimed at, it could have been expected to extend to all of the 'simple appetites'.

There is a second reason for thinking that the theory of the passions fails as an empirical theory. Among other things, Hobbes is trying to explain how a sentient creature develops an elaborate stock of pursuit- and avoidance-behaviour. Or, what amounts to the same thing in his terms, he is trying to explain how individuals come over time to discriminate in detail between what seems good and what seems bad. The explanation given is roughly that the fine discriminations are learnt by trial and error. Each person learns what to pursue and avoid largely on the basis of a long succession of pleasant and unpleasant encounters with different objects of sense. It is a highly individualistic account of the way judgments of good and bad are formed, and it helps Hobbes to explain why valuations differ in one person over time and between people at the same time. The reason there can be this variation is that different people have different constitutions, are affected sensually in different ways by different objects, and can encounter different objects as they follow their different spatio-temporal paths. Given equal times and equally diverse sets of experiences, different human beings can work out equally elaborate discriminations between good and bad things. But their discriminations need not agree, because they are differently constituted and because of the differences in their experiences.

The trouble with this highly individualistic account is that it does not seem to fit the case of creatures whose passions Hobbes is most concerned to catalogue, namely creatures like us. He usually neglects the ways in which appetites and aversions are formed by training or conditioning; consequently, he seems to leave out of account the ways in which patterns of training can enforce a single pattern of values that prevails in a wider community. Hobbes does of course admit that it is possible to have one's passions influenced by the eloquence of others (*EL*, Pt. 1, ch. 13, vi–vii. 67-68; *L*, ch. 6, E III 49–51; ch. 25, E III 242f), and by the teaching of others (*De Hom.*, ch. 13, vii. 67f), but he typically regards this as only one influence among others when it can plausibly be claimed to be pre-eminent. He is typically over-individualistic in his account of how people develop their systems of valuation. In his attempt to tie together the effects of sense with the first beginnings of voluntary motion, he seems to look for causes mostly inside the agent and not around him.

4 The succession of the passions and action

The theory of motivation is not confined to an account of the origins and types of passions. Hobbes also considers practical deliberation and acting at will. The main lines of this account can be readily stated. We act at will or voluntarily when an action concludes a process of deliberation (cf. *L&N*, E IV 243). A process of deliberation occurs when

> in the mind of man, appetites and aversions, hopes, and fears, concerning one and the same thing, arise alternately; and divers good and evil consequences of the doing, or omitting the thing propounded, arise successively in our thoughts (*L*, ch. 6, E III 47).

A process of deliberation *ends* when the 'thing propounded' is either done, omitted, or thought impossible (E III 48). And what makes the resulting action or omission voluntary is its relation to the particular appetite or aversion that calls a halt to the deliberation. This appetite or aversion is the one not only immediately preceding, but 'immediately adhering' to the action or omission (E III 48). It is the agent's will on the basis of deliberation, and it necessitates the performance of the action that follows. Of an agent who does what he wills, it is not true to say that he could have done otherwise; an agent is only free as long as his deliberation has not reached a conclusion (*L&N*, E IV 273); once he ceases to consider the pros and cons of a propounded action, what happens next is bound to happen. Freedom is not a matter of being able to confound or cancel one's choices at the last moment; it is a matter of making a choice and not being hindered in its execution (*L&N*, E IV 273).

Criticism of this doctrine from Hobbes's day to our own has tended to focus on the idea that to act at will is to perform an action that is necessitated. But in Hobbes's own exposition the stress is often laid elsewhere. In *De Corpore*, for instance, he underlines the point that the type of deliberation he describes is as much within the capacity of beasts as of men (ch. 25, xiii, E I 409). And in *Leviathan* he stresses that on his view, an action can be voluntary though it is prompted by fear and other aversions (ch. 6, E III 49). This last point looks forward to his arguments concerning the covenant that establishes the commonwealth. The covenant is entered into and kept going voluntarily, but it is entered into and kept going for fear of the consequences of doing otherwise. The other point, that a succession of appetites and aversions can occur in the minds of living creatures other than men, helps him to distinguish between two types of deliberation. One kind comes naturally to us, and tends to reflect the balance of pleasure and pain we have experienced in the past in the pursuit of what is gratifying; the other kind is informed by the dictates of reason or laws of nature, and is available only to those, i.e. men, who are fitted to discover the causes of war and peace.

By contrast with the matters just mentioned, the point that actions are necessitated seems to be put over as if it were uncontroversial. Even in *Of Liberty and Necessity*, where Hobbes considers the issue at some length in reply to criticisms from Bishop Bramhall, he ends up by saying that much of what he says about free will is no more than a distillation of what we ordinarily mean when we say that an action is spontaneous, that a man deliberates, that something is a man's will, or that an agent is free.[1] Probably Hobbes exaggerates the innocence of his views, but even if that is so, the exaggeration does not seem to be serious. He goes wrong not so much in what he says about the necessitation of action as in what he takes for granted about deliberation, action and aversion.

Here is how he puts over what I take to be his crucial contention in the free will controversy:

> I conceive that nothing taketh beginning from *itself*, but from the *action* of some other immediate agent without itself. And that therefore, when first a man hath an *appetite* or *will* to something, to which before he had no appetite nor will, the *cause* of his will, is not the *will* itself, but *something* else not in his own disposing. So that whereas it is out of controversy, that of *voluntary* actions the *will* is the *necessary* cause, and by this which is said, the *will* is also caused by other things whereof it disposeth not, it followeth, that voluntary actions have all of them necessary causes, and therefore are *necessitated* (*L&N*, E IV 274).

This is little more than an application of a principle we have seen Hobbes invoke many times before: there is always a local external cause of any effect or species of motion in a given thing. In the case under discussion, the principle holds that there is a local external cause of a given internal motion, such as an appetite, in a sentient thing. Whatever exactly the cause of the appetite, it must be some aggregate of accidents such that the aggregate being present, the appetite cannot but be created or under-stood to be formed at the same time. (This much follows from the definition of 'cause' (cf. *De Corp.*, ch. 9, iii, E I 122).) Since the appetite in question is identical with the agent's will, the cause, being external to the appetite, must be something outside the will, and so not in the agent's disposing. No doubt Hobbes's argument as quoted contains an illicit step from 'There is something outside the will that causes it' to 'There is something outside the agent's control that causes the will', but it does not seem to jeopardize the independently plausible conclusion, which is that actions done at will are partly determined to happen by events we do not will to happen.

If Hobbes were only claiming that actions are wholly the outcome of their causes, and that some parts of the total cause of an action are things we have no control over, his view would be exactly as innocent and uncontroversial as he claims it is. Yet his position does seem to be stronger, and somehow implausible. When a voluntary action is necessi-tated in Hobbes's sense, it not only occurs but is such that it couldn't have failed to occur. This seems wrong, but in a way it is hard to capture. One possible objection is that Hobbes's account seems unfaithful to what it is actually like to weigh up pros and cons, choose and act. When an agent is for a time of two minds about what to do, then decides, he may have the vivid sense of being able to back out even as he is poised to do as he has chosen. Perhaps what is wrong with Hobbes's account is that it seems to deny that there is a real possibility of backing out where the agent thinks there is. But it is not clear that Hobbes must deny the possibility of backing out in the sense just described; all he need deny is that where this possibility exists the agent has really made up his mind. So long as the option of not doing as he has chosen is still a factor in his deliberation, the agent's deliberation is not at an end.

Though the objection just considered is easy for Hobbes to deflect, it does gesture at a genuine area of difficulty in his general treatment of action. The account tends to fasten on actions as events that have occurred rather than as things that, while still the topic of deliberation, are merely possible and contemplated in prospect. Yet it is as things so contemplated that actions seem contingent to agents. And it is as things we can imagine being so contemplated that actions, once they have been performed, can seem less than inevitable to us as observers. Though Hobbes may be right to hold that our actions are determined down to the last detail by preceding events, he seems to misdiagnose the source of our impression of their contingency. It is not that we cling to the idea that there is a special class of actions that are uncaused. It is not that, being ignorant of the chain of causes that led up to an action, we feign a gap in the chain or some lack in what is otherwise a total cause: it is that we are able imaginatively to reconstruct a process in which options other than the one decided for were real options for the agent.

The misdiagnosis is unsurprising given that Hobbes's theory of action is weak on the topic of agency.[2] It is not exactly true that Hobbes ignores the relation between agents and actions, but to the extent the relation is acknowledged, it tends to be reduced to a relation between events that take place *in* an agent, and their effects. The idea of an agent's being the source of his actions is incompletely recovered: at best room is made for the idea of an agent's being the *site* of the causes of some effects. Hobbes mistrusts the idea of a power of willing from which a great many actions are mysteriously elicited (*L&N*, E IV 266). But in reducing the power of willing to the collection of acts of will, and in construing acts of will as episodes that merely terminate a certain succession of appetites and aversions, Hobbes deprives himself of the framework he needs if he is to make what he claims are perfectly familiar connections between the concepts of deliberation, voluntary action, liberty and spontaneity. He depicts deliberation as a process that begins and ends and involves a succession of appetites and aversions; but it does not seem to be a process an agent initiates; and it does not seem to involve any articulated notion of the *weighing* of considerations pro and con. The agent does not *conclude* that all things considered, such and such is the thing to do; the succession of appetite and aversion merely stops and the agent acts accordingly. He is more the medium than the controller of the process of deliberation, and so not much like the deliberator we are apt to conceive pre-theoretically.

VIII

The Pursuit of Felicity and the Good of Survival

What is the connection between Hobbes's theory of the things that move people to act, and his claim in the moral and political treatises that people who act freely will come into conflict with one another? He is often read as saying that when people act freely they are moved by self-interest alone. And at times he seems to say that each person has an overriding interest in having the largest share of the goods everyone pursues. If these are points that Hobbes makes, then they give a simple connection between the theory of motivation and the claim about conflict. They do so, however, at the cost of saddling Hobbes with a psychological doctrine, namely egoism, it is hard to credit. People *can* be expected to come into conflict with one another if what matters most to each is getting ahead of everyone else in the race for goods. And the desire to be foremost makes sense if one acts only for one's own benefit. What is hard to believe is that people do act only for their own benefit. Does Hobbes claim as much?

No. According to the interpretation to be given here, he holds that it is possible, though unusual, for people to act benevolently. But he also holds that in a situation of total liberty it is so dangerous to act benevolently as to be against reason to do so. One may feel like promoting the good of someone else, one may even see that it is necessary to do so if it will not put one's life at risk. The trouble is that in a situation of total liberty, or in the state of nature, every benevolent action *is* highly risky, and foreseeably so. The only thing it is rational and therefore permissible to do is to pursue one's good at the expense of everyone else. Not to act ruthlessly is to hasten one's own death, according to Hobbes, and no-one can be blamed for not hastening his own death. Considerations about survival are always supposed to be overriding in clearheaded practical reasoning, and it is considerations about survival that recommend ruthlessness. But they can come into one's deliberation alongside strongly felt benevolent impulses, or alongside clearly recognized hypothetical

96

imperatives enjoining the helpful gesture. Hobbes does not deny the power of benevolence to move us, only the rationality of acting benevolently no matter what.

1 Egoism

Bishop Butler is one famous exponent of the view that Hobbes denied the reality of human benevolence, and traced its appearance to the operation of selfish forces. In a long footnote to the first of his *Fifteen Sermons Preached at the Rolls Chapel*, Butler reports Hobbes as claiming that the principle in the mind underlying anyone's display of apparent benevolence is 'only the love of power, and delight in the exercise of it.'[1] To support this reading Butler cites chapter 9, section 17 of *Human Nature*, the book made up from Part One of *The Elements of Law* and published in 1650. Butler seems to have in mind the opening sentences of section 17, where Hobbes writes,

> There is yet another passion, sometimes called *love*, but more properly *good will* or *charity*. There can be no greater argument to a man, of his own power, than to find himself able not only to accomplish his own desires, but also to assist other men in theirs: and this is that conception wherein consisteth *charity* (E IV 49).

As I read it this does *not* identify charity with the love of power or the delight in exercising it. The passage identifies charity with finding oneself able to assist others in accomplishing their desires, and it also says that what one finds, when one finds oneself able to help others, is power greater than is needed just to fulfil one's own desires. The passage says nothing about taking delight in exercising the power one finds one has, and nothing about love of power.[2] So Butler's criticism is ill-founded.

Instead of denying that there is such a thing as benevolence or charity, Hobbes denies that benevolence ever operates outside one's inner circle of family and friends. The 'affection wherewith men many times bestow their benefits on *strangers*, is not to be called charity, but either *contract*, whereby they seek to purchase friendship, or fear, which maketh them to purchase peace' (*HN*, ch. 9, xvii, E IV 49). He has doubts, too, about the reality of charity in the form of Platonic love. But these doubts leave ample room for a recognizable if unextensive charity. Even in Hobbes's famous, largely cynical comparison of life to a race, charity does not appear to be reduced to a self-regarding attitude. To be charitable in the race is to carry someone to whom you are bound by love (*HN*, ch. 9, xxi, E IV 53).

Pity is another attitude one would expect Hobbes to reconstruct as narrowly self-regarding if he were a psychological egoist. But again, when he characterizes pity in terms afforded by his race metaphor, he

THE PURSUIT OF FELICITY AND THE GOOD OF SURVIVAL

says that it is to 'see one out-gone whom we would not' (*HN*, ch. 9, xxi, E IV 53) i.e., to see a fellow racer overtaken whom we would not. There is nothing particularly selfish about pity so described. How is it with the more formal treatment of pity in *Human Nature*? Chapter 9, section 10, says that pity is

> imagination, or *fiction* of *future* calamity to ourselves, proceeding from the sense of *another* man's calamity.

Butler complains that if this were correct, 'fear and compassion would be the same idea' and that the phrase 'pity for one's friends' would make no sense, the object of pity being always oneself. Both objections are muddled. Hobbes does not mention fear, nor is 'imagination or fiction of future calamity' short for 'fear' as Hobbes uses the term. As he uses it 'fear' signifies aversion in relation to a thing from which one *expects* displeasure (*HN*, ch. 7, ii, E IV 32). Accordingly, for pity to involve fear, the 'sense of another's calamity' would have to create the *expectation* of the same calamity's befalling oneself; Hobbes says plainly enough that another's plight can cause pity if we merely *imagine* ourselves similarly placed. Again, though he does not suppose that pity is a selfless attitude, though he holds that it is by way of imagining a calamity befalling oneself that one feels pity for another, it does not follow that the *object* of the pity can only be oneself: the object of the pity can be the very person whose misfortune makes one picture oneself similarly placed.

Compatibly with his other glosses on the passion-words in *Human Nature*, Hobbes could have said, perfectly unexceptionably, that pity is *grief* at another's calamity. For grief is the kind of pain we feel when, though we are not physically hurt, we feel hurt by something none the less (*HN*, ch. 7, viii, E IV 34). In chapter 6 of *Leviathan* he does adopt 'grief at the calamity of another' as the relevant gloss (E III 47). Similarly, in *De Homine*, he says that to be compassionate is to 'grieve because of another's evil and to suffer with him' (ch. 12, x. 61).

The theory of the passions may not be egoistic in letter, but isn't it egoistic in spirit? Many commentators concede the charge of egoism is well-founded when it is directed against *The Elements of Law* or *Human Nature*, but they deny that *Leviathan*'s account of motivation can sustain a similar interpretation.[5] I doubt that Hobbes's published views about the passions changed very much, and so I doubt that *Leviathan*'s non-egoistic theory is really a departure from the one in *The Elements of Law* or *Human Nature*. If psychological egoism holds that people never act to benefit others,[6] then Hobbes was never a psychological egoist. Even when he says that the life of man is well compared to a race in which each racer's goal is to be foremost, this does not exclude one racer's helping another to come a close second, or suffering with someone whom one wishes to come a close second, but who has fallen behind.

In short, having the goal of being foremost does not rule out one's wishing or helping others to do well. Hobbes doubted the possibility of extending one's good wishes and good offices to perfect strangers, but his remarks about charity suggest that it was quite natural to offer them to friends and family. To that extent it is not even clear that in *spirit* Hobbes's doctrine falls in with psychological egoism.

'Egoism' may be the right label for Hobbes's position if the term is defined broadly enough. A formulation that provides the necessary breadth is Thomas Nagel's:

> Egoism holds that each individual's reasons for acting, and possible motivations for acting, must arise from his own interests and desires, however those interests may be defined. The interests of one person can on this view motivate another or provide him with a reason only if they are connected with some sentiment of his, like sympathy, pity or benevolence.[7]

This is wide enough to accommodate both Hobbes's belief in at any rate limited benevolence, and his saying that 'of the voluntary acts of every man, the object is some *good to himself*' (*L*, ch. 14, E III 120; *EL*, Pt. 1, ch. 14, vi. 71; *De Cive*, ch. 2, viii, E II 19; *De Hom.*, ch. 11, vi. 48). The question is whether this wider form of egoism is objectionable. Nagel thinks that psychologically speaking it would be very peculiar in practice,[8] and he tries to show that quite apart from how it would operate in regard to other people, 'it is objectionable in its application by each person to his own case, and to his own reasons for action'.[9] More generally, Nagel holds that if egoism were the truth about reasons for action, then would-be moral requirements would not have the inescapability they ought to have. Their having the power to motivate would depend on the presence of desires or interests an agent could conceivably lack, or have without being required to accept them.[10] If Hobbes is an egoist in the broad sense, then, according to the line of thought just sketched, he threatens to deprive himself of a genuine ethical theory.

Since it is possible to have doubts about the thesis that moral requirements are inescapable or else not moral requirements,[11] Nagel's line of thought may itself require a defence. But even if his Kantian intuitions are allowed to pass unchallenged, it is not obvious that Hobbes falls foul of them. It is true that for him all reasons for action are traceable ultimately to a desire or interest one is merely subject to, and which it would not make sense to say one was required to accept: on the other hand, the relevant desire or interest, namely the desire to preserve one's life, is such that one could not conceivably lack it and be a rational, living animal, i.e., a human being. Hobbes's theory of motivation does cater for *that* sort of inescapability. What it does not do, as we shall see, is capture the inescapability in the way Kantians would like. It does not disentangle the foundations of morals from what Kant called 'anthropology'. It does not make the motivation for being moral a distinctively moral motivation.

2 War and the free pursuit of felicity

Though Hobbes is no psychological egoist, he may well be committed to the 'ethical egoism' Nagel takes issue with. But is anything wrong with ethical egoism? And is it this version of egoism that connects Hobbes's theory of motivation with his claim that people will come into conflict if allowed to do what they like? To answer these questions it is necessary to look in more detail at Hobbes's theory of motivation. What emerged in the last chapter was only part of the theory, the part designed to show, among other things, that the different passions were no more than varieties of motion. It remains to see which of the passions typically animate human behaviour, especially the behaviour of men in groups. More generally, we need to discover which factors, according to Hobbes, make it both difficult and necessary for men to combine into civil societies. These matters belong to what we may call his substantive theory of motivation. The key to the theory is the concept of felicity.

Felicity is the smooth and orderly achievement of the many distinct desires one has in a lifetime. Hobbes emphasizes that it is an active condition, and not one of repose after a long run of success. To experience felicity *is* to have had success in the past, but it is also to be too occupied with a current project to look back. The 'great grief' of not knowing what to do next is no part of felicity (cf. *EL*, Pt. 1, ch. 7, vii. 30). Instead, felicity involves continual success (*L* ch. 6, E III 51) relative to a series of desires in which one desire shows the way to the next (*L*, ch. 11, E III 85). Hobbes sometimes requires for felicity that in the passage from one success to another the agent should meet with little hindrance (*De Hom.*, ch. 11, xv. 54), implying that felicity is marred rather than enhanced when consistent success involves a lot of effort. The core idea, however, is that of continually getting what one wants.

Since individuals can differ markedly in what they want (*L*, ch. 6, E III 40–41), one person's felicity may not be another's. And since individuals can differ markedly in how they go about getting what they want (cf. *L*, ch. 11, E III 85), even when they want the same thing, one person's *pursuit* of felicity need not be another's. What, then, can be said in general about felicity and the pursuit of it? One thing Hobbes manages to say in *Leviathan* is that the desire for power, the more the better, goes with the pursuit of felicity (*L*, ch. 11, E III 85–6). By 'power' he means some present means to a future good (*L*, ch. 10, E III 74). He has in mind not only special strengths of body and character a person may naturally possess, but also things that can be acquired, such as riches, reputation and friends (*L*, ch. 10, E III 74). These are things people want and have reason to pursue no matter what their ultimate ends are.

Also, and crucially, these means to future goods are things people can never have enough of. The reason is not that people are always greedy for power, but that they are competitors, and any advantage in power one competitor has over another can be short-lived unless he constantly increases his power (cf. *L*, ch. 11, E III 86). Take natural advantages in power. Hobbes does not deny that some people are born to be quicker witted or physically stronger than others, but he doubts that there are any insuperable natural advantages. If one person is brawnier than another, for example, the difference can usually be made up by the powers of a few weaker people who join forces (cf. *L*, ch. 13, E III 110). In a similar way, it is possible for naturally clever people to be outwitted by competitors who, though duller, have longer experience (*L*, ch. 13, E III 110). Advantages in respect of riches, friends, servants and reputation are also assailable – by force, fraud, bribery and defamation (cf. *L*, ch. 13, E III 115). Unless special efforts are made to consolidate it, practically any advantage can be eaten away by determined competitors who know what they are doing.[12]

Can people be blamed for consolidating a personal advantage by foul means, or weakening the position of a competitor through force and fraud? Not if the only thing that governs anyone's activity is the goal of felicity in Hobbes's sense. Felicity is continual success in one's undertakings. If what one undertakes is to do down one's competitors, then any means that achieves that will be permissible. Or if, as is more likely, one aims at something else, doing down one's competitors can still often promote one's goal. Even the moderate man who wants only a small share of the good life can have reason to resort to foul means if he thinks he will lose everything by playing fair with rivals. In general, the goal of felicity requires one to get an advantage and keep it. One way of doing this is by disabling other people. And the most effective way of disabling other people is to kill them. So long as it is common knowledge that people will try to get or increase an advantage over others, perhaps by disabling others, no-one can be sure that he is not on someone else's hit list. So survival becomes a thing one has consciously to struggle for.

Struggling for survival is far removed from felicity, but the demands of pursuing felicity threaten to reduce one to struggling for survival. This is the message of each of the moral and political treatises, where the so-called state of nature is discussed (*EL*, Pt. 1, ch. 14; *De Cive*, ch. 1, *L*, ch. 13). Hobbes argues that if no common power exists to prevent them doing so, vainglorious people will pursue felicity ruthlessly. Moderate people, concerned with safety before felicity, will have reason to act violently to pre-empt the attacks of the vainglorious. And in any case people will be set against one another by the mere fact of having to compete for goods everyone wants. Whether they are vicious, virtuous or morally indifferent, people who pursue felicity, and who have no common power to fear, must suffer from a general insecurity Hobbes calls 'war'.

By 'war' he does not mean only open fighting between large numbers of men. It is enough that most men show they are *willing* to come to blows (*EL*, Pt. 1, ch. 14, xi. 73; *De Cive*, ch. 1, xi, E II 11; *L*, ch. 13 E III 113). Hobbes recognizes what we would now call 'cold war', and he does not under-estimate its costs. When most people show that they are willing to enter a fight that can be foreseen to be a fight to the death, most people are unlikely to channel their efforts into production. If people agree to work at all while under the threat of all-out war, then according to Hobbes they will tend to produce things on their own and for themselves. War, even cold war, threatens production by the division of labour, and indeed threatens to halt production of any kind (*EL*, Pt. 1, ch. 14, xi. 73; *De Cive*, ch. 1, xi, E II 11; *L*, ch. 13, E III 113). It also threatens to impede the development of the arts and sciences. And the effects of open as against latent war are of course much worse. Besides the loss of the good of society, open war brings with it the loss of the good of assured survival and the probable loss of life itself.

Hobbes's main negative conclusion, when he describes man's prospects for felicity in the state of nature, is that the prospects are poor. What comes naturally to human beings, what they will do if there is nothing to prevent them, is wage war in the pursuit of felicity, and thereby make themselves miserable. Hobbes thinks he is able to *demonstrate* that the seeds of war are present in the behaviour of pre-political or totally free men; but he claims his conclusion is also borne out by the behaviour of people who live in civil societies, people such as his readers. In *Leviathan* he invites anyone to test his 'inference from the passions' against experience.

> Let him therefore consider with himself, when taking a journey, he
> arms himself, and seeks to go well accompanied; when going to
> sleep, he locks his doors; when even in his house he locks his chests;
> and this when he knows there be laws, and public officers, armed,
> to revenge all injuries shall be done him; what opinion he has of his
> fellow subjects, when he rides armed; of his fellow citizens, when he
> locks his doors; and of his children, and servants, when he locks his
> chests. Does he not there as much accuse mankind by his actions, as
> I do by my words? (*L*, ch. 13, E III 114)

A similar question rounds off a similar line of thought in *De Cive* (Pref. to the Reader, E II xv). But the answer to the question is in fact not the one Hobbes wants.

Someone who takes the precautions described does not show by his actions that he has a certain view of human nature, for the thoughts that inform his actions need not be about mankind or every human being or most human beings. The man who locks his doors and chests need only live in the fear that some people or other – he doesn't know which – are disposed to attack and rob him; he need not believe that everyone is prepared to attack and rob. It is true that the locks on the cautious man's chests and doors present an obstacle to everyone indifferently: it does not follow that he locks his chests and doors against everyone. Hobbes's main negative conclusion is not proved twice over. It has only the backing of his abstract argument from felicity and the passions of man.

3 Egoism and the avoidability of war

How good is the abstract argument? Does it show that men will come into conflict if left to pursue felicity unhindered? It is tempting to dismiss the argument as uncompelling, on the ground that it leans heavily on uncompelling egoistic assumptions. But in fact the argument does not assume that strong selfish drives are part of the human make-up, and it does not *have* to assume as much in order to connect war in the required way with the pursuit of felicity.

In *Leviathan* (ch. 11) and *De Homine* Hobbes freely admits that human behaviour displays a great variety of settled inclinations or 'manners', in their turn underpinned by a great variety of appetites. Some of these, notably the appetite for 'knowledge and arts of peace' are definitely unselfish, and certain dispositions, such as the disposition to worship an invisible power, are not necessarily selfish. Again, even in the work in which Hobbes is at his most cynical about people, *The Elements of Law*, he recognizes that there are moderate or temperate men (*EL*, Pt. 1, ch. 14, iii. 71; *De Cive*, ch. 1, iv, E II 7), men who neither credit themselves with more power or worth than anyone else, nor want for themselves a larger share of goods than anyone else. These men, presumably unselfish, can nevertheless be as much disposed to fight as others in the state of nature, for though they are content with a moderate share of goods, vainglorious men drive them into protecting this moderate share by force. Temperate men go to war reluctantly, but they go to war all the same, and they do not lose their claim to be temperate by having a show of force wrested from them. So not all parties to the war in the state of nature have to be assumed to be selfish for Hobbes's abstract argument to work.

Hobbes does of course claim that whenever human beings act, they act for what they take to be their own good, and this claim is egoistic, in the wide sense of 'ethical egoism'. I doubt, however, that this claim bears any of the weight of the argument for the inevitability of war in the state of nature. The crucial premises are that felicity requires power enough to assure an accrued well-being, and that the power required has always got to be more than the power competitors can muster. Whether or not these premises are disputable, they do not seem to display a bias toward egoism. To see this it will help to consider an example involving an unselfish, indeed a self-sacrificing, character. Imagine a Mother Teresa figure whose work in life is curing people of heroin addiction. Let us stipulate that she has no end of good will. So strong is her love of humanity, in fact, that she wishes no harm to come even to heroin dealers. What she wants most of all is a state of affairs in which heroin dealers are ineffectual; what she does not want is a situation in which heroin dealers are ineffectual because they are deprived of their life or liberty. Compatibly with her scruples could she not wish for a state of affairs in which those trying to prevent and undo heroin addiction had such powers of dissuasion and cure as to make all future dealers' efforts come to nothing? If so, then we have a case in which a strongly non-egoistic life's work can be scrupulously pursued without compromising Hobbes's assumptions about power. The Mother Teresa figure wants heroin dealers to lose nothing but their incentive to stay in the heroin trade, and she gets what she wants if the powers ranged against the dealers are always more than a match for them. It does not suffice for her felicity that the powers on her side are only temporarily more than a match for those of heroin dealers. She wants, in conformity with Hobbes's assumptions, the power permanently to have the advantage over her adversaries. There is no reason to think, then, that Hobbes's premisses are only at home in the setting of egoism.

Egoistic premises do come into Hobbes's general theory of conflict, but they operate not in the argument for the inevitability of war in the state of nature, but in the argument for the avoidability of war once the state of nature has been left behind. Officially, of course, this is the argument that matters most. For whatever else Hobbes's political writings are supposed to do, they are supposed to show to an audience of malcontents living under government that the costs of getting rid of government are greater than the costs of suffering with one. A subject who wills an end to government violates a covenant, it being by a covenant that a civil society can be understood to be established and maintained. To violate a covenant is to act unjustly, and to act unjustly is morally wrong, because it tends to disturb the peace. Any action that tends to disturb the peace must be omitted, on pain otherwise of increasing the chances of war and premature death. Actions that increase the chances of premature death must be omitted, because it is against reason not to take all reasonable steps to preserve one's life.

That, of course, is only a sketch of an argument Hobbes states very elaborately, and in more than one way, in *The Elements of Law, De*

Cive and *Leviathan*. Still, the sketch shows how the justice of remaining under government depends on something else – self-preservation – that anyone can be assumed to care about whether or not he cares about the claims of his co-covenanters upon him. Hobbes offers what is ostensibly a moral argument, and yet he allows its persuasive power to arise from an agent's clear-headed view of what is in his own interest. Someone who is moved by the argument to bear with the inconveniences of government, can be moved to go on submitting to a sovereign power only because there is something in it for him. Considerations of justice thus seem to be bent to the requirements of what was earlier called 'ethical egoism'. Doesn't this mean Hobbes's argument is not a moral one after all?

In order to counter insinuations of egoism, or the general charge that Hobbes offered no moral argument for living under government, commentators sometimes call attention to evidence in the text of a possible duplication of reasons for civil obedience, some prudential, others moral.[13] Or if not a duplication of moral and prudential reasons, then a duality of systems of motives and obligations, the system of motives geared to the supreme principle of self-preservation, the system of obligations geared ultimately to the need to 'obey natural law regarded as the will of God'.[14] With many others, I doubt that these interpretations make good sense of Hobbes's texts. But I am suspicious of them for another reason, too, which is that they read into Hobbes a strict distinction between prudential and moral motivation he does not seem to have been sensitive to at all. Like the claim that he flouted the distinction,[15] or the claim that he tried to collapse it,[16] the claim that he actually drew the distinction in the case for civil obedience, or that he devised a moral theory in a sense of 'moral' that contrasts with 'prudential' and excludes egoism, seems to me to be mistaken.

4 Hobbes's sense of 'moral'

The argument for obedience to the prevailing political power does purport to be a moral argument, but in a sense of 'moral' that is far less pointed than latter-day commentary sometimes assumes. The argument justifies obedience to a sovereign, or to a sovereign's laws, by reference to obligations people have under the laws of nature.

One law of nature enjoins the performance of covenants (*L*, ch. 15, E III 130; ch. *EL*, Pt. 1, ch. 16, i. 81f.; *De Cive*, ch. 3, i. E II 29), and it is by covenants that sovereigns are empowered to promulgate whatever laws they in fact promulgate, so long as they are promulgated with a view to the security of the commonwealth. Another, more fundamental law of nature, justifies one's entering into the relevant covenants. Covenants are acts by which rights are laid down now for the sake of some good later, and one is obliged by the more fundamental law of nature to lay down, under certain circumstances, any rights that endanger peace or prolong war (*L*, ch. 14, E III 118; cf. *EL*, Pt. 1, ch. 15, ii. 75; *De Cive*, ch. 2, ii. E II 17). This law of nature is justified by the most fundamental law of nature of all, which enjoins people to seek peace by all means, where there is any hope of getting it (*L*, ch. 14, E III 117; cf. *EL*, Pt. 1, ch. 14, xiv. 74; *De Cive*, ch. 2, ii, E II 16). Ultimately, Hobbes's case for civil obedience rests on an appeal to the fundamental law of nature; but the incentive to do what the fundamental law says, is created by a general desire for avoiding harm and doing oneself good. As for the general desire, it is inescapable if one is human, for it is inescapable if one is a living creature.

The argument for civil obedience is supposed to be a moral argument, because the laws of nature the argument invokes are supposed to be moral laws (cf. *EL*, Pt. 1, ch. 18, i. 95; *De Cive*, ch. 3, xxxi, E II 47). 'Moral' in what sense? 'The laws mentioned in the former chapters,' Hobbes writes in *The Elements of Law* (Pt. 1, ch. 18, i. 95), '[are called] moral laws, because they concern men's manners and conversation one towards another'. In *De Cive* it is because the natural law 'commands also good manners or the practice of virtue' that it is called 'moral' (ch. 3, xxxi, E II 48). In *Leviathan*, Hobbes's ground for calling the doctrine of the laws of nature 'moral philosophy' is that 'the science of virtue and vice, is moral philosophy' (ch. 15, E III 146). These comments suggest that if we are to fix the sense 'moral' had for Hobbes, we should do so within the context of what he had to say about manners, or about vice (bad manners) and virtue (good manners).

In this connection it pays to begin with Hobbes's remarks about the ways in which he innovates in moral philosophy. He taxes previous writers with having failed to say in what the goodness of actions called virtuous consists (*L*, ch. 15, E III 146–7; *EL*, Pt. 1, ch. 18, xiv. 94; *De Cive*, ch. 3, xxxii, E II 48). He claims to make good the omission in his doctrine of the laws of nature. In his own doctrine, he points out, what makes it good to act charitably, modestly, justly and so on, is that actions of those kinds promote unity and peace. Symmetrically, what makes it bad to act unjustly, vaingloriously, etc., is the tendency of those actions to produce war or discord.

Hobbes always contrasts his own proposal about the ground of vice and virtue with what he claims is Aristotle's rival suggestion that the goodness of virtue consists in keeping to a mean between extremes (*L*, ch. 15, E III 146–7; *EL*, Pt. 1, ch. 18, xiv. 94; *De Cive*, ch. 3, xxxii, E II 48). In fact, Hobbes is closer to Aristotle than he realizes. His criticism of the doctrine of the mean is misdirected, and misdirected in a way that matters to fixing Hobbes's sense of 'moral'. The doctrine of the mean is Aristotle's attempt to define the moral virtues, not an attempt to say what makes them good. Aristotle's views on the latter topic are to be found where he connects the moral virtues with happiness or flourishing. The moral virtues are good, according to Aristotle, because a flourishing or happy life cannot be had without them, and a flourishing or happy life is one in which one has as many of the external and bodily goods as help one to enjoy to the full the goods of the soul.[17] Now Aristotle's flourishing life is defined differently from Hobbes's safe or secure life within the state. But each is supposed to be the best sort of life it is possible for human beings to lead. And in Aristotle and Hobbes alike, what are called the moral virtues are precisely the qualities or characteristics that are appropriate for leading the best sort of human life.

The fact that Hobbes identifies the moral virtues with ones that contribute to the social good of peace, is sometimes taken as evidence that his moral philosophy is genuinely other-regarding, and so pointedly 'moral', 'moral' in a sense that contrasts with 'prudential'.[18] On the other hand, the fact that Hobbes is careful to reconcile the practice of virtue, especially the practice of justice or covenant-keeping, with self-interested voluntary action (cf. *L*, ch. 14, E III 120), is sometimes taken to show that no genuinely moral motivation is catered for in Hobbes's doctrine.[19] Both interpretations are to be expected if Hobbes's moral philosophy is, like Aristotle's, systematic guidance for living well or doing well: the concept of doing or living well is neither definitely self-regarding nor definitely other-regarding, and a concept of moral virtue geared to doing or living well inherits this indefiniteness.[20]

Is it correct to regard the doctrine of the laws of nature as a doctrine of virtue roughly comparable to Aristotle's? Hobbes's legalistic language obscures, but does not rule out, similarities. Sometimes he makes it seem as if virtue consisted in unconditional obedience by the will to divine decrees or commandments, a way of putting things that seems far removed from Aristotle's talk of forming the right habits and developing the right dispositions in order to make the right choices. On the other hand, there are passages in *Leviathan* and elsewhere that make it clear that 'law of nature' is in more than one way a figure of speech, and that it is not to be interpreted strictly. Usually these passages call attention to a difference between a rationally-discovered precept, which is not really a law, and the command of someone who has the right to have his will done, which *is* a law (cf. e.g. *L*, ch. 15, E III 147). But there are also places where Hobbes says that by 'laws of nature' he means certain dispositions. Thus, in chapter 26 of *Leviathan* he says that 'the laws of nature, which consist in equity, justice, gratitude, and other moral virtues on these depending, in the condition of mere nature, . . . are not really laws, but qualities that dispose men to peace and obedience' (E III 253). Hobbes seems to think that these qualities are put in men by God, and that considerations about war make men conscious of what the qualities dispose them to do, namely seek peace, transfer rights, keep covenants, and so on. This view of the moral virtues as dispositions latent in the human make-up, which it takes reasoning about war to disclose and activate, and a sovereign's commands to channel into specific types of activity, has a counterpart in Aristotle's view about natural virtue and virtue in the full sense.[21]

Despite that, it might be thought that Hobbes cannot be putting forward a doctrine of virtue in which the virtues are means to the good life. 'For surely,' the objection runs, 'if what the virtues are for is living peaceably, then given how austere Hobbes allows the life of peace or the secure life within the state to be, it can happen that though it is the best sort of life available to men, it is not recognizably a good life.' There is something in this complaint, for Hobbes does write at times as if life in civil society were good only relative to the condition men would be in if they were stateless. When he deals in *Leviathan* with the objection that life under a sovereign power would be very miserable for the sovereign's subjects (*L*, ch. 18, E III 169–70), he seems to concede that it *could* be very miserable, but, even so, not nearly so miserable as life with no sovereign power. Elsewhere, however, he denies that sovereign power serves its purpose when all it effects is a 'bare preservation' of the people who agree to live under it (*L*, ch. 30, E III 322). The safety of the people, which is the *raison d'être* of the state, must be interpreted to contain 'all other contentments of life, which every man by lawful industry, without danger, or hurt to the commonwealth, shall acquire to himself' (*L*, ch. 30, E III 322).[22] This sort of comment seems calculated to make the secure life coincide pretty well with a standard idea of a good life, and the comment seems to be characteristic (cf. *EL*, Pt. 2, ch. 5, i. 137–8; ch. 9, i. 178–9; *De Cive*, ch. 13, iv, E II 167).

5 An acceptable concept of morality?

Even if Hobbes does cater, and cater consciously, for a convergence of the secure with the good life, is his case for doing whatever will prolong the secure life acceptable as a moral argument? We are back to the question of whether his argument appeals to self-interest in a way that undercuts its claim to be a moral argument. Perhaps in a modern sense of 'moral', one we cannot unlearn, the argument is unacceptable. The possibility is not ruled out by Hobbes's appeal to what *he* calls 'moral virtues' or 'moral obligations'. If Hobbes's critics in our own day are right, his system of obligation is consciously devised so that e.g. the obligation to act justly *never* conflicts with self-interest, and in the sense of 'moral' that matters to the critics, no obligation that invariably coincides with self-interest deserves to be called 'moral'.[23] At times the claim that Hobbes excludes the possibility of a conflict between moral obligation and self-interest, is connected with the claim that only selfish reasons for action weigh with the Hobbesian agent.[24]

The second of these claims seems to me to be clearly incorrect. Though it is probably true that any action a Hobbesian agent performs is done in his self-interest, it is important that an action can be self-interested without being purely selfish. Actions done out of what Hobbes calls 'charity' are cases in point, since they are done to help people other than the agent. But more important are things done in self-defence. If Hobbes insists on anything, it is the point that no-one can be blamed for actions in defence of one's life and limbs. Surely this is generally true, notwithstanding the fact that Hobbes may count far too many things acts of self-defence. If it is generally true that there is no stigmatizing acts of self-defence, then there is no stigmatizing them as selfish. They are self-interested, but, in general, blamelessly so.

What about the critics' other claim, that since Hobbes never allows a conflict between moral obligation and self-interest, he deprives himself of any concept of moral obligation? Consider the first part of this claim, that Hobbes never allows a conflict between morality and self-interest. If what this means is that Hobbes never allows a case in which discharging a moral obligation costs one something, then it is false. Discharging one's obligation to keep the peace, for example, can involve suffering not only 'words of disgrace and some little injuries' (L, ch. 27, E III 286), but also outright intimidation (L, ch. 27, E III 285). So fulfilling one's moral obligations *can* cost one something. What, then, becomes of the claim that Hobbes does not allow for the possibility of a conflict between morality and self-interest? If it means that Hobbes arranges things in his theory so that from a rational agent's point of view there is always *more* to be got out of discharging one's moral obligations than out of not doing so, then it is a correct reading of Hobbes. It is also a plausible reading of other philosophers (notably Plato in reply to Thrasymachus) who no-one would dream of claiming had deprived themselves of a concept of moral obligation or moral motivation. I think that in order to arrive at a formulation that fits some of his text and gives him a case to answer concerning the conflict between moral obligation and self-interest, Hobbes's rational self-interest has got to be collapsed into selfishness. But when this is done, the text suffers distortion. What gives content to rational self-interest in the text is the good of self-preservation, or self-defence, or survival, which it is in general *not* selfish to promote. So the line of criticism we are considering seems to fizzle out.

Hobbes's views *are* vulnerable to attack if there is something wrong with appeals in ethics to self-interest, or personal interest of any kind. They are vulnerable if ethical requirements are necessarily universalistic in form or impersonal in content. Since I think both things are true of ethical requirements, I do not think that in the end Hobbes has an acceptable concept of morality. What I deny is that it is obviously unacceptable, or that what is wrong with it is close to the surface in the exposition of his moral philosophy. Neither his definition of the other-regarding attitudes, nor his assumption that voluntary action is self-interested, leads directly to a refutation of his views. To refute Hobbes one would need no less than a knock-down argument for impersonal morality in the face of the claims of self-interest, and such an argument is notoriously difficult to construct.[25]

IX

Absolute Submission, Undivided Sovereignty

1 The dangers of visible virtue

Hobbes's moral philosophy calls attention to a purpose or 'end' all rational people can agree is good, and it specifies types of behaviour that are means to that end. The end and the means are supposed to be discoverable even in the state of nature. Each pre-political person can agree to call peace 'good', for each can see that peace is a means of self-preservation. Seeing that peace is good, each can see the good in virtuous types of behaviour – charity, equity, complaisance, forgiveness – enjoined by the laws of nature. But seeing *only* this much, each person is not unequivocally obliged to act virtuously, for each person must be sure it is safe to do so, and it may be dangerous if the next person is prepared to act iniquitously or in contravention of the laws of nature. The next person *may* be prepared to act iniquitously: in the state of nature he may think it is unsafe to act in any other way. And there is no gainsaying him. Since each man in the state of nature is entitled to preserve himself by any means he thinks suitable (*L*, ch. 14, E III 117; *EL*, Pt. 1, ch. 14, viii. 71; *De Cive*, ch. 1, x, E II 9), and since this entitlement may be a matter of common knowledge (*De Cive*, ch. 1, ix, E II 9), it is not necessarily safe to abide openly by the laws of nature. One is always obliged to try to abide by the laws, to give them due weight in one's practical deliberation, but giving them due weight may be done in private or *in foro interno*: one is not always obliged to abide by the laws openly, i.e. in one's actions or *in foro externo*.

There is a problem, then, of publicly implementing the knowledge of right and wrong one gets from the laws of nature. At the root of the problem is each person's possession of the 'right of nature'. Hobbes defines this right in *Leviathan* as

the liberty each man hath, to use his own power, as he will himself, for the preservation of his own nature, that is to say, of his own

111

life, and consequently, of doing any thing, which in his own judgment, and reason, he shall conceive to be the aptest means thereunto (ch. 14, E III 116).

In other words, what is naturally permitted or all right for a man to do is anything that in his judgment promotes his survival. Hobbes goes on to say that since anything a person finds a use for may help somehow in preserving his life in the state of nature, anything a person finds a use for is all right for him to use (E III 117). This comes down to saying that in the state of nature 'every one has a right to every thing, even to one another's body' (L, ch. 14, E III 117; EL, Pt. i, ch. 4, x. 72; De Cive, ch. 1, x E II 9–11).

What does the right of each to every thing amount to? The answer can be gathered from Hobbes's explanation of what it is to lay down a right (L, ch. 14, E III 118f; EL, Pt. 1, ch. 15, iii. 75–6; De Cive, ch. 2, iv. E II 17). To lay down a right to a thing is to give way to another in his pursuit or enjoyment of a thing. If one lays down by renouncing a right, one gives way to anyone else's pursuit or enjoyment of the thing. If one lays down by transferring the right to someone else, then it is that person only one agrees not to hinder in his pursuit or enjoyment of the thing. All of this implies that not to lay down a right to a thing – to keep or have a right to a thing – is to be free to hinder anyone else's pursuit or enjoyment of it. And to have a right to every thing, is to be free to hinder anyone else's pursuit or enjoyment of any thing at all.

Given how he describes the right, it is no wonder Hobbes calls it 'unprofitable'. 'For the effects of this right are the same, almost, as if there had been no right at all. For although any man might say of every thing, This is mine, yet could he not enjoy it, by reason of his neighbour, who having equal right and power, would pretend the same thing to be his' (De Cive, ch. 1, xi, E II 11). The effects of the right cancel out when everyone has it. Little or nothing is lost, then, if everyone lays down the right, and the second law of nature recommends that it be laid down to the extent that peace requires it (L, ch. 14, E III 118).

The second law of nature recommends this, however, subject to one's exercising the right of nature. One is to lay down one's right to every thing for the sake of peace, if, in one's judgment, doing so is necessary for one's self-defence (E III 118). This is to make compliance with the second law of nature hang on a big 'if', for people in the state of nature may well judge that laying down the right to every thing is not necessary for self-preservation. Or, people may go through the motions of laying down the right, and then afterwards go back on what they have agreed to, because in their judgment going back on the agreement is necessary for their preservation.

The right of nature threatens to annul any ostensible laying down of

112

right. It licenses anyone's breaking any covenant or promise in the state of nature. A covenant is made when two people agree not to hinder one another in the pursuit or enjoyment of something, and one stands aside now, trusting the other to stand aside later (*L*, ch. 14, E III 121). A covenant is broken when the trust of the performer is betrayed by the other party. A promise is just like a covenant except that neither party is expected to perform immediately: each trusts the other to perform in the future (*L*, ch. 14, E III 121). A promise is broken when there is failure to perform.

Can promises so much as be made in the state of nature? People can of course produce the familiar form of utterance beginning 'I promise', but to no effect if Hobbes is right (*L*, ch. 14, E III 124). For when a 'promise' in the relevant sense is made, it is made between two parties, each of whom is supposed to gain something by the future performance of the other. In the state of nature neither can perform first in the full assurance that the other will perform after. In fact, whoever performs first betrays himself to the other (*L*, ch. 14, E III 125). Since neither can safely perform first, Hobbes argues, the contract apparently created by going through the motions of promising is void.

He takes a similar view of covenant-making in the state of nature. When two people mutually transfer rights, and one performs first, there is no counting on the other -- call him the 'second party' – to do his part later, for the second party is held to performing only by the signs or words by which he entered into the covenant, and as in the case of promises, 'the bonds of words are too weak to bridle men's ambition, avarice, anger and other passions . . .' (*L*, ch. 14, E III 124). To put it another way, the performer's fear of being taken advantage of by the second party is always well-grounded, which makes his performing first unreasonable. Indeed, until there is a power sufficient to compel the second party to perform and render groundless the fear of the one who performs first, all covenants are invalid. Hobbes goes so far as to say that until there is a *civil* power instituted that is capable of compelling performance, no covenant is valid (*L* ch. 15, E III 131).

He does not claim that in the absence of a civil power the second party to a covenant is not *obliged* to perform: an obligation exists, all right, created by the act of transferring right. It is not even against reason for this obligation to be discharged in the state of nature. It might seem to be against reason, for doing things to one's disadvantage is against reason, and on the surface it might seem to be to the disadvantage of the second party to keep his part of the bargain rather than enjoy for free the benefit that accrues from his co-covenanter's performing first. But in fact, Hobbes argues, any immediate benefit to the second party from not doing his part would be wiped out by hostility and distrust from those who counted on performance and were disappointed (L, ch. 15, E III 133–4).[1]

It is not Hobbes's view, then, that in the state of nature second parties act rationally and break no real obligation when they fail to perform. They *do* break obligations, and they can work out that it *is* reasonable to perform. Despite this, however, they can be carried away by their passions and not keep faith. Indeed, this possibility of not keeping faith is a probability until there is a civil power to keep people to their undertakings (L, ch. 15, E III 131). So a party to a covenant who considers doing his part, but who draws back for fear of non-performance on the other side, has a well-grounded fear and a well-grounded reluctance. It is this justifiable fear of non-performance that voids covenants in the state of nature.

Covenants being invalid in the state of nature, there can be no such thing in the state of nature as an act of injustice, that is, an act of breaking a valid covenant. Symmetrically, there can be no such thing as a just action. There *can* be virtuous actions of other kinds, e.g. acts of gratitude, complaisance, forgiveness and modesty, for these do not presuppose valid covenants. But though such actions are possible in the state of nature, and though reasons for performing them are discoverable pre-politically, there is no reason to expect they will be performed: performance is simply unsafe while each retains the right of nature. When people are all more or less equal in the ability to hinder one another, and each is entitled to decide when and how to channel this ability in the interest of security, anything goes. In particular, the omission of virtuous action may be seen as necessary for living longer.

Hobbes needs to explain how just action can ever be possible, and also how it can ever be safe to display the other virtues. He accounts for both of these possibilities simultaneously, but in a way that is at first sight question-begging. For he invokes a certain kind of covenant in order to explain how, in general, there can be valid covenants presupposed by just action. More explicitly, he invokes the kind of covenant that institutes a commonwealth, to explain how covenants that would otherwise be voided by fear of non-performance are valid.

2 Making it safe for morality

Hobbes's problem about justice arises from the reasonable fears of people in the state of nature. When they think of entering into covenants, and wonder whether to trust people they would be agreeing not to hinder, they are right to fear that they would be taken advantage of, if the terms of the covenant call on them to perform first. They right to fear this so long as words alone bind people to the performance of covenants. Hobbes's task is to describe arrangements under which it is unreasonable to fear non-performance by second parties. One possibility he considers is an arrangement under which people fortify their promises with oaths sworn before God (*L*, ch. 14, E III 128–9; ch. *EL*, Pt. 1, ch. 15, xv. 80; *De Cive*, ch. 2, xx, E II 27). Oaths add weight to promises because they call God's revenge on the oath-maker if he breaks his promise, and it comes naturally to men to fear God: religion, or a fear of 'invisible spirits' concentrated on an object called 'God' is as natural a human passion as the desire to know causes (*L*, ch. 12, E III 94; cf. *EL*, Pt. 1, ch. 11, ii, 53–4). But are oaths effective?

It all depends. It depends, for example, on whether people swear by what they sincerely think is God (*L*, ch. 14, E III 129–30; cf. *EL*, Pt. 1, ch. 15, xvi. 80–1; *De Cive*, ch. 2, xxi, E II 27). If they 'swear' by anything else, nothing is in fact sworn at all. If they are atheists and go through the motions of swearing, then once again the oath is empty. On the other hand, if they sincerely and piously swear, adding a real oath to a promise, it is nevertheless possible for them to be taken as insincere, so that the force of the oath is cancelled out by disbelief. Hobbes says that in the state of nature an oath strengthens the force of a promise if anything can, but this falls short of saying that an oath ever does keep a person to his promise. In fact, it seems clear that even when oaths by second parties are sincere and taken at face value by people who have to perform first, those who have to perform first *still* have reason to fear second parties will not perform. This is because the oaths are taken in the state of nature, where a second party is allowed to cry off if doing so seems required in the interest of personal security.

If fear of a second party's non-performance is really to be unreasonable, then non-performance itself must go against a second party's interest in his security. In fewer words, non-performance must be dangerous and be seen to be dangerous. Non-performance is unlikely to seem dangerous enough to second parties if covenants are made between people of equal strength, and if the disappointed person alone is the dispenser of retaliation for a breach of covenant. Unless the second party can reasonably expect to be overpowered on breaking his word, there is no relying on the fear of the consequences to keep him to his agreement. On the other hand, if he knows that he *will* be pitted against stronger forces than he can muster if he breaks the covenant, then either that is because he will face an assisted co-covenanter, or some formidable third party acting as enforcer. But for a disappointed party to a covenant to call upon assistants or an enforcer, he must be able to trust the assistants or the enforcer, and the question then is, 'What keeps *them* on his side?' If it is an agreement in the form of a promise or covenant, we seem to be back where we started. If it is a tie of friendship or kinship, then surely there is no assuming in advance that the second party lacks friends and family of his own.

Hobbes does in fact invoke the device of an enforcer of covenants, an enforcer who plays that role by virtue of an agreement made in the state of nature. And yet it is not, as it might seem, a question-begging solution to the problem of making agreements binding in the state of nature, for the agreement that creates the role of enforcer is so framed as to abolish the state of nature, and with it the obstacles the state of nature puts in the way of binding agreements. Foremost among these obstacles is an unrestricted right of nature, the freedom of each person to judge for himself what must be done for his security.[2] In making the special agreement Hobbes describes, the many in the state of nature each agree to be governed in matters of security by someone else, charged with seeing to the security of them all. In practice, agreeing to be governed by someone else means carrying out his positive commands and omitting what he prohibits. Parties to the agreement undertake to submit to the one charged with collective security, i.e., to lend their power as agents to whatever courses of action his deliberations recommend for the public safety. Or, to put it in more familiar political terms, the many form themselves into a state or commonwealth, as subjects of some man or body of men they collectively agree to regard as head of state or sovereign.

What is the content of the agreement by which the many bring about their subjection to the one or the few? There are discrepancies between the version of the agreement given in *Leviathan*, and those set out in *The Elements of Law* and *De Cive*,[3] but all three are agreements between the many which make a free gift of the power of each to a designated man or body of men. The power of each is freely made available for security from everyone else, and it is freely made available by any one of the many on the condition that every other one do the same (*L*, ch. 17, E III 158; *EL*, Pt. 1, ch. 19, vii. 103–4; *De Cive*, ch. 5, vii–viii, E II 68–9; ch. 6, xx, E II 91).

Since the alternative to entering the agreement is continued war in the state of nature, everyone has reason to become party to it. If many covenant together, they all perform simultaneously; there is no need for some to perform now and trust others to perform later. But perhaps more important, given present concerns, is the fact that no-one can safely break the agreement once the many are sticking to it. Breaking the agreement would consist in open and consistent disobedience to the commands of the sovereign as declared in his laws. Any one person who disobeyed, or any disobedient minority, would always make an enemy of a sovereign in control of the formidable power of the majority. Any non-performer or minority of non-performers would almost certainly be overcome if that formidable power were unleashed. Since the knowledge of the possible uses of majority power is made available to anyone who enters the agreement, everyone has reason to find the consequences of breaking the agreement supremely fearful.

So there is no difficulty about the bindingness of the agreement or covenant that sets up the commonwealth. There would be no problem about the bindingness of other agreements either, if not to perform *them* was to invite penalties for disobeying the sovereign. And such penalties would be in force, if it were the sovereign's law to keep all lawful covenants. This in outline is Hobbes's solution to the general problem of binding covenants. He first describes a covenant there is every reason to enter in the state of nature, and every reason not to break once it has been widely entered into; he then makes the breaking of any other lawful covenant sufficient for breaking the original covenant to obey the sovereign. In this way the consequences of non-performance of covenants within a civil society can be sufficiently fearful to make fears of being betrayed on the part of those performing first, unreasonable. Nothing more is needed to create conditions for valid covenants, and so conditions for just actions once the commonwealth exists.

The general theoretical strategy for explaining how justice is possible also helps to show how it can be safe to display the other virtues. Hobbes need only postulate for each of the precepts of reason or laws of nature enjoining a kind of virtue, a corresponding sovereign command with the same content. And this is the approach he seems to adopt. 'When a commonwealth is once settled,' Hobbes says in chapter 26 of *Leviathan*,

> then are [the laws of nature] actually laws, and not before; as being
> then the commands of the commonwealth; and therefore also civil
> laws: for it is the sovereign power that obliges men to obey them.
> For in the differences of private men, to declare what is equity,
> what is justice, and what is moral virtue, and to make them binding,
> there is the need of the ordinances of the sovereign power, and
> punishments to be ordained for such as shall break them; which
> ordinances are therefore part of the civil law. The law of nature is
> therefore a part of the civil law in all commonwealths of the world
> (E III 253).

The effect of allowing for enforceable positive laws corresponding to the laws of nature, is to explain how doing the virtuous thing can always be safe. For anyone who acts as directed by the sovereign can expect protection against anyone who, contrary to law, seeks to harm or disadvantage him.

The creation of the commonwealth makes it safe for people to do the virtuous thing, and so encourages the overt practice of virtue. But the creation of the commonwealth does not thereby make people virtuous, for more than outward compliance with the laws of nature is required for a virtuous character. Hobbes makes the point clearly in the case of justice, distinguishing in a number of ways between people whose actions are just, and people who are just themselves. According to *Leviathan*, a just man is someone who takes great care to make all his actions just (ch. 15, E III 135), and who so hates the idea of owing his contentment to fraud or breach of promise, that he does not need fear to hold him to his word (ch. 15, E III 136). An unjust man is someone who does not care whether his actions are just, but who may invariably carry out his undertakings because he thinks that doing so will cause him less trouble than breaking his word.

Hobbes reserves the term 'guiltless' for people whose actions are just, but who aren't wholehearted in acting justly (*L*, ch. 15, E III 136). What the creation of the commonwealth is supposed to promote is general guiltlessness: it is too much to hope that it will make just men of individuals who are otherwise aggressive pursuers of felicity. Similarly with the other virtues.[4] When people behave outwardly as the laws of nature advise, and make the just, or modest or grateful gesture, they are doing all that the laws of nature ask when the laws of nature function as laws of the commonwealth. Making the relevant gestures may not, however, be enough for compliance with the laws of nature *qua* laws of a God who can see into hearts, and who commands that the virtuous thing be done wholeheartedly. The laws of nature may be upheld as civil laws, binding only *in foro externo*, and at the same time be broken as laws binding *in foro interno*. When that happens, an agent sins but commits no crime (cf. *L*, ch. 27, E III 278–9), and it is only crimes that are punishable by civil law.

One would not expect the commonwealth to exact purity of heart as well as good behaviour, for the purpose of the commonwealth is to give people relief from war, and no more than good behaviour is required for that. Besides, there is no bending one's intentions to the laws of nature, for intentions are only appetites that occur before deliberation ends (*LNC*, E V 362), and neither one's appetites nor their position in a train of deliberation is in one's control.

3 Safety at what price?

The covenant that creates the commonwealth obliges men twice over: once to one another, once more to the man or body of men empowered to act for all in matters of security. In obliging themselves to one another, parties to the covenant are supposed to create for themselves real unity, where real unity is a cut above consent or concord (*L*, ch. 17, E III 158). Consent between men is achieved in practical matters, when their actions separately promote a good that each makes the object of his will (*De Cive*, ch. 5, iii, E II 65; *EL*, Pt. 1, ch. 12, vii. 63). Union reduces many different wills to one will. It is the condition people are supposed to enjoy when they agree to let one man or one body of men choose for them the means of staving off war and living commodiously. By making themselves subject to one judgment and one will – that of the person to whom the right of self-governance is transferred – they do more than minimize the risk of contention: they rule out the *possibility* of contention. For it is only where there are many different wills that there can be a contention of wills.

Reasons for preferring unity to concord double as reasons for preferring undivided to divided sovereignty. Though Hobbes concedes that monarchy has its difficulties, especially in regard to sustaining for long enough the perpetual peace the many trade for their submission (cf. *L*, ch. 19, E III 176ff), the shortcomings of sovereignty in one man are, in principle, fewer than those of sovereignty in few or many men (aristocracy or democracy). The more sovereignty is distributed, the more scope there is for contention among those with power, and so the more scope there is for a limited version of the war of all against all. Monarchy is the form of government Hobbes preferred, but nothing in his theory of sovereignty depends on the preference. Whether one man is responsible for the public security, or a body of men, the subject's obligations are the same.

The obligations are special. For unlike the obligations that tie them to one another, the obligations of subjects to their sovereigns are entirely one-sided. By the covenant that institutes the commonwealth each of the many makes a free gift of his right of self-governance to whomever becomes the sovereign, but since this person transfers or lays down no right himself, he can enjoy the benefit of the transfer of right from the multitude without having to give up some right in return.

Not that a free gift creates no constraint at all on the receiver. The fourth law of nature calls on anyone who benefits by free gift to omit actions that would make the giver reasonably regret his good will (*L*, ch. 15, E III 135; cf. *EL*, Pt. 1, ch. 16, vi. 84–85; *De Cive*, ch. 3, viii, E II 35). This means that a sovereign who accepted the rights transferred to him by the many, would be guilty of the sin of ingratitude if he did not do his best to make the many secure. On the other hand, the sovereign's obligations *to* the many are no more binding than obligations *between* the many before there is a sovereign to over-awe them. For there is no one to enforce the sovereign's obligation to be grateful, no-one but God or perhaps the head of some other, more powerful state. The sovereign never gives up *his* right of self-governance; so he is rightfully his own judge of which obligations to discharge, and also of the occasions appropriate for discharging them. In any case, he does not answer to the many for his actions. He is responsible *for* them, not *to* them, and his actions do not fall within the scope of the civil laws.

The one-sidedness of binding obligations in the commonwealth is

119

underlined by Hobbes's description of the just powers of the sovereign by institution (*L*, ch. 18; cf. *EL*, Pt, 2, ch. 1. 107ff; *De Cive*, ch. 6, E II 71ff). It is as if the sovereign has all the rights and the subjects all the duties. Thus, it is for the sovereign to judge what shall be done or omitted for the sake of peace, what doctrines shall be publicly taught, what laws there should be, how the laws apply in particular cases, who should hold office, who should get rewards and punishments, who will have what rank, and so on. Added to these are the powers of raising taxes, regulating the money supply, overseeing commerce in general (cf. *L*, ch. 24). Even the power of life and death is in the hands of the sovereign, subject to the inalienable right of self-defence on the part of anyone who is commanded to be killed (cf. *L*, ch. 21, E III 204f).

Isn't this too much power, and power only too likely to be used unjustly? To take the worry about excessive power first, Hobbes's reply is that each right of the sovereign is deduced from the purpose of instituting the commonwealth, and that each is necessary for keeping the peace and making it last. Since the sovereign has responsibility for securing the end or goal of peace, he has a right to the means of doing so (*L*, ch. 18, E III 163). As for the question of whether the sovereign is liable to use his power unjustly, Hobbes's answer is that toward his subjects a sovereign *cannot* act unjustly:

> [B]ecause every subject is by [the] institution [of the commonwealth] author of all the actions, and judgments of the sovereign instituted; it follows, that whatsoever he doth, it can be no injury to any of his subjects; nor ought he to be by any of them accused of injustice. For he that doth anything by authority from another; doth therein no injury to him by whose authority he acteth: but by this institution of a commonwealth, every particular man is author of all the sovereign doth: and consequently he that complaineth of injury from his sovereign, complaineth of that whereof he himself is author, and therefore ought not to accuse any man but himself; nor himself of injury; because to do injury to one's self is impossible. It is true that he that have sovereign power may commit iniquity; but not injustice, or injury in the proper signification (*L*, ch. 18, E III 163).

The sovereign *can* do wrong, *is* capable of iniquity. But he cannot act unjustly toward his subjects. The reason is that in covenanting to create the commonwealth, each of the many makes himself the author of anything the sovereign, or more strictly the 'sovereign representative', does.

The notions of an author and of a representative are peculiar to *Leviathan*, and *Leviathan*'s theory of sovereignty by institution. In chapter 16 of the book Hobbes defines a *person* as someone whose actions are either his own or representative of those of another man.

One person's actions are representative of those of another when he is *authorized* by the other to act on his behalf, and it is in this capacity of authorized representative that a sovereign acts, his actions being representative of those of each of the many who transfer their right of self-governance to him. Or, in other words, the many are *authors* of anything the sovereign representative does (cf. *L*, ch. 17, E III 158). This is what is supposed to make it impossible for the sovereign to commit an injustice or do an injury to his subjects. Anything he does to any one of the many is authorized by that one, and the effects are suffered by consent of the sufferer, who therefore cannot complain of injury (cf. *L*, ch. 15, E III 137).[5]

Though it may look that way, Hobbes does not help himself to the assumption that there can be no self-inflicted harm, and then conclude that since what the sovereign does to a subject is indirectly self-inflicted, there is nothing for the subject to complain about. He thinks an agent *can* do harm to himself, and he even mentions some laws of nature that prohibit the infliction of the more typical forms of such harm (cf. *L*, ch. 15, E III 144). What he denies is that there can be self-inflicted injury. He uses the term 'injury' in a narrow sense, applying it to any act that breaks a valid covenant (*L*, ch. 14, E III 119), and more generally to any act the agent does not have the right to do (cf. *L*, ch. 15, E III 137). The sovereign representative, whoever he is, makes no covenant with his subjects, retains the right of nature, and knows by the terms of the gift made to him by the many, that the many are willing to have done whatever he does for their protection. Whatever he does for their protection, then, he has a right to do; so the conditions of injury can never be satisfied.

Hobbes seems to have an answer to worries about unjust uses of power, but the answer seems pat. Given the extent of the sovereign's power, what is to stop him doing anything he likes in the name of public protection? In particular, what is to keep him from passing off as for the subjects' safety, measures that only promote his own glory and enrichment? After all, whoever occupies the office of sovereign is only human, and subject to the irregular passions that rule any human being in his pursuit of felicity. What is more, as holder of a position that lawfully attracts signs of honour from all who are subjects in the commonwealth, the sovereign is perhaps more likely than the ordinary mortal to over-value himself and regard too much as his due. Surely this probable vainglory can work disastrous effects when allied with so much power?

In dealing with this question, it is important not to be carried away by talk that Hobbes himself is careful to acknowledge as metaphorical. Though he describes the commonwealth as a mortal god with great power (*L*, ch. 17, E III 158), a god that sovereign man or assembly personifies, the god's powers are only as great as the number of people willing to join forces in obedience to the sovereign. The power evaporates if the loyal become incapacitated or die, or if, albeit unjustly, they transfer allegiance to someone else. So a sovereign risks everything if he makes the life of his subjects too miserable. Misery cannot only provoke disobedience, it can actually make disobedience all right. For example, if the distribution or production of basic goods in the commonwealth is so mismanaged that many subjects do not have enough to eat, and can only get enough to eat illegally, they commit no crime when they break the law and steal to feed themselves:

> When a man is destitute of food, or other thing necessary for his life, and cannot preserve himself any other way, but by some fact against law; as if in a great famine he take food by force, or stealth, which he cannot obtain for money or charity; . . . he is totally excused (L, ch. 27, E III 288).

Totally excused because not to break the law would mean co-operating in cutting short his life, and 'nature compels him' to live as long as possible (E III 288).

Hobbes draws no very firm boundary between misery that totally excuses crime, and misery that is no more than a justifiable 'inconvenience' of government for the governed. But it is clear from what he says in *Leviathan* concerning the office of the sovereign (ch. 30), and in parallel chapters concerning the duties of heads of state in *The Elements of Law* (Pt. 2, ch. 9) and *De Cive* (ch. 13), that it is for the sovereign to procure for his subjects as much of what they would regard as the delightful life as is consistent with their security. This means not overburdening them with taxes, not multiplying unduly the laws that regulate their actions, being lenient in punishment where security permits, and so on. A sovereign who does not do his best to minimize the intrusions of government or who makes his subjects miserable and provokes civil disobedience, is like an individual in the state of nature who is not moderate in eating and drinking: his excesses lead to his physical disintegration. A sovereign with immoderate habits can also become an easy target for a stronger government in a war of conquest. These risks make it unreasonable for a sovereign to exploit his subjects for merely personal gain or glory.

Though it may seem at first that by submitting to the sovereign the many obtain their safety at a high price, it turns out that in a well-ordered state they need not suffer impoverishment, rough justice, or an intolerable curtailment of their liberty. The sovereign who owes his position to the free gift of his subjects either does well by them or invites the state's and his own ruin.

It is not significantly different for a man who becomes sovereign by force or acquisition. He too is empowered by the many to act for them in matters of security, and he, too, owes his sovereignty to acts of authorization on the part of each (*L*, ch. 20, E III 185).[6] Again, no less than someone instituted as sovereign, someone who takes over by force enjoys sweeping rights, and a near total immunity from accusations of injury when he exercises the rights as he likes. But like the solo pursuer of felicity in the state of nature, whose successive gains demand larger and larger reserves of power if he is to keep what he has already got, a sovereign who has started to build an empire must be able to count on obedience from ever larger numbers of subjects. Widely dispersed, probably only governable by proxy, these colonials pose formidable problems of control unless they remain willing subjects. Once more, the sovereign's dependence on the will of his subjects acts as a safeguard to the quality of life of his subjects.

4 Citizenship without judgment, civil society without civilization

Suppose a sovereign's subjects have reasonable security and enough to eat, are left free to profit from trade, and feel reasonably content. May not the price of life in the commonwealth *still* be too high? The transfer of right that creates the commonwealth is the laying down of liberty, and a renunciation by each person of policies of action in accordance with his own judgements about what is best for him. In submitting to the will of the sovereign one agrees to be bound by the value judgments embodied in the civil laws that declare the sovereign's will (cf. *L*, ch. 21, E III 198). In whatever sphere of daily life the civil laws pronounce, they make redundant the capacities for practical deliberation and judgment that are indispensable in the state of nature. Finding out what would be the right thing to do becomes no harder than finding out what the law prescribes and doing that, or finding out what the law prohibits and omitting that. Once the commonwealth is in place there is at the same time the true and certain rule of our actions that Hobbes taxes the old moral philosophers with failing to specify. Moral and practical decision become algorithmic for citizens.

But isn't that a travesty of the idea of citizenship? The subject in Hobbes's commonwealth is someone who makes himself the vehicle for the sovereign will in all the areas of life that matter most. Can such a subject be a citizen? Here it is worth contrasting Hobbes's view with the Aristotelian position he often says he is trying to inter (*L*, ch. 46, E III 669). According to Aristotle, it is essential to being a citizen that one have a turn at holding political office and a hand in the state's judicial functions.[7] A subject in Hobbes's sort of commonwealth fulfils the requirements of membership in the body politic by obeying the sovereign, and definitely not by pressing into service a capacity for practical judgment and decision-making. Life in Aristotle's state is supposed to prepare one for virtuous conduct at its fullest, and this is the conduct of someone who, as a ruler, channels the virtue and practical wisdom that makes him a good man into obtaining the good for the polity as a whole.[8] In its ideal form the state makes men good, and enables men as a result to be both good subjects and good rulers. But because becoming and being a good man is not a matter of following strict rules,[9] because it is a matter rather of having the wisdom to see which demands a given situation makes of one, neither is being a good subject or a good ruler a matter of following codifiable precepts. When Hobbes holds, to the contrary, that 'strict theorems of moral doctrine' equip men to govern and obey (L, ch. 31, E III 357–8), that may look like a claim appropriate only to a denatured citizenship and rulership, citizenship and rulership geared to making people survive rather than to helping them to perfect themselves.

In one way this impression is correct, and in another not. It is true that Hobbes's state does not help men to perfect themselves in Aristotle's sense. It does, however, help men toward salvation, for following God's laws is necessary to salvation (cf. e.g. L, ch. 43, E III 599; De Cive, ch. 28, ii, E II 300), and the state makes it safe to follow God's laws in one's outward behaviour. The state indeed does more, for it encourages (without enforcing) the development of intentions in keeping with the laws of nature (cf. L, ch. 30, E III 330). Of course, the state cannot provide for everything that salvation requires, since all men are sinners and it is the office of the Saviour to redeem the sins of men. But it counts for something that the state is an answer to certain evils. Or so Hobbes strongly implies in Leviathan where he explains the signification of salvation or being saved:

> To be saved, is to be secured, either respectively, against special evils, or absolutely, against all evils, comprehending want, sickness, and death itself. And because man was created in a condition immortal, not subject to corruption, and consequently to nothing that tendeth to the dissolution of his nature; and fell from that happiness by the sin of Adam; it followeth, that to be *saved* from sin is to be saved from all the evil and calamities that sin hath brought upon us (ch. 38, E III 451).

The state does not save men from all the evil and calamities consequent on sin. It does not, for example, protect them from death, only from dying prematurely. But it can do something directly to secure men against want, and, through the encouragement of science, it is supposed to help to remedy sickness.

There is another way in which the state can be understood to be a response to the 'sin of Adam'. Adam forfeited everlasting life when he broke God's commandment, and with Eve, ate from the tree of knowledge of good and evil. In eating Adam and Eve tried to become judges of good and evil in their own right, rejecting government by God for the false attractions of self-government. In the acts by which any of Adam's descendants show that they are willing to be governed, they show that they have no wish to become private judges of good and evil. What is more, they can submit to another's judgment in the knowledge that only contention and war result from trying to remain judges of good and evil. Once acquainted with the main features of the state of nature, they have their eyes opened to the nature of self-government. In rejecting it they can be interpreted as making a sign that they wish to atone for the Fall. They can be interpreted as repudiating Adam and Eve's proud and pointless rebellion against God's dominion. And since submission can be seen as a means of repentance, the seemingly denatured citizenship that leaves all the important judgments to someone else is quite compatible with a kind of human improvement.

It must, however, be an improvement within very narrow limits. Hobbes cannot make great claims for the power of the state to transform people for the better, and hold at the same time that were the state to dissolve, its people would immediately revert to savagery. If competitiveness and the hunger for glory are causes of quarrel indelibly engraved in human nature, then there cannot be a state made up of men who are free of the hunger or of the urge to compete. Either the truths about men that Hobbes states are scientific, or they are not. If they are not, they cannot endow an argument for absolutism in sovereignty and quiescence in subjection with any scientific authority. If they *are* scientific truths, on the other hand, then being 'general, eternal and immutable' (cf. *L*, ch. 46, E III 664), they must hold no matter what political arrangements men live under. Of course, compatibly with all of that, political arrangements may change things on the surface. They may make men behave *as if* they were reformed. What political arrangements cannot do, it seems, is go so far as to alter the dispositions of citizens so that men *are* reformed. The state can inhibit the dispositions, make it dangerous for people to behave aggressively. But it seems that at bottom subjects in the commonwealth must always be the uncivilized and warlike creatures they start out as.

If that is right, and people remain aggressively inclined however peacefully they behave, perhaps their nature is so unfortunate that their being left free to kill themselves off in the state of nature would be, from a sufficiently detached point of view, no bad thing. If all the commonwealth does is to keep at bay creatures who deep down are only arrant wolves, and if it is a constant struggle to keep this wolfishness from coming out, perhaps it is better to have done with it and let the species perish at its own hands. It is ironic that Hobbes's scientific perspective on human nature allows this thought to arise naturally, for officially the scientific perspective is supposed to assist men to see the necessity of treating one another as if they were *not* arrant wolves.

This comes close, I think, to revealing the main source of weakness in Hobbes's morals and politics. It is not that the sort of commonwealth Hobbes describes is too oppressive for people who end up as its subjects. It is not that the arrangements Hobbes describes are too generous to heads of state. It is that just below the surface, subjects and sovereigns are human, and therefore discoverably unattractive as specimens of living creatures. So unattractive do they turn out to be, in fact, that it is a question why their survival should seem desirable from any point of view but their own, pre-scientific one.

X

Sedition, Submission and Science

Hobbes often proclaims the merits of his civil science by pointing out some advance he thinks it makes on the shoddy theories of his predecessors. As if the doctrine of *De Cive* and *Leviathan* were prompted by his distaste for false ideas in old books. In fact, false ideas in the heads of his contemporaries worried him more, and brought his views to public notice sooner than he would have liked. He described *De Cive* as a work 'ripened and plucked' from him by the years before the English Civil War, when 'my country . . . was boiling hot with questions regarding the rights of dominion, and the obedience due from subjects' (*De Cive*, Pref. to the Reader, E II, xx). *Leviathan*, too, was occasioned by the 'disorders of the present time' (Rev. and Conc., E III 713), though these were no longer the same as the ones that had prompted *De Cive*. Between the composition of the second and third of Hobbes's political treatises monarchy gave way in England to the Commonwealth. But it remained a timely question whether any *de facto* holder of civil power could justly command obedience.[1] Issues surrounding the submission of subjects were very much alive, and as Hobbes thought, still liable to be exploited by demagogues.

No chapters in the political treatises engage the ideological disorders of the Civil War period more directly than those on sedition, or the break-up of states. In these chapters Hobbes purports to be giving the causes of the dissolution of bodies politic in general, but there is a close match between what he says in *The Elements of Law* (Pt. 2, ch. 8), *De Cive* (ch. 12), and *Leviathan* (ch. 29) in this connection, and what he says at the beginning of *Behemoth* (E VI 166f), where he lists the causes of the English Civil War itself. In all four books he is mainly concerned with the causes of sedition in popular ideology. Though there are differences in emphasis, he consistently singles out for attack at least the following opinions: that each person is his own judge of right and wrong, that it is never right to act against one's conscience, that sovereigns are subject to their own laws, that sovereign power is divisible, and that subjects have property outside the control of the sovereign.

In *The Elements of Law* and *De Cive* he rounds off his attack on these ideas with an argument against the kind of 'eloquence' that propagates them. *Leviathan* contains a counterpart of this discussion, devoted to the differences between counsel and exhortation (ch. 25, E III 240f). Hobbes's criticism of what is in effect political rhetoric raises questions about the status of his own treatises on government. Why aren't *they* open to precisely the criticisms he directed against rhetorical works? The answer depends on an alleged incompatibility between eloquence and wisdom on the one hand, and a supposedly intimate connection between wisdom and science on the other. Pursuing these matters helps to make clear what Hobbes means by 'civil science' and also how he was for a time inclined to view science in general. After running through Hobbes's objections to seditious ideas and the breeders of sedition, I shall discuss the view of civil science his objections against rhetoric lead up to. It was perhaps his best effort at arriving at a view of science that was timely without being time-bound.

1 'Heads of pretence to rebellion'

Hobbes always reduced to about a half dozen the number of opinions that lead to popular rebellion, and except in *Behemoth*, he always begins with the opinion that each person, or each person's conscience, is the best judge of what to do, and in particular the best judge of whether he ought to obey a sovereign's commands. This opinion, he says, is quite correct as regards people in the state of nature, but it is out of place in a commonwealth, where 'the measure of good and evil actions is the civil law, and the judge the legislator, who is always representative of the commonwealth' (*L*, ch. 29, E III 311; cf. *EL*, Pt. 2, ch. 8, v. 171; *De Cive*, ch. 12, i, E II 150). It is a simple consequence of his general doctrine that no-one but the sovereign can simultaneously be a party to the commonwealth and retain the right of nature, the right to govern himself as he thinks best.

Sometimes, as in *Leviathan*, Hobbes treats as interchangeable the view that conscience is decisive in political matters, and the view that there can be legitimate, private value-judgments; at other times, he takes up the nature of conscience in relation to religion (*EL*, Pt. 2, ch. 8, v) and the role assigned to it in the thinking of Protestant sects. When it is attacked in the second way, the opinion about conscience is considered in relation to a general moral epistemology Hobbes wants nothing to do with.

It is a mainly Protestant moral epistemology, and it provides for sources of information about right and wrong that are independent of

the civil laws. One source is the individual conscience; the other is private
interpretation of scripture. Each, as Hobbes realizes, can generate reasons
for illegal actions and omissions, reasons that will seem morally authori-
tative to the agents who have them. Hobbes thinks that agents cannot
effectively be prevented from consulting their consciences (*EL*, Pt. 2,
ch. 6, iii. 146), and that it is anyway wrong to penalize people for the
beliefs they hold (*L*, ch. 46, E III 684). Yet if conscience can make men
flout the civil law by making them think that the civil law or a part of
it is immoral, then conditions can obtain for civil disobedience, the
dissolution of the commonwealth and a return to war in the state of
nature. Hobbes's way out of the problem is to put in question the
authority of deliverances of conscience, and show that obedience to civil
law does not worsen a man's chances of salvation.

How conscience is deprived of its authority is by stipulative definition.
By definition, conscience is only a faculty for knowing what one believes
(*EL*, Pt. 1, ch. 6, viii. 27). So if your conscience tells you that p, you
don't thereby know that p: p need not even be true. At best you think
you know that p, or you are prepared to say (possibly incorrectly) that
you know that you know that p. Either way, it is only an opinion
concerning p you have, an 'opinion of evidence' as Hobbes puts it in
The Elements of Law. Leviathan's treatment is not significantly different.
Conscience is knowledge of what one thinks or is strongly held opinion
(*L*, ch. 7, E III 53), but it is not knowledge or a source of knowledge.
This deflationary account, however, leaves Hobbes with the problem of
explaining why 'it was, and ever will be reputed a very evil act, for any
man to speak against his conscience' (E III 53). Hobbes's explanation (E
III 53) posits an ambiguity in common talk of conscience. Sometimes
'conscience' means the knowledge of what one thinks; sometimes it
means the knowledge of witnessed fact. It is in this second sense of
'conscience' that speaking against one's conscience is an evil act: it is a
case of bearing false witness. But it is in the first sense of 'conscience'
that appeals to conscience are usually made, and it is this sort of appeal
Hobbes wishes to deprive of authority. In this sense of 'conscience' it is
false that 'whatsoever a man does against his conscience is a sin'. Hobbes
says that this dictum 'dependeth on the presumption of making himself
judge of good and evil' (*L*, ch. 29 E III 311). And no-one can presume
to do that, 'for a man's conscience and his judgment is the same thing,
and as the judgment, so also the conscience may be erroneous' (ibid.),
however much one is in love with one's opinions (*L*, ch. 7, E III 53).

The reduction of deliverances of conscience to individual opinions is
not supported by argument, and it is unlikely that someone who already
believed that conscience was a faculty for obtaining objective knowledge,
would be won over. But though what he says is not particularly
persuasive, Hobbes does manage to shift the burden of proof somewhat.

He is able to explain the moral lore about conscience without supposing that objective knowledge can be got from conscience, and his opponents, who do suppose as much, are left having to explain the workings and provenance of the faculty. Since it is hard to see how this could be done by a method Hobbes would regard as belonging to genuine science, and since Hobbes does do something to reconcile both piety and morality with genuine science, his efforts at defusing the authority of conscience do not come to nothing.

What about problems surrounding the private interpretation of scripture? Since Hobbes thought it was dangerous for particular men to suit their actions to particular understandings of the Bible, he might have been expected to disapprove of the Bible's having been widely available in the vernacular in England during his lifetime. But in *Behemoth*, he denies that 'it is needless, or perhaps hurtful, to have the Scriptures in English'. 'There are so many places of Scripture easy to be understood,' he says,

> that teacheth both true faith and good morality . . ., of which no seducer is able to dispossess the mind of any ordinary reader, that the reading of them is so profitable as not to be forbidden without great damage to them and the commonwealth (Pt. 1, E VI 230).

So there is nothing wrong with making the Bible generally available: the state is threatened only if the Bible is taken to have authority as the word of God and if there are too many legitimate interpreters of scripture. The question, then, is whether the scriptures are in fact the word of God, and if so, who is to interpret them.

Hobbes sometimes says that they may be the word of God, while insisting that it is impossible to know that they are. In *Leviathan* he claims that men can at most believe that they are the word of God (*L*, ch. 43, E III 589), but he sometimes allows that the word of God can be known to be such by revelation (*EL*, Pt. 1, ch. 11, viii, 58). This may not be much of a concession, however, since it is also Hobbes's view, at least in *Leviathan*, that God stopped revealing his word to particular men at the time of the Old Testament prophets (ch. 42, E III 516). People afterwards who thought that God had spoken to them, were more likely to have been dreaming or hallucinating, and Hobbes thinks the same is true of his contemporaries. That leaves faith as the sole means of knowing that the scriptures reveal the word of God, and faith, or belief-in, is something that attaches to what another man says (*L*, ch. 7, E III 53). To the question of which man's sayings are to be trusted on matters of scripture, Hobbes thinks there are only two possible answers: the civil sovereign or a putative 'vicar of Christ', i.e., a pope (*L*, ch. 33, E III 380).

To exclude the second possibility he devotes many chapters in Part

III of *Leviathan* to interpreting central points of Christian doctrine in the light of the scriptures. He reaches many striking conclusions. One is that the world to come is this world (*L*, ch. 38, E III 456). Salvation will be experienced by the righteous here on earth in a kingdom centred at Jerusalem (E III 454). A second crucial conclusion is that salvation will be experienced by the righteous formed into a commonwealth, with a returned Christ as sovereign (E III 444). Still relying on scripture, Hobbes turns to the question of the authority of the church. There is a passage in Chapter 40 of *Leviathan* in which he extracts evidence that, as a matter of historical fact, the authority of priests was circumscribed by that of kings at the time of Saul (E III 469-71). Much later, he says, after the time of the apostles, not just supreme power, but also supreme ecclesiastical power, was vested with Christ's approval in princes (*L*, ch. 42, E III 491). Hobbes concludes that it is never right to 'obey any minister of Christ, if he should command us to do anything contrary to the command of the king, or other sovereign representant . . .' (E III 492). Indeed, Christ has appointed as ministers only those who obey civil authority (E III 492).

He cannot conclusively justify the concentration of ecclesiastical power in the sovereign by reference to scripture, for he admits that the interpretation of scripture is controversial. But he can and does add to the case built on scripture by saying that it costs the faithful nothing to obey the sovereign (*L*, ch. 43, E III 585ff). Here he trades on the point that obedience to Christ or God is assured merely by a sincere effort at obeying, by the will to obey. That will can be present when we are coerced to do things against our will by an iniquitous sovereign's laws; so by outwardly obeying against our will we invite neither the sovereign's punishment nor Christ's. This leaves a problem about whether martyrdom can have a point, which Hobbes tries to resolve by restricting the proper application of the term 'martyr' to those killed among the men Christ sent to convert the infidels (*L*, ch. 42, E III 496). The idea is that not every Christian can be a martyr, and that not every believer is obliged to run the risks that may attach to professing the faith openly.

Again and again in his writings Hobbes attacks political arrangements which multiply authorities, divide obedience, and water down the sovereign power. Provisions for an autonomous clergy belong to a wide range of measures he objects to. In *De Cive*, for example, he considers an arrangement vesting the power of making war in a monarch and the power of raising taxes in an independent authority (ch. 12, v, E II 156). He claims the set-up is muddled: since only those who can raise the money can wage wars, the monarch is not really in a position to decide about military campaigns. He objects on similar grounds to the detachment of legislative from executive powers. No-one could really own all the powers of sovereignty *except* that of law-making, for the legislature

131

could restrict or outlaw the exercise of the powers that remained, at its pleasure (*EL*, Pt. 2, ch. 8, vii. 173). In the same vein Hobbes says that people who believe in the separation of powers are guilty of misunderstanding the nature of the body politic: a body politic is no loose association of individuals, but a whole entity with the unity of a person (*EL*, Pt. 2, ch. 8, vii. 173): there is no considering a hiving off of powers without forgetting about the kind of unity the commonwealth has.

Mistakes about the nature of sovereignty in the commonwealth underlie other seditious opinions. For example, the idea that it is for the sovereign to abide by the laws he makes for his subjects, is a misunderstanding of the sovereign's power of making laws. If the sovereign really is supreme legislator, then he has the power of making any and all actions legal or illegal, and therefore has the power of making any of his own actions legal (*L*, ch. 24, E III 252; *EL*, Pt. 2, ch. 8, vi. 172). This argument may seem defective, for it allows for a type of law that can be altered or broken when it proves an inconvenience to a particular agent, and it might be thought essential to a law that if it prohibits a type of action, it should do so categorically, without the possibility of escape by one person and no others. Hobbes's concept of a law does not seem to cater for this consideration. A law in his sense is simply whatever someone in authority commands to be done by someone previously obliged to him. What is commanded can vary or be restricted according to the will of the one in authority.

In trying to overturn the opinion that a sovereign is subject to the laws he makes, Hobbes calls attention to the special freedom enjoyed by the sovereign as law-maker, and also the absence of a person (other than God) to sit in judgment over the sovereign and punish him (*L*, ch. 29, E III 312). The special position of the sovereign is invoked once more when Hobbes confronts the view that sovereigns have no right of ownership that excludes a subject's right to his goods. In this connection he recurs to the authority of the sovereign's judgment. It is the measure not only of good and evil, right and wrong, but also of *meum*, *tuum* and *suum*, i.e., the distribution of property. Since it is among the terms of the covenant that a sovereign's decision, whatever it is, is final in matters of ownership, then since his decision can be that a certain good is his, there is no rightfully withholding anything from him. Of course, it can happen that the sovereign decides iniquitously when he decides whom a thing should belong to. He can be biased in favour of a third party, violating the law of nature enjoining equity (*L*, ch. 15, E III 142; *EL*, Pt. 1, ch. 17, vii. 91; *De Cive*, ch. 3, xxii, E II 42), or biased in favour of himself, in contravention of the ban in natural law on deciding issues in which one is an interested party (*L*, ch. 15, E III 143; *EL*, Pt. 1, ch. 17, vii. 91; *De Cive*, ch. 3, xxi, E II 42). The fact that a sovereign may abuse his power to decide what belongs to whom, however, does not show that he does not have the power by right, and to the exclusion of rights of private ownership.

The list of seditious opinions Hobbes deals with could be extended, but enough are before us to show how he goes about rebutting them. In each case he takes something initially plausible that might be said by a demagogue to justify rebellion; he then translates what is plausibly said into the well-defined terms of his theory of sovereignty and subjection. In the process of translation some of the plausible contentions are reduced to incoherence, others are rendered doubtful or shown to need further defence. For example, the idea that a king is subject to his own laws is strictly incoherent if the monarch is a sovereign in Hobbes's sense, while it is at least doubtful, once Hobbes has finished considering the matter, that any passage from the Bible could decisively justify rebellion. Or take an 'inconvenience of government' Hobbes thinks is perennially exaggerated by the rabble-rouser, the inconvenience of having less than total liberty. 'This is really no inconvenience,' he says, because what is given up by a citizen, namely the right of each to 'govern his actions according to his own discretion and judgment, . . . or conscience' is what creates war (*EL*, Pt. 2, ch. 5, ii. 139; cf. *De Cive*, ch. 10, i, E II 127; *L*, ch. 21, E III 198f). The reason loss of liberty seems an inconvenience, is that people have a false conception of what it would be to be free. Each one imagines himself at perfect liberty to do what he likes, while everyone *else* is bound. But this is not to imagine liberty: it is to imagine something like government over others (*EL*, Pt. 2, ch. 5, ii. 139). If people only operated with well-defined or properly worked out senses of terms like 'freedom', he is suggesting, no-one would ever say they wanted a state of total liberty.

2 Reason, eloquence, and persuasive civil science

The general strategy of referring what one hears or reads to definitions, and then seeing whether contradictions or implausibilities follow, is foreshadowed in Hobbes's account of scientific method. The last thing one should do if one has scientific pretensions is to become a mouthpiece for what one hears and reads; the last thing someone should do, if he pretends to be rational, is just accept what seems plausible or allow himself to be overwhelmed by a demagogue's eloquence. Hobbes shows how the persuasiveness of a demagogue's case can evaporate when its content is critically examined, and in his chapters on sedition he tries to establish how the very practice of the demagogue – the 'habit of putting together passionate words, and applying them to the present passions of the hearer' – taints anything the demagogue conveys.

We shall see in a moment how he casts doubt on the rabble-rouser's habit; but it is as well to note in advance a risk Hobbes runs in pressing

133

his doubts. If he is to put forward his own political treatises as answers to sedition, he must credit *them* with some persuasive power. They must be able to move people to obedience at the same time as they impart knowledge of the causes of war and peace. If Hobbes's attack on persuasive speech is too sweeping, it undercuts his own political treatises, while if it is not sweeping enough it does not expose the typical passion-stirrer for what he is. In *The Elements of Law* Hobbes's argument tends to be too sweeping, discrediting eloquence of all kinds. But he does better in the two subsequent political treatises. In all three, he starts by explaining why seditious speech often convinces. The reason, he says, is that it is natural for audiences to suppose that people who speak well are wise. But in fact, as he tries to show, there is no necessary connection between being eloquent and being wise, and there can be no such figure as the wise and eloquent spokesman for rebellion.

In *The Elements of Law* (Pt. 2, ch. 8, xii–xiv. 175–8), Hobbes's argument is two-staged. He first argues that wisdom is a kind of knowledge, either prudence or science, and that the 'movers and authors of sedition' can have neither. If they were prudent they would not attempt sedition, knowing from history that attempts to foment rebellion much more often fail than succeed. If they had knowledge in the form of science, on the other hand, they would be guided in their speech and thought by what was commonly called 'good', 'bad', 'right' and so on. But they cannot be guided in that way without calling 'good' precisely what they hate, the maintenance of government, and they cannot call whatever breaks the peace 'unjust' without condemning themselves. Instead of being guided by 'general agreement' over how to name things, the breeders of sedition must suit their evaluative judgments to their own passions, or those of the authorities they admire. By bending their judgments to measures of right and wrong that are subjective and vacillating (their own passions), or to the posturings of authorities, they must not only settle for belief rather than knowledge about what is good or bad: they must settle, according to Hobbes, for false belief about what is right and wrong (*EL*, Pt. 2, ch. 8, xiii. 177). He adds that since it is by eloquence that the breeders of sedition try to produce rebellion, they must be all the more lacking in wisdom. For eloquence is only a power to persuade, not a power of showing people the truth. It wins belief by exploiting what people think already, and by manufacturing and manipulating passions. It owes none of its force to evidence, which it has to do if it is to convey knowledge and so stand a chance of expressing wisdom.

In *De Cive* (ch. 12, xii, E II 161–2), a similar line of thought is trailed. Hobbes distinguishes between eloquence bent only on persuasion, and eloquence used to demonstrate truth. The art of the former sort of eloquence is 'rhetoric', of the latter 'logic'. One kind of eloquence, the kind whose art is logic, 'is never disjoined from wisdom' but the other kind 'almost ever'. And the reason? Rhetorical eloquence is 'a commotion of the passions of the mind, such as *hope, fear, anger, pity,*' and derives from a metaphorical use of words fitted to the passions (E II 161). Logical eloquence, on the other hand, is 'an elegant and clear expression of the conceptions of the mind, and riseth partly from the contemplation of the things themselves, and partly from an understanding of words taken in their own proper and definite signification' (E II 161). It is suitable, then, for the expression of truth and knowledge, while rhetorical eloquence is not.

As in *The Elements of Law*, so in *De Cive*, Hobbes insists there is a tension between rhetoric on the one hand, and wisdom and science on the other. But in *De Cive* he leaves room for a respectable type of eloquence, the kind that can serve as the vehicle for a persuasive science of morals and politics. By the time he brought out the last of the political treatises, he was prepared to relax his former strictures on powerful speaking still further. *Leviathan*'s Review and Conclusion mentions, only to pronounce resoluble, the conflict between reason and eloquence. In 'all deliberations, and in all pleadings, the faculty of solid reasoning is necessary, . . . and yet if there not be powerful eloquence, which procureth attention and consent, the effect of reason will be little. But these [reason and eloquence] are contrary faculties . . .' (E III 701). Contrary, that is, in some connections. For Hobbes goes on to say that 'reason and eloquence, though not in the natural sciences, yet in the moral, may stand very well together' (E III 702). He still distrusts exhortation and dehortation, the vehement urging of people to actions or omissions that are mainly for the benefit of the ones doing the exhorting or dehorting (cf. *L*, ch. 25, E III 242ff). But he takes a favourable view of 'counsel' – imperative speech addressed to someone for his benefit – and he evidently thinks of counsel as the kind of imperative speech that not only can but must be supported by reasons (*L*, ch. 25, E III 245–6).

So by the time of *Leviathan* he ceased to condemn all kinds of eloquence. It may even be that he wished his political works to be read as extended pieces of counsel to subjects and sovereigns. But it is a question whether the marriage of reason and eloquence in moral philosophy is really catered for by his general view of philosophy or science. The idea of science, together with the cognate ideas of knowledge, logic and teaching, are better defined for speculative than for practical matters, and it is the same for Hobbes's concept of reason or ratiocination. In its primary sense, Hobbes's term 'ratiocination' means theoretical, not practical reasoning. Similarly, 'speech' usually means propositional speech – the sort designed to state what is the case rather than what ought to be done. When Hobbes tries to make room for an alternative to passion-stirring prescriptive speech that is still prescriptive but also rational and scientific, and material for deductive reasoning, it is not immediately clear he has the resources to do so. After Hume, it may even seem that the resources *cannot* be available, there being, it is often claimed, no sound passage from 'is' to 'ought'.

In fact, Hobbes faces no very formidable difficulty in this latter connection. Any prescriptions he deduces or gives reasons for in his moral philosophy are straightforward instances of other prescriptions – the precepts called the law of nature. So in his reasoning he passes from one 'ought'-statement to another. Nor is there anything wrong with holding, as he seems to, that statements of the laws of nature, though not indicative in grammatical mood or assertive in force, explicate or define the meanings of the virtue-words as the words are commonly used.

A more serious problem, perhaps, arises in connection with the concepts of authorization and union on which Hobbes's arguments for obedience and against rebellion so often depend. These concepts are worked out with reference to people in a hypothetical state of total freedom. Yet the arguments employing these concepts were addressed to people in an entirely different case. They were addressed to people who lived under government, who suffered its inconveniences, who were apt to interpret the inconveniences as injustices, and who therefore felt justified in resisting the sovereign. What is more, they were people who had always lived under civil government, or at least people who had never covenanted as free agents for protection against one another. Why should *they* have been persuaded by arguments referring to acts hypothetical agents could have made in a hypothetical situation? Why should Hobbes's case for quiescence, which reinterprets the costs of government as inconveniences willingly incurred by founders of a commonwealth, have persuaded people who had never been party to the creation of their government?

The reason Hobbes could expect his readers to be persuaded was that they were people. Whether or not they had experienced the 'unfruitful liberty' of the state of nature – and Hobbes's theory implies that some readers of *Leviathan*, having lived through the Civil War, *had* experienced this liberty – his readers were human beings, subject to the very impulses that led to war in the state of nature. They would see as much, moreover, if they candidly examined themselves. 'Read Thyself' was the motto Hobbes adopted for the First Part of *Leviathan*, the Part on Human Nature (cf. *L*, Intro, E III x-xi), and long before *Leviathan* it was a slogan mentioned favourably in *The Elements of Law* (Pt. 1, ch. 5, xiii. 24). If citizens only considered in their own case the passions they were subject to, they would be able to read in themselves the ingredients of the warlike behaviour that a total freedom would unleash.

Finding in themselves the causes of war, they would be willing, once the nature of war was made explicit to them, to avoid it, and for the same reasons people in the state of nature would end their war.

It was not necessary to experience war to see that war was as contrary to the exercise of the right of nature as suicide. Anyone would see that war could be nobody's means of preserving life. Anyone would thereby be able to see that it was right to keep the peace if it was right to preserve one's life. Anyone would also see that it was right to obey and not resist one's sovereign if to disobey was to start a war. Having both reason and passion in common with agents in the state of nature, Hobbes's readers were able to accept, as people who had left a fictional state of nature could accept, the inconveniences of government. Without necessarily having helped to create a commonwealth out of chaos, Hobbes's readers were able to keep it from degenerating into anarchy. They had only to behave as if they were keeping to the sort of covenant made explicit in Hobbes's writings. In practice this would mean no more than abiding by civil laws.

3 Civil science as exemplary science

Hobbes's civil science succeeds after all in marrying reason with 'eloquence'. Not only does it show that the alternative to life under government is extremely fearful, thus enlisting the aid of a strong passion in persuading people to obey a sovereign power: it also adduces arguments from the definitions of terms like 'right' and 'just' to show that rebellion against the sovereign power can be neither just nor right. So its case for quiescence under any government strong enough to keep the peace, has two distinct but complementary strands. The reason-engaging strand, distinguished by its method of passing step-by-step from clear definitions to evident conclusions, or from controversial claims back to the meanings of the relevant terms, was supposed to have the rigour of geometrical synthesis and analysis. Indeed, for a time, Hobbes was prepared to call nothing 'science' that did not enjoy this measure of rigour. Even when he changed his mind about this, recognizing in the natural sciences the need for hypotheses in addition to the composition and decomposition of terms and speeches, he retained the view that because of its departures from geometrical method, natural science was a lesser specimen of science than civil science.

Political phenomena he saw as the products of many human wills. Their causes were immediately discoverable in any one human will, much as the causes of geometrical figures could be discovered in the wills of their constructors. Natural phenomena he thought were ultimately caused by the divine will, with 'secondary causes' that could only be fathomed indirectly and with no certainty (cf. *SL*, Ep. Ded., E VII

SEDITION, SUBMISSION AND SCIENCE

183–4). Civil associations or bodies politic were human artifacts, fully intelligible as solutions to a distinctly human problem: unsociableness. Natural bodies, on the other hand, were not fully intelligible, and to the extent their constitutions could be worked out, they could not be understood as the solution of a problem, or the realization of a purpose, divine or otherwise. Thus the idea that a scientific understanding of bodies politic would surpass the understanding supplied by physics.

At its most explicit the idea comes out in a line of thought concerning grades of demonstrative science developed repeatedly in Hobbes's writings. Perhaps as early as 1646, in a Latin optical treatise,[2] Hobbes had begun to distinguish between the kind of demonstration that was possible in physics, and the kind that was available in 'other sciences', meaning, probably, geometry and pure mechanics. By the time of the *Six Lessons* and *De Homine*, he was still observing such a distinction (*SL*, Ep. Ded; *De Hom.*, ch. 10, iv–v. 41–43). Only it had become, if it was not originally, a distinction between the kind of demonstration possible in physics, and the kind that could be carried out in geometry *and* civil philosophy.

In civil philosophy there is supposed to be *precognition* of 'the causes, generation and construction' of the body politic, and so civil philosophy is fully demonstrable (*SL*, Ep. Ded., E VII 183–4; *De Hom.*, ch. 10, iv–v. 41–3). Instead of having to reason from observed properties to their causes, and from the causes back to the properties, as in physics, the civil philosopher can by-pass the effect-cause stage of reasoning completely. Synthesis, composition or demonstration of effects from causes is possible with no preliminaries. The reason is that the causes of the properties of bodies are our own 'operations'. We make or keep a certain pact or covenant from which all of the institutions of the state and the distribution of rights and duties within the state can be deduced. Everything there is to be known about the commonwealth is put into it by ourselves as makers or keepers of the covenant that institutes it. That is how there can be precognition of causes and with it full demonstrability of effects or properties.

It is supposed to be similar in geometry. When someone proves a theorem about the properties of a geometrical figure, the properties of an equilateral triangle, say, he knows in advance that such a figure can exist, because he actually constructs it. And any properties it has once it is constructed must result, as the whole figure does, from the motions he has gone through in constructing it. So nothing more than the operations have to be known for the properties to be deducible. As Hobbes says in *De Homine*, 'the reason many theorems are demonstrable about quantity, the science whereof is geometry', is that

the causes of the properties that individual figures have belong to them because we ourselves draw the lines; and since the generation of the figures depends on our will; nothing more is required to know the phenomenon peculiar to any figure whatsoever, than that we consider everything that follows from the construction that we ourselves make in the figure to be described (ch. 10, v, 41).

Theorems are demonstrable in the science of the just and unjust for the same reason: 'because we ourselves make the principles – that is, the causes of justice (namely laws and covenants) – whereby it is known what *justice* and *equity*, and their opposites . . . are' (*De Home.*, ch. 10, v, 42–43).

There is an upshot for sciences in which the principles are *not* dependent on our will. These are sciences that lack certain and infallible principles, and they cannot be counted upon to be rigorously demonstrable. Now physics is among these second class sciences. Its principles are not of our own making, and for that reason they are not known in advance. They have to be worked out by ratiocination from effects or sensory appearances (*De Corp.*, ch. 25, i, E I 388). And the ratiocination has to be assisted at places by hypotheses (ibid., ch. 30, xv, E I 531), hypotheses rather than known truths (ibid.). Because hypotheses come into the demonstrations of natural effects from their causes, the causes cannot be assumed to be the actual causes of the phenomena demonstrated to flow from them. At most they are possible causes. Accordingly, the synthesis or reconstruction of effects out of causes is at best probabilistic.

If a physicist specifies causes of the phenomena of gravity or heat, or of the causes of movements of celestial bodies, one is not to take it that he has discovered for certain how those things work. Other explanations may be proposed that are equally plausible, and many plausible explanations may be proposed without any being faithful to the actual generation of the phenomena in question. The reason there can be this contest of equally plausible theories, the reason that no one explanation can conclusively be demonstrated, is not just that the demonstrations invoke hypotheses; there is the further fact that natural effects are traceable ultimately to God. His power being unlimited, there is 'no effect which [He] cannot produce by many several ways' (*SPP*, Ep. Ded., E VII 3; cf. *DP*, ch. 2, E VII 88).

Hobbes has more than one reason for claiming that physics is the lesser science, but the point that he usually stresses is that its demonstrations depend on hypotheses, and that its principles 'contain not the generation of the subject'. One of his worries is that the demonstrations of physics can be disputed, whereas proper demonstrations ought to be incontrovertible. He took the demonstrations of geometry to live up to this ideal, and partly by reference to the strange analogy between geometrical things and bodies politic, he argued that demonstrative knowledge in politics could approximate to demonstrative knowledge in geometry.

Just as his demand for incontrovertible demonstration explains the lowly status of physics in his scheme of science, so the same demand explains why he allows into that scheme so little of what passed in his day for science or philosophy. He was writing at a time when 'philosophy' was the name for arts learned by formal disputation in the universities. Genteel controversy in Oxford and Cambridge, focussed on abstrusely formulated 'questions' out of Aristotle or Aquinas, co-existed in England with bitter public disagreements over religion, over the authority of the common law, and over the division of powers between King and parliament. These apparently different sorts of contention Hobbes saw as connected. He thought 'madness' was the right word for the clamour outside the universities, 'the seditious roaring', as he called it, of 'a troubled nation'. But another kind of madness was 'incident to none but those, that converse in questions of matters incomprehensible, as the School-men; or in questions of abstruse philosophy' (L, ch. 8, E III 69). As an antidote to both sorts of insanity Hobbes prescribed philosophy: true philosophy, not university dogmatics or lawyer's cant. This is what would end some of the controversy and silence some of the clamour. This was his remedy for madness.

4 Hobbesian science and latter-day philosophy

The idea that philosophy cures various sorts of mental disorder is a special case of Hobbes's bigger idea that science or philosophy ought to do people good, that it ought to improve the human condition. Superficially similar ideas have been put forward by others, in Hobbes's day and our own. Thus Descartes claimed that his own metaphysics was good therapy for the intellect. Much more recently, a certain philosophical method has been prescribed by Wittgenstein as a cure for a sickness of the understanding that afflicts us all as users of language. Hobbes's idea is closer to the Baconian one that philosophy or science can contribute to the 'relief of man's estate' – alleviate the worst features of the life of Fallen human beings. It has relatively little to do with up-to-date views of science. It has still less in common with certain current views of philosophy. For at its most distinctive and at its most philosophical, i.e., in application to ethics and politics rather than to astronomy or optics, Hobbes's science manages to be at once coercive, revisionary, and bent on pronouncing the last word. I want to conclude by indicating how this is so, and why it is no bad thing.

(i) In describing the form philosophy assumes when it is pursued in orderly fashion, Hobbes, as we have seen, emphasizes its 'synthetic' or 'compositive' character. Philosophy starts from the definitions of meanings of words, and proceeds truth by truth, syllogism by syllogism, part of science by part of science, from first philosophy to ethics and politics. The main vehicle of doctrine is supposed to be the syllogism. And in a syllogism a proposition

> is said to *follow* from two other propositions, when these being granted to be true, it cannot be denied but the other is true also (*De Corp.*, ch. 3, xviii. E I 42).

Another way he puts it is by saying that when a proposition follows from others it 'cannot but be understood' that its predicate is the name of everything the subject-term names: it is psychologically necessary for the proposition to be taken as true (E I 42). Or in other words, by winning assent to the premisses the teacher or demonstrator *forces* belief in the conclusion on the part of the student. This is how someone learns or acquires knowledge by teaching (*De Corp.*, ch. 6, xii, E I 80).

Nozick has coined the term 'coercive philosophy' for the practice of using arguments to compel belief, and he has objected that forcing people to believe things is self-frustrating as a means of improving people. 'Just as dependence is not eliminated by treating people dependently, and someone cannot be forced to be free, a person is not most improved by being forced to believe something against his will, whether he wants to or not'.[3] It is better for someone to learn out of a willingness to be taught than to learn because argumentative bludgeoning happens to penetrate the barriers put up against it. Agreed. But Nozick seems to me to run together being got to believe something against one's will, with being got to believe something whether one wants to or not (which may involve no resistance on the part of the believer). And he overlooks the frequency with which philosophical arguments state reasons for what most people believe anyway.

Further, and unlike Hobbes, Nozick does not seem to take into account unsavoury motives for putting up resistance to argument, especially moral argument. Pretty clearly, one reason for putting up barriers can be an unwillingness to face up to the errors of one's beliefs or practices. Hobbes thinks that certain unfortunate but powerful passions will always block a philosophical message as soon as the message is seen to take away from one's self-love or go against one's short-term advantage. In some parts of philosophy, notably the 'doctrine of lines and figures', i.e., geometry, the truth conflicts with people's interests only rarely, and so in those areas even a conclusion that is far from obvious has a chance of winning assent so long as it is rigorously derived (cf. *L*, ch. 11, E III 91; *EL*, Ep. Ded.). But in civil philosophy things are different, and special measures are needed to demonstrate one's findings. Hobbes is describing the special measures when he says in the Epistle Dedicatory to *The Elements of Law* that 'he puts down such principles

for a foundation, as passion not mistrusting, may not seek to displace.'
It is a way of saying that he engages the self-interest of his readers from
the start, and shows why war can never be in their interest. Of course,
it is their *rational* self-interest he engages; he is not pandering indiscrimi-
nately to the passions in his hearers, but trying to give them as much
detachment from the passions as is needed for a clear-headed self-interest
to come into operation. If Hobbes's measures work, and otherwise
resisting passions are disarmed by the operation of rational self-interest,
then his demonstration can be both compelling and yet encounter less
resistance then it might have. It can also, if its conclusion is adopted,
improve people. But it has this power not despite but on *account* of its
overcoming some natural defence-mechanisms in the people to whom it
is addressed.

(ii) Hobbes's science of morals and politics is supposed to *correct*, not
just assemble and make clear, people's untutored beliefs concerning right
and wrong. Hobbes speaks of the 'prospective glasses' civil philosophy
makes available to counteract our natural shortsightedness in matters of
morals and politics (*L*, ch. 18, E III 170). He thinks the unforeseen
consequences of pursuing felicity only come to light by way of his
demonstration of the connection between war and the gratification of
appetite or passion. Other passages suggest that people are not only
naturally ignorant of the rules of peace, but are wrong about where their
duty lies when it comes to avoiding war, the error being due to passions
and self-love (cf. e.g. *L*, ch. 15, E III 144–5). Hobbes's deduction of
the laws of nature is supposed to change all of that. It is a self-consciously
revisionary civil philosophy.

But it is not revisionary in the wrong way. As I tried to suggest in
the first two chapters, Hobbes realizes that in order to expound a
doctrine that will influence Everyman's actions, the doctrine must not
surpass Everyman's understanding. Everyman must be able to see in
himself what disposes people to come into conflict with one another,
and he must be able to see that the existence of a strong government keeps
these aggressive forces in check, but he need not be able to understand the
causes of the forces, or command a clear view of the various offices and
departments of strong government. He must simply be able to see strong
government as a security device, and his fellow men, were they
ungoverned, as subject to passions that could make them his enemies.
Beyond being able to grasp this residue of theory he is only called upon
to know which civil laws he must abide by, and to see abiding by them
as insurance against war. It is not much to take away from Hobbes's full-
blown theory, but it is plausibly quite enough to transform Everyman's
understanding of his obligations and give Everyman something like
general knowledge of his fellow men. Certainly no prior excursion into

physics is necessary or relied upon, to get people to see their political position in a new way.

Hobbes sometimes seems to disclaim any interest in revisionary philosophy, remarking in *The Elements of Law* that he intends only 'to put men in mind of what they know already, or may know by their own experience' (Pt. 1, ch. 1, ii. 2). But this is a remark about principles or starting points, not about what is deduced from them. When he derives the rights that sovereigns ought to enjoy, and the duties that subjects ought to fulfill, he knows he is describing arrangements no-one has experienced (cf. *L*, ch. 20, E III 195f; ch. 30, E III 324–5); but he makes no apology for this, pointing out that when civil societies are organized along lines that *are* familiar, they are never long free of civil war. He takes his task to be one of showing how sovereigns and subjects could better conduct themselves, and he does not shrink from recommending, albeit at an extremely high level of generality, novel precepts they would have to follow to bring about this improved conduct. In some ways his work looks forward to writing in applied ethics that has come to be prominent in moral philosophy in the English speaking world. This, too, seeks ways of improving and not just of interpreting the practices it describes. But there is perhaps something less absurd about Hobbes's criticisms of public policy and his recommendations of reform than those in the professional philosophers' journals. Hobbes had the ear of influential noblemen in England all of his life, and free access to the king after the Restoration.

(iii) He aimed at conclusive demonstrations in civil philosophy. By contrast with his work in the hypothetico-deductive science of physics, which he openly conceded could be rivalled or bettered by other theories of an anti-scholastic kind (cf. *De Corp.*, ch. 30, xv, E I 531), his civil philosophy was taken as definitive on those topics it dealt with at the foundations of the subject. Indeed, Hobbes was committed to holding as much by his self-consciously labelling his subject 'civil philosophy': to be that it had to be made up of 'general, eternal and immutable truths' reached exclusively by reasoning aright.

The idea that there can be a true, definitive and scientifically methodical morals and politics is often dismissed in our own day as resting on a deep confusion. Indeed, it is sometimes suggested that until notions of objectivity and scientific method are abandoned in favour of categories appropriate to understanding speech or literature, deep confusions will linger about the kind of illumination social and political theory can provide.[4] Rorty has argued more generally that until philosophy ceases to be in the thrall of these notions, and starts to become an activity in which objectivity and definitiveness are not ideals, a bad and long-lived self-image in the subject will be perpetuated.[5]

The ideals Rorty thinks philosophy ought to adopt are those of making inventive and suggestive additions to an activity of conversation, which the participants try to prolong rather than conclude. But the fact that in his own day Hobbes's moral and political treatises prompted further, very refined speculation by Spinoza, in Holland, as well as a host of works by writers on politics, morals and religion in England,[6] the fact that there has continued to be discussion down to our own day, shows that trying to pronounce the last word may be one of the more effective ways of keeping the conversation going.

Notes

Chapter I The Science of Politics and the Unity of Science

1 For more detail, see G. C. Robertson's *Hobbes* (Edinburgh: W Blackwood, 1886). Robertson is generally reliable on matters of chronology, and is good on the early editions and early reception of *De Cive*.

2 By the time of *Leviathan* and *De Corpore*, Hobbes's claims about the influence of Aristotle were probably out of date. In the last of the *Six Lessons*, Less. 6, E VII 348, there is an aside that indicates his Oxford critics had tried to point this out.

3 The Epistle Dedicatory of *De Corpore* softens *Leviathan*'s condescending line on experimental results. Before Copernicus, Galileo and Harvey, he says, 'there was nothing certain in natural philosophy *but* every man's experiments to himself . . .' (E I ix – my emphasis). Previously he had been inclined to exclude experimental results from natural philosophy.

4 See e.g. Peters' *Hobbes* (Harmondsworth: Penguin, 1956), p. 87; Macpherson, *The Political Theory of Possessive Individualism* (Oxford: Clarendon Press, 1962), p. 10. Macpherson cites chapter 6 of *De Corpore* as asserting the possibility of this deduction. Gauthier, in *The Logic of Leviathan: The Moral and Political Theory of Thomas Hobbes* (Oxford: Clarendon Press, 1969), writes, 'Had Hobbes succeeded in his grand design for a unified science, questions of morals and politics would be treated in a purely synthetic manner, by derivation from the supreme relations or principles established through an analysis of body' (p. 3).

5 Hobbes's identification of science with a knowledge of truths in the context of demonstrations, is clear from his earliest political treatise (*EL*, Pt. 1, ch. 6, iv. 26; cf. also the opening pages of TW) as well as from *Leviathan* (ch. 5, E III 35). The idea that his morals and politics was a science because it was demonstrative, is put over indirectly in the last chapter of the Six Lessons. Hobbes is trying there to rebut the charge that he expressed conceit when he claimed (in *De Corpore*) that civil philosophy or civil science was no older than his book *De Cive*. He replied to this criticism by pointing out that someone else's summary of *De Cive* in French had been given a title which

145

indicated the summarizer's belief in its scientific status. The title was *Ethics Demonstrated* (cf. E VII 333).

Chapter II The Parts of Science and the Methods of Science

1 The fullest and most influential statement of this position is J.W.N. Watkins's. See his *Hobbes's System of Ideas* (London: Hutchinson, 1965), chs. 3 and 4, pp. 47–81. A broadly complementary interpretation can be found in M.M. Goldsmith's *Hobbes's Science of Politics* (New York: Columbia University Press, 1966). See esp. chs. 1 and 7. Like Watkins, Goldsmith is inclined to read Hobbes as extending a method of understanding natural bodies to bodies politic. Note especially the opening sentence of ch. 7, p. 228.

2 Instead, it seems to be an application of a precept Hobbes keeps separate from his official account of method in chapter 6 of *De Corpore*. The precept comes over in a remark in *De Corpore*'s Epistle to the Reader, where he urges the reader to 'imitate the creation' (E I, xiii). He has in mind a speculative construction from scratch of the 'most universal things' – space, time, body, accident, motion – out of which the world is composed. It is a construction from scratch of those components of the world, not a construction of the world from those components as revealed by analysis or resolution. And similarly, when Hobbes proposes to consider the rights and duties as 'dissolved' it is arguably a counterpart of the method of imaginary annihilation. Goldsmith, who has recognized the parallel between the imaginary annihilation of the world in *De Corpore* and the imaginary dissolution of rights in *De Cive* (op. cit., p. 85), nevertheless seems to run annihilation together with resolution or analysis (p. 229).

The assumption that Hobbes was urging resolution of the commonwealth into individuals and not the annihilation of rights and duties so as to reveal bare human nature, has led to the claim that Hobbes was the first exponent of what is now called 'methodological individualism', a reductive thesis to the effect that truths about states as wholes reduce to truths about the individuals who make them up. For this (I think mistaken) interpretation and references to others along similar lines, see Stephen Lukes's 'Methodological Individualism Reconsidered', reprinted in A. Ryan, ed., *The Philosophy of Social Explanation* (Oxford: University Press, 1973), pp. 119–29.

3 According to chapter 1 of Nozick's *Anarchy, State and Utopia* (Oxford: Blackwell, 1974), the idea of a state of nature is particularly well suited to 'explanatory political theory', the sort of theory that specifies in non-political terms how 'the political realm' could have been generated, though it was not generated that way. Watkins's interpretation suggests that Hobbes's use of the state of nature was motivated by an interest in some Paduan, resolutive/compositive counterpart of what Nozick calls 'explanatory political theory', but considerations to be reviewed in this chapter make the suggestion doubtful. Hobbes's use of the state of nature is best understood, I think, as contributing to a venture in *rhetoric*, broadly conceived. He wants to persuade people that remaining obedient to a *de facto* protective power is for the best. In order to win his readers over to this point of view, he thinks he has to overcome the operation of strong passions, notably avarice and ambition (cf.

De Cive, Ep. Ded., E II iv), which incline them to opportunistic rebellion. The strong passions arise in his readers from their experience of political arrangements in an actual state. To induce detachment from this experience and blunt the effects of the associated passions, Hobbes tries to conjure up in his readers a vivid conception of anarchy or statelessness, a conception calculated to bring into operation passions *favourable* to obedience, namely fear of death and hope of enjoying a moderately-scaled good life. These passions aid his readers to discover, or at least see the point of, the laws of nature, which in turn give them a rationale for obedience.

Rawls's device of the 'original position' in *A Theory of Justice* (Cambridge, Mass.: Harvard University Press, 1972), is sometimes claimed to function in *his* contractarian theory as the state of nature does in Hobbes, Locke and Rousseau (cf. Daniels's Introduction to *Reading Rawls* (Oxford: Blackwell, 1975), p. xviiif). Leaving aside the question of whether Hobbes, Locke and Rousseau subscribed to a way of thinking that was reasonably homogeneous, the affinities between Hobbes and Rawls seem to me to be very slight, even when what is being compared is the original position and the state of nature. One thing that keeps the two views apart is Rawls's assumption that occupants of the original position are ignorant of who they are and of what they think is good. Enveloping each party to a social contract in a veil of ignorance is supposed to facilitate their opting unanimously in fair circumstances for principles that should govern real institutions and social practices. Now Hobbes makes no special provisions for unanimity, indeed says outright that if only a majority of those involved in instituting a commonwealth designate a particular man or assembly sovereign, he or it still acts for them *all*, and is authorized by each so to act (*L*, ch. 18, E III 159, 162). Nor does Hobbes think of the covenant as being entered into in conditions that would intuitively count as fair: for one thing, each person in the state of nature can be assumed to fear and distrust everyone else. These departures from the thinking behind the original position make it a question whether it can have the same *point* as the state of nature.

Dworkin has suggested that 'the ignorance of the parties in the original position might . . . be seen as a kind of limiting case of the ignorance that can be found, in the form of a distorted or eccentric ranking of interests, in classical contract theories and that is natural to the contract device' ('The Original Position' in *Reading Rawls*, op. cit., p. 47). Dworkin illustrates the point by reference to Hobbes's state of nature, where, as Dworkin thinks, Hobbes's prior assumptions about the primacy of the right to life, lead to a 'contract situation' in which the parties have put a secure life above all other individual goals (ibid.). But this is a misleading way of putting it. People in the state of nature certainly think that security must be seen to *before* the goods each thinks important to felicity can be pursued with any hope of success. But the good or felicitous life is what each wants security for the sake of. In that sense the good life is prior to security as a goal, though only security is covenanted for. The upshot is that there is nothing distorted or eccentric about the ranking of interests in the state of nature, and the parallel with Rawls's veil of ignorance seems to collapse.

4 Alan Ryan, who is impressed by what he takes to be a parallel between

Millian and post-Millian approaches on the one hand, and Hobbes's on the other, sees in *Leviathan* an outright assimilation of politics to physics. See *The Philosophy of the Social Sciences* (London: Macmillan, 1970), p. 15.

5 This suggestion, or one very similar to it, has also been made by Michael Oakeshott, in his Introduction to *Leviathan*, reprinted in *Hobbes on Civil Association* (Oxford: Blackwell, 1975). See esp. pp. 16ff. Oakeshott's general development of the suggestion is different from my own, and defective, I think, in at least its contrast between philosophy and science or reason and empiricism (p. 18f). For my own account, see the opening section of chapter 3, below.

Chapter III Knowledge and Power in Fallen Man

1 This line of thought may at first appear to anticipate Hume. Hobbes does not, however, think that constant conjunctions are all we can discover. Necessary connections turn out to be accessible to people because they can acquire a capacity for reasoning.

2 Experience sufficed only to acquaint people with the workings of the passions themselves. The consequences of their unrestricted operation, namely the horrors of war, were for reason to disclose.

3 Bacon before Hobbes, and Locke after him, took up the story of the Fall in their writings, Bacon in expounding a theory of science markedly more optimistic than Hobbes's. For some telling quotations from Bacon and comments on their significance in relation to the period leading up to the Civil War, see Hill's *Intellectual Origins of the English Revolution* (Oxford: Clarendon Press, 1980), pp. 87-90. Other uses of the story of the Fall in the Civil War period come out in Hill's *The World Turned Upside Down* (London: Temple Smith, 1972), ch. 8. John Dunn's *The Political Thought of John Locke* (Cambridge: University Press, 1969), contains scattered remarks on the attention Locke paid to the story. See chs. 6 and 9.

4 See his early *Discourse on the Moral Effects of the Arts and Sciences* and *A Discourse on the Origin of Inequality*, in G.D.H. Cole, trans., *The Social Contract and Discourses* (London: Dent, 1973).

5 This and more seems to be implied by Rousseau's claim that the savage or primitive 'lives within himself'. See the concluding paragraphs of *Inequality*. It is also implied by Rousseau's claim that in his natural state man is self-sufficient (ibid., pt. 2, p. 103).

6 As a matter of fact, Hobbes makes it clear that there is something wrong with a civilization in which men have, or spend all of their time procuring, unnecessary riches. In general, he seems to prefer, with Rousseau, the kind of society that is *not* tainted by luxury. Keith Thomas assembles relevant textual evidence in defending Hobbes against the Marxist accusation that he is a mouthpiece for a *bourgeois* social outlook. See Thomas's excellent article, 'The Social Origins of Hobbes's Political Thought' in K.C. Brown, ed., *Hobbes Studies* (Oxford: Blackwell, 1965), pp. 216ff.

7 On the point that Hobbes had no intention of framing a full-blown philosophy of language my interpretation is broadly in agreement with Hacking's *Why Does Language Matter to Philosophy?* (Cambridge: University Press,

1975), ch. 2. See esp. p. 23. Hacking does not, however, seem to consider the way a theoretical interest in science motivates Hobbes's remarks about language.

8 For illuminating discussion of the relevant chronology and careful discussion of the text that first announces his belief in hypothetico-deductive science, see Brandt, *Hobbes's Mechanical Conception of Nature* (London: Hachette, 1928), ch. 5, esp. pp. 191f.

Chapter IV Two Problems with Demonstrative Science

1 Hobbes has often been taken to be a conventionalist about the truth of all propositions, not just the propositions of science. Leibniz was one of the first to interpret him in this way. See Loemker's edition and translation, *Leibniz: Philosophical Papers and Letters* (Chicago, 1956), I, p. 199.

2 Singular propositions have a use in science in analysis or the method of discovery but *not* a use in the syllogisms or chains of reasoning that are supposed to be used to teach science.

3 *Discourse on the Method for Rightly Conducting the Reason and Seeking for Truth in the Sciences*, in E. Haldane and G.R. Ross, trans., *The Philosophical Works of Descartes* (Cambridge: University Press, 1970), vol. 1, p. 91.

4 *Posterior Analytics*, II, i.

5 Officially Hobbes is non-committal about whether motion is essential to all bodies; but he does go so far as to say that as a matter of fact, no body is ever at rest (*DP*, ch. 2, E VII 87).

6 'Concepts of Cause in the Development of Physics', reprinted in Kuhn, *The Essential Tension* (Chicago: University Press, 1977), p. 24.

Chapter V First Principles, First Causes, and the Sciences of Motion

1 See the Fifth of the *Meditations on First Philosophy*, in Haldane and Ross, op. cit., pp. 183–4.

2 See e.g. Geach, *Mental Acts* (London: Routledge & Kegan Paul, 1957), ch. 6.

3 As Descartes, Berkeley and Reid saw, notions of what exists independently of the senses must either be non-sensory notions (Descartes, Reid) or else notions of things that do not after all exist independently of sensory experience (Berkeley).

Chapter VI Motion, Phantasms and the Objects of Sense

1 Haldane and Ross, op. cit., vol. 2, p. 65.

2 Haldane and Ross, op. cit., vol. 1, pp. 128–9.

3 The problem may not face Hobbes only. Panpsychism seems to follow from premises that are commonplaces of current physicalist literature in the philosophy of mind. See Thomas Nagel's *Mortal Questions* (Cambridge: University Press, 1979), pp. 181–95.

4 Though he is sometimes saddled with a representative theory of perception

in the course of being saddled with an ideational theory of meaning, there is very little evidence of his holding that we are immediately acquainted with ideas and only indirectly in touch with things ideas represent. Peters, op. cit., p. 134, seems to believe that Hobbes held to both a representative theory of perception and an ideational theory of meaning. Watkins mentions others, including his former self, who agree with that interpretation. See op. cit., p. 140f. Hacking, op. cit., ch. 2, shows that any attribution of an ideational theory to Hobbes must be extremely doubtful.

5 *Pace* Peters, op. cit., pp. 107f.

Chapter VII Sense, Thought and Motivation

1 Hume remarks in Section 7 of the *Enquiry Concerning Human Understanding* that 'men have ever agreed in the doctrine both of necessity and of liberty, according to any reasonable sense which can be put on those terms'. This remark seems to echo Hobbes.
2 'Agency' in the sense of the relation of an agent to his actions.

Chapter VIII The Pursuit of Felicity and the Good of Survival

1 T. A. Roberts, ed., *Butler's Fifteen Sermons* (London: SPCK, 1970), p. 19n.
2 Why does the discussion of charity in *Human Nature* mention power at all? The answer is given in chapter 8 of the book. Hobbes points out that some passions involve the expectation of pleasure, and not just experience of pleasure in the present. But there is a problem about expected pleasures, because Hobbes's theory of experience rules out conceptions of things in the future in general (*HN*, ch. 4, vii, E IV 16). There can be conceptions of things in the future only if there are conceptions of things in the present capable of producing certain effects in the future (*HN*, ch. 8, iii, E IV 37). And there can be conceptions of pleasure to come only if there can be a conception by an agent of some power in himself capable of producing the pleasure (*HN*, ch. 8, iii, E IV 37). How an agent comes to know what powers he has is by observing what he does (*HN*, ch. 8, v, E IV 38), and when he observes himself being charitable he finds he has power to spare, power he can therefore channel into the pursuit of a remote good. Charitable actions, then, given an agent evidence of surplus power needed to bring about future pleasure. Now finding out that he has power to spare may delight an agent, but if it does, it is not, as Butler's argument requires, the self-regarding delight in power Hobbes calls 'glory', for glory is the feeling of triumph that proceeds from discovering that one has more power than a competitor. Being gratified at one's charitable acts is not glory, for it is gratification without reference to a competitor.
3 Op. cit., Fifth Sermon, 49n.
4 Ibid., 50n.
5 See F. S. McNeilly's *The Anatomy of Leviathan* (London: Macmillan, 1968), pp. 117-19 and D.D. Raphael, *Hobbes: Morals and Politics* (London: George Allen & Unwin, 1977), pp. 64f. Gert's Introduction to *Man and Citizen*,

op. cit., cites passages from *De Cive* that seem to commit Hobbes to egoism, but Gert's conclusion, based on passages taken from a variety of Hobbes's works, but predominantly from *De Homine*, is that 'the evidence against his holding psychological egoism overwhelmingly outweighs the evidence for his holding it' (p. 3).

6 Gert, op. cit., p. 5, characterizes psychological egoism in this way.

7 *The Possibility of Altruism* (Oxford: Clarendon Press, 1970), p. 84.

8 Ibid., p. 85.

9 Ibid.

10 Ibid., pp. 3–5.

11 See Phillipa Foot, 'Morality as a System of Hypothetical Imperatives', *Philosophical Review* 81 (1972).

12 And since one person's advantages can be compensated for by his competitors, competition is in effect between equals, at least in the state of nature. For enlargement on this point, see *L*, ch. 13, E III 110–11.

13 A. E. Taylor, 'The Ethical Doctrine of Hobbes', *Philosophy* 13 (1938).

14 Howard Warrender, *The Political Philosophy of Hobbes* (Oxford: Clarendon Press, 1957).

15 See S. M. Brown, 'Hobbes: The Taylor Thesis', *Philosophical Review* 68 (1959), Thomas Nagel, 'Hobbes's Concept of Obligation', *Philosophical Review* 68 (1959), and Watkins, op. cit., ch. 5.

16 Watkins, op. cit., p. 84.

17 *Nicomachean Ethics* I, 9, 1099b25f.

18 Warrender, op. cit., p. 218.

19 Nagel, 'Hobbes's Concept of Obligation', loc. cit., p. 74.

20 For the application of the point to Aristotle, see Kathleen Wilkes's 'The Good Man and the Good for Man in Aristotle's Ethics', *Mind* 87 (1978). Phillipa Foot notes a difficulty in saying in general who benefits from the possession of moral virtue, the virtuous man himself or his companions. See the title essay in her *Virtues and Vices* (Oxford: Blackwell, 1978), p. 3.

21 *Nicomachean Ethics* VI, 13, 1144b1–25. Aristotle's point is that unless there is something to guide the practice of virtue – namely a practical wisdom or intelligence united with the possession of virtue – the virtues a man naturally has can be misused. Hobbes agrees, but holds that the locus of practical wisdom in the state is the sovereign, not the individual.

22 In 'A Hobbesian Minimal State', *Philosophy and Public Affairs* 11 (1982), Michael Levin seems to overlook completely chapter 30 of *Leviathan* when he argues that being intended only for the security of those who institute it, the Hobbesian commonwealth is 'minimal' in Nozick's sense. 'It is no part of the Hobbesian bargain,' Levin says, 'to gain security against hunger, cold, ignorance or poverty' (p. 341). This way of putting it comes of an unduly minimalist understanding of Hobbes's concept of public safety.

23 Nagel, 'Hobbes's Concept of Obligation', op. cit., pp. 74, 81.

24 Ibid., p. 74.

25 For the best attempt at constructing such an argument, and an unparalleled appreciation of the difficulties, see D. Parfit's *Reasons and Persons* (Oxford: Clarendon Press, 1984).

Chapter IX Absolute Submission, Undivided Sovereignty

1 In *The Logic of Leviathan*, op. cit., Gauthier depicts the problem of keeping or not keeping the covenant as a Prisoner's Dilemma. Presenting the problem game-theoretically does not seem to me to throw light on it, and as a device for expounding Hobbes's reasoning the Prisoner's Dilemma has the major drawback of abstracting completely from the way the actions of the parties are related in time, something Hobbes repeatedly refers to.

2 Hobbes usually describes the unrestricted right of nature as an obstacle in the way of peace, rather than justice (cf. e.g. *L*, ch. 26, E III 254), but there is no tension in saying it is an obstacle in the way of both.

3 For accounts of the differences, see Gauthier, op. cit., chs. 3 and 4, and Goldsmith, op. cit., pp. 156f.

4 Keith Thomas has suggested in 'The Social Origins . . .', loc. cit., p. 202, that Hobbes envisaged the development of a genuinely virtuous character in only a select few, probably drawn from 'the leisured minority of the population'. The inspiration for his just man may have been one or more of the group, mainly aristocrats, who met at Great Tew before the Civil War (p. 206).

5 Critics of Rawls who note that *A Theory of Justice* lacks an abstract defence of contractarianism, sometimes ask why in the theory of justice as fairness, or any comparable theory, so much should be thought to be justified by people's agreeing to submit to institutions. As Nagel puts it, 'it is not the agreement that justifies what has been agreed to, but rather whatever justifies the agreement itself' ('Rawls on Justice', reprinted in *Reading Rawls*, op. cit., p. 5). Applied to Hobbes, the point would be that the acts of a sovereign toward his subjects are justified not by the subjects' authorization, but by whatever justifies the authorization. Is the point missed by Hobbes in the passage just quoted? Certainly the passage seems to say that when subjects lend their wills to policies decided by the sovereign, that by itself makes the policies all right, even when the policies are found unpleasant in practice by the authorizers. And this does seem to leave out the important matter of why subjects lend their wills to the policies in the first place. In fact, however, Hobbes makes it perfectly clear in *Leviathan* and elsewhere that subjects lend their wills in the interest of security. This is the good that ultimately justifies the acts of the sovereign toward his subjects, not the authorization *tout court*.

But a problem remains. The sovereign is the sole judge of what conduces to security, and in particular of what must be given up for the sake of security. If the things he thinks have to be given up are constitutive for subjects of their felicity, then that is too bad; they must abide by what the sovereign decides or break a covenant they have made for the sake of security. Since they will the end, they will the means, and since they leave decisions about means to the sovereign, they must will *his* choice of means. So Hobbes seems to argue. But since people in the state of nature sue for peace and submit their wills to the sovereign's not as an end in itself, but in the hope of enjoying the good life peace is necessary for, what is in a sense their ultimate goal, namely leading the good life or experiencing felicity, can be betrayed at the same time as the lesser good of peace they explicitly covenant for is procured for them by the sovereign. Because what explicitly justifies their authorization of the sovereign's acts understates what they want as the result of those acts, and since those acts can actually conflict with their ultimate goal, it is not clear that just any acts the sovereign performs for the sake of peace really are done with the agreement of the covenanters. In a sense, the good they 'really' covenant for is not the one that justifies their authorization.

6 Indeed, Hobbes thinks the parallel between sovereignty by institution and sovereignty by acquisition goes further, for acts of authorization in both cases are prompted by the same type of passion, namely fear. Only the object of the fear serves to distinguish the acts of authorization of the conquered from those of free men in the state of nature. In the case of sovereignty acquired by force, what men fear is death or imprisonment at the hands of the conqueror. In the other case they fear death or subjection at one another's hands.

Probably Hobbes exaggerates the parallel between the two kinds of sovereignty: the fear that drives people into civil society from the state of nature is mutual fear on the part of individuals who by and large are equal in power. In the case of conquest, the fear is of someone whose power has prevailed in a fight against a whole commonwealth. An individual who refuses to submit to this power, and who tries with all his might to resist it, is a much more puny obstacle for a conquering sovereign power than he is for another individual. The position of someone in a conquered commonwealth is better likened to the position of a free rider, or perhaps an outlaw, in an instituted commonwealth. Where the parallel as Hobbes draws it *is* exact enough, is in respect of the rights of the two types of sovereign and the frailty of their power.

7 *Politics*, III, 1, 1275a22–23.
8 See *Nicomachean Ethics*, X, 9; *Politics*, III, 5.
9 *Nicomachean Ethics*, II, 2, 1104a5–10.

Chapter X Sedition, Submission and Science

1 See Skinner's 'The Ideological Context of Hobbes's Political Thought', *The Historical Journal* 9 (1966), pp. 295f. Also relevant is Dewey's 'The Motivation of Hobbes's Political Philosophy' in R. Ross, H. Schneider and T. Waldman eds., *Thomas Hobbes in His Time* (Minneapolis, Minn.: University of Minnesota Press, 1974), pp. 12ff.

2 Excerpts from this treatise appear as Appendix II in Tönnies's edition of *The Elements of Law*, op. cit. Hobbes distinguishes physics from other sciences in chapter 1, article 1, pp. 211–12 of Tönnies.

3 *Philosophical Explanations* (Cambridge, Mass.: Harvard University Press, 1981), p. 5.

4 See Rorty, 'Method, Social Science, and Social Hope', reprinted in his *Consequences of Pragmatism* (Brighton, Harvester Press, 1982), pp. 191–210. For an indication of the background to the demand for interpretive categories in social science, and many useful references, see Christopher Lloyd's Editor's

Introduction to *Social Theory and Political Practice* (Oxford: Clarendon Press, 1983).

5 Rorty, *Philosophy and the Mirror of Nature* (Oxford: Blackwell, 1980), chs. 7 and 8.

6 Skinner, op. cit., *passim*. See also Samuel Mintz, *The Hunting of Leviathan* (Cambridge: University Press, 1970).

Select Bibliography

The most up-to-date list of works by and about Hobbes is William Sacksteder's *Hobbes Studies* (1879-1979). This was published in 1982 by the Philosophy Documentation Centre at the Bowling Green State Universtiy. The items below are cited in the Notes, and exclude works by Hobbes already listed at the beginning of this book.

Aristotle, *Nicomachean Ethics*, M. Ostwald (trans.) (Indianapolis, Indiana: Bobbs Merill, 1962).

Aristotle, *Politics*, in A. Smith and W.D. Ross (eds), *The Works of Aristotle Translated Into English* (Oxford, 1912–52).

Aristotle, *Posterior Analytics*, in Smith and Ross (eds).

Brandt, F., *Hobbes's Mechanical Conception of Nature* (London: Hachette, 1928).

Brown, S. M., 'Hobbes: The Taylor Thesis', *Philosophical Review* 68 (1959).

Daniels, N., Introduction to *Reading Rawls* (Oxford: Blackwell, 1975).

Descartes, R., *Discourse on the Method for Rightly conducting the Reason and Seeking for Truth in the Sciences*, in E. Haldane and G.R. Ross (trans.), *The Philosophical Works of Descartes* (Cambridge: University Press, 1970).

Descartes, R., *Meditations on First Philosophy*, in Haldane and Ross, op. cit.

Dewey, J., 'The Motivation of Hobbes's Political Philosophy', in R. Ross, H. Schneider and T. Waldman (eds.), *Thomas Hobbes in His Time* (Minneapolis, Minn.: University of Minnesota Press, 1974).

Dunn, J., *The Political Thought of John Locke* (Cambridge: University Press, 1969).

Dworkin, R., 'The Original Position' in Daniels, *Reading Rawls*, op. cit.

Foot, P., *Virtues and Vices* (Oxford: Blackwell, 1978).

Foot, P., 'Morality as a System of Hypothetical Imperatives', *Philosophical Review* 81 (1972).

Gauthier, D., *The Logic of Leviathan: The Moral and Political Theory of Thomas Hobbes* (Oxford: Blackwell, 1978).

Goldsmith, M., *Hobbes's Science of Politics* (New York: Columbia University Press, 1966).

Hacking, I., *Why Does Language Matter to Philosophy?* (Cambridge: University Press, 1975).

Hill, C., *Intellectual Origins of the English Revolution* (Oxford: Clarendon Press, 1980).

Hill, C., *The World Turned Upside Down* (London: Temple Smith, 1972).

Kuhn, T., 'Concepts of Cause in the Development of Physics' in Kuhn, *The Essential Tension* (Chicago: University Press, 1977).

Leibniz, G., *Philosophical Papers and Letters*; Loemker (ed. and trans.) (Chicago, 1956).

Levin, M., 'A Hobbesian Minimal State', *Philosophy and Public Affairs* 11 (1982).

Lloyd, C., (ed.), *Social Theory and Political Practice* (Oxford: Clarendon Press, 1983).

Lukes, S., 'Methodological Individualism Reconsidered', reprinted in A. Ryan (ed.), *The Philosophy of Social Explanation* (Oxford University Press, 1973).

Macpherson, C. B., *The Political Theory of Possessive Individualism* (Oxford: Clarendon Press, 1962).

McNeilly, F. S., *The Anatomy of Leviathan* (London: Macmillan, 1968).

Mintz, S., *The Hunting of Leviathan* (Cambridge: University Press, 1970).

Nagel, T., 'Hobbes's Concept of Obligation', *Philosophical Review* 68 (1959).

Nagel, T., *The Possibility of Altruism* (Oxford: Clarendon Press, 1970).

Nagel, T., *Mortal Questions* (Cambridge: University Press, 1979).

Nozick, R., *Anarchy, State and Utopia* (Oxford: Blackwell, 1974).

Nozick, R., *Philosophical Explanations* (Cambridge, Mass.: Harvard University Press, 1981).

Oakeshott, M., *Hobbes on Civil Association* (Oxford: Blackwell, 1975).

Parfit, D., *Reasons and Persons* (Oxford: Clarendon Press, 1984).

Peters, R., *Hobbes* (Harmondsworth: Penguin, 1956).

Raphael, D. D., *Hobbes: Morals and Politics* (London: George Allen & Unwin, 1977).

Rawls, J., *A Theory of Justice* (Cambridge, Mass.: Harvard University Press, 1972).

Roberts, T. A. (ed.), *Butler's Fifteen Sermons* (London: SPCK, 1970).

Robertson, G.C., *Hobbes* (Edinburgh: W. Blackwood, 1886).

Rorty, R., 'Method, Social Science, and Social Hope', reprinted in Rorty, *Consequences of Pragmatism* (Brighton: Harvester Press, 1982).

Rorty, R., *Philosophy and the Mirror of Nature* (Oxford: Blackwell, 1980).

Rousseau, J. J., *The Social Contract and Discourses*, trans. G.D.H. Cole, (London: Dent, 1973).

Ryan, A. (ed.), *The Philosophy of Social Explanation* (Oxford University Press, 1973).

Ryan, A., *The Philosophy of the Social Sciences* (London: Macmillan, 1970).

Skinner, Q., 'The Ideological Context of Hobbes's Political Thought', *The Historical Journal* 9 (1966).

Taylor, A. E., 'The Ethical Doctrine of Hobbes', *Philosophy* 13 (1938).

Thomas, K., 'The Social Origins of Hobbes's Political Thought', in K.C. Brown (ed.), *Hobbes Studies* (Oxford: Blackwell, 1965).

Warrender, H., *The Political Philosophy of Hobbes* (Oxford: Clarendon Press, 1957).

Wilkes, K., 'The Good Man and the Good for Man in Aristotle's Ethics', *Mind*, 87 (1978).

Index

absolutism, 125
abstraction, 63, 65
action, 2, 9–10, 15–16, 30, 56, 90, 92–5, 103, 104, 106, 109, 110, 120, 128, 135, 142, 150
Adam, 34, 35, 36, 54, 124, 125; *see also* Fall
aether, 76, 77
agent, 37, 94–5, 150
agreement, 47, 48, 115–17, 152–3; of men and commonwealth-making, 14; and significations of names, 41, 134; *see also* conventionalism
agriculture, 32
air, 70, 78
almanacs, 5
ambiguity, 39, 56, 61
analysis, 18, 46, 48, 56–7, 73; *see also* method; resolution
analytic truth, 31
anarchy, 21, 137, 147
anger, 6, 91, 113, 135
animals, 37
animate-animation, 15, 25, 50, 74, 85; animate matter, 74–5
annihilation, hypothesis of, 62, 66, 146; *see also* dissolution
antecedents, 30
anxiety, 54
apostles, 131
appearance(s), 24, 50, 51, 55, 60, 62, 63, 69, 74, 78; natural, 48; neutral, 88; pure, 79; and reality, 12, 78; *see also* subjectivity
appellations, 45, 56, 59; *see also* names
appetite(s), 6, 25, 68, 87–8, 89–90, 91–4, 95; simple, 91; and war, 10
approach, 88, 89, 91
Aquinas, St T., 140
architecture, 27, 32
aristocracy, 119, 152
Aristotle, 2, 4, 7, 50–3; 57, 59, 106–7, 108, 123, 140, 151; categories in natural science, 50–3; causes, 54; explanation in,

best suited to condition of man before the Fall, 54; moral philosophy and rhetoric of, rejected by Hobbes, 2–3; physics of, Hobbes's departures from, 52–4: virtue, doctrine of, compared to Hobbes's, 106–8
artifact, *see under* body
artificial man, 20
astronomy, 76, 77
atheists, 115
attribute, *see* properties
avarice, 113, 146
aversion, 6, 68, 87–8, 89, 90, 91, 93, 95
axioms, 23

Bacon, F., 140
bad, 9, 29, 33, 34, 88, 91, 134; *see also* good
beasts, 35, 85; *see also* animals
bees, 37
belief(s), 129, 134, 141–2; *see also* judgement
benevolence, 32, 68, 96–7, 99; and action, 97; Hobbes's alleged egoistic reduction of, 97
Berkeley, G., 149
body (bodies), 4, 14–15, 17–18, 20, 23, 25, 46, 47, 48, 49, 50, 51, 52, 54, 55–6, 57–8, 59–61, 62–6, 69, 70–2, 74–5, 76–7, 78–9, 80, 82, 84, 85, 87, 146, 149; animate, 25; artificial, 18, 137, 138; celestial, 139; differentiated, 25; experienced, 21; external, 75, 80, 81, 84; functionally organized, 20; in general, 17, 19, 25; inanimate, 85; intersideral, 77, 78; natural, 14, 15, 22, 146; politic, 15–17, 18, 19–20, 24, 124, 132, 138, 139–40, 146; *see also* commonwealth; property of, defined, 15; self-moving, 72; types of, two chief, 22; whole, 18
brain, 78, 83, 87, 91
Bramhall, Bishop, 93
Brandt, F., 149
Brown, S. M., 151
Butler, J., 97–8, 150

calamity, 98, 124
carnality, 34
cause, 16, 17, 23, 24, 29, 32, 37, 51, 53, 57, 58, 59, 61, 70, 71, 73, 80, 81, 84, 92–4, 95, 115, 127, 134, 137, 138–9, 142; constitutive, 18; efficient, 15, 23, 24, 54; final, 24; formal, 53; material, 53; secondary, 55, 137; universal, 60
change, 53, 61, 70–1; sensible, 71
charity, 97, 99, 109, 111, 122, 150
civic duty, 6, 25–6, 27
civilization, 31, 33, 36, 148
civil law, see under law
civil philosophy/science, 2, 3–4, 5, 6, 7, 11, 12–13, 14–16, 17–18, 19, 20–3, 24–6, 30, 33, 42, 44, 127, 128, 137, 138, 141, 143, 145–6; autonomy of, 7, 13, 14, 15; and decision-procedure, 9–10; normative character of, 16; and method of resolution and composition, 17–22; and progress from primitiveness to civilization, 33; and rhetoric, 2–3, 133–7; scientific status of, 12–13, 137–9; useful science par excellence, 33
civil society, 16, 100, 102, 108, 143, 153; see also commonwealth
civil war, 2, 143; English, 127, 136, 148, 152
choice, 34, 93
Christ, 124, 131
circulation, 75, 87
coercion, see under power; sovereign
cognitive capacity, 31, 37, 26, 84–5, 87, 90
colour, 78–80, 81, 83, 85
command(s), 16, 107, 116, 117
common law, 1, 140
common sense, 8, 11, 12
commonwealth, 14, 17, 18, 19–21, 24, 32, 33, 93, 105, 108, 114, 116–20, 121, 123, 125–6, 128, 130–1, 132, 136, 138, 146, 147, 153; acquisition of, 123, 153; as artificial body, 14, 137–8; institution of, 8–9, 116; obligation to maintain, 9, 116; opinions leading to dissolution of, 2, 19, 128–33; parts of, 20; personified by sovereign, 120, 121–2; as union of the multitude, 118–19, 132
communication, 38, 86
comparison, 83, 86
competition, 151
concepts, 74, 85–7, 100, 107, 110
conclusions, 39, 41, 48, 49, 52, 94, 137, 141
concord, 118
conditioning, 92
conjecture, 32
conquest, 153
conscience, 128, 130, 133
consciousness, 38, 63, 88; stream of, 83
consent, 47–8, 118, 135
constant conjunction, 148; see also cause
contentment, 108, 118; see felicity
contract(s), 11, 97, 113, 152; see covenant, promise

controversy, 44, 140
conventionalism, 44–7
Copernicus, N., 76
counsel, 128, 135
covenant(s), 3, 9, 19, 45, 105–6, 108, 112–13, 116–17, 118–19, 121, 132, 137, 138, 139, 147, 152; binding with abolition of right of nature, 116; defined, 113; invalid in state of nature, 113, 114; justice and, 3, 9, 114; and promise, 113
crime, 118, 122

death, 32, 96, 120, 124, 153
decomposition, 19, 20, 21, 48, 137; see also analysis; method
deduction, 8, 9, 11, 12
definition(s), 16, 41–2, 44–5, 45–8, 49–50, 52, 56, 58–60, 61, 63–5, 89, 133, 140–1; stipulative, 129
dehortation, 135
deliberation, 10, 12, 16, 90, 92–3, 95, 96, 111, 116, 118, 123, 135
demagogue(s), 127, 133
democracy, 119
demonstration(s), 38, 42, 43, 44, 45, 48–9, 50, 57, 65, 72–3, 138, 139–40, 143; see also syllogism; teaching
density, 77, 78
Descartes, R., 8, 50, 57, 58, 68, 73, 140
desire(s), 36, 89, 91, 97, 99–100
Dewey, J., 153
discourse, 58, 85, 86
disobedience, 19, 117, 122, 129
dissolution, 21, 33, 127, 129, 146; method of, in civil philosophy, 21
division of labour, 102
dogmatici, 44
doubt, 47
dreaming, 84, 130
Dunn, J., 148
duty (duties), 7, 19–20, 26, 142, 146; civic, 27; distribution of, 19, 20–1; of rulership, 17; of subjects, 4, 18–19, 20–1
Dworkin, R., 147

Eden, 34, 35, see also Adam; Fall
effect(s), 23, 24, 31, 32, 35, 41, 51, 54–5, 57–8, 68, 70, 78, 84, 88, 95, 138, 139
egoism, 96, 97–100, 103–4, 105, 106, 150–1
eloquence, 92, 128, 135; see also counsel
endeavour(s), 69, 70, 73, 77, 83; as small motions (def.), 76
equity, 9, 132, 139
error, 2, 19, 91, 127, 141
essence, 55, 56, 59, see under cause, formal; see also definition, genera and species
ethics, 6, 12, 25, 68, 110, 140, 143, see also moral philosophy; passions
Euclid, 64–5
event, 43, 85, 94–5; types of, 30
Everyman, 26, 142
evil(s), 2, 8, 30, 34, 98, 150

expectations, 30, 84, 89, 98, 150
experience(s), 7, 10, 11, 21, 29, 29–33, 40, 45, 48–9, 78, 79, 87, 88, 91, 101, 102, 148, 150
experiments, 23–4, 42
explanations, 55, 58, 60, 72, 76, 78, 112, 139; mechanistic, 58
explications, 49, 61

faith, 130; the faithful, 131
Fall, 34, 35, 36–7, 54, 124–5, 140
false witness, 129
fear(s), 6, 32, 54, 93, 98, 113, 114–15, 117, 135, 147
felicity, 100–2, 104–5, 118, 142, 147, 152
Foot, P., 151
force(s), 87, 101, 123, 142
forgiveness, 111
freedom, 92, 116, 133; total, 136; see also liberty
free will controversy, 93–5
friends, 97, 99, 101, 115, 145

Galileo, 8, 27, 76; Law of Fall, 47
Gauthier, D., 145, 152
Geach, P., 149
genera and species, 50, 52, 79
generation(s), 15, 16, 18, 21, 64–5, 139; of a circle, 65; of a commonwealth, 20; discoverable, 15
geometry, 1, 5–6, 22, 25, 27, 33, 47–8, 57–8, 60, 64, 65–6, 67, 68, 138, 140, 141; and commodious arts, 27; comparable to civil science, 1, 42, 137–40; construction in, 57, 66; figures in, 44, 67, 137; as first part of natural philosophy, 5; as first part of philosophy, 7, 8; indispensability of, 67; and motion, 63–6; principles of, and the will, 138–9; and simple motion (motion in the abstract), 25, 66; truth of theorems in, 47–9
glory, 34, 36, 101–2, 121, 122, 125, 150
goals, 29
God, 24, 27, 34, 58, 107, 115, 119, 130, 132, 139; first cause, 58; infinite power, 77; knowledge of his properties, 58; will of, 106; word of, 230
Goldsmith, M. M., 146, 152
good, 2, 8, 9, 10, 12, 29, 33, 34, 88, 125; genuine science of, 7; the, 7, 9, 12; the good life, 101, 108, 147; the real, 12
goods, 29, 33, 89, 96, 101, 102, 103, 147; the race for 96; of the soul in Aristotle, 107
government, 9, 11, 12, 30, 33, 104–5, 122, 133, 134, 136, 137; by God, 125; see also body politic; civil society; commonwealth; sovereign
Great Tew, 152
grief, 98

Hacking, I., 149–50
heart, 75, 87; as innermost organ of sense, 77

heat, 51, 55, 139
Hill, C., 148
honour, 121
human nature, 18, 54, 103, 146
Hume, D., 136, 150
hypothesis/hypotheses, 27, 32, 45, 73, 75, 80, 137, 139–40

idea(s), 56, 62–3, 66, 70, 71, 82, 83, 150; clear, 58; geometrical, 64, 65; universal, 62; see also phantasm
identity, 61
iniquity, 120
injury, 102, 120, 121
injustice(s), 10–11, 12, 120, 121, 135; real/ apparent, 12; supposed, and kingly power, 19; see also justice
intentions, 118, 124
introspection, 7, 26, 70–1; passions and, 7
invisible spirits, 115

justice, 9, 10, 19, 104, 117–18, 139, 152; demands of, 20; genuine science of, 7, 139; just action, 117; just distribution of rights and duties, 20; just man, 117–18; see also virtue
judgement(s), 34, 82, 102, 125, 134
Jerusalem, 131

Kant, I., 99
kindness, 90
king(s), 2, 19, 20, 133; decrees of, 2; grounds for deposing, 19; see also sovereign
knowledge, 26, 33, 45, 58, 135; demonstrative, 45, 52; experience only one source of, 45; experimental, 42; of law, 16; in politics, 140; tree of, 34, 54; see also philosophy; science
Kuhn, T., 149

language, 27, 38, 58, 85, 86, 149; see also names; proposition; speech
law, 9–10, 15–16, 17, 117, 120, 122, 123, 132; laws, 8–9, 11, 107, 127–8, 139; civil, 117, 119, 123, 128, 137, 142; common, 1, 140; king's, 133; -maker/-making, 131–2; moral, 106; of nature, 9, 17, 105, 106, 107, 111, 117–18, 121, 124, 136, 142; positive, 117
Law of Fall, 47
Levin, M., 151
life, 75, 104, 108, 109; everlasting, 124; the good, 108, 152; of man, compared to a race, 98; quality of, 123; at risk, 96; secure vs flourishing, 107
light, 51, defined 77–8, 79; propagation of, 78; solid rays of, 78; source, 77
line(s), 64–65
liberty, 8, 95, 122, 133, 136; loss of, 30, 133; of preserving life, 32, restricted, 9; total, 96, 133; see also anarchy; freedom; state of nature

Lloyd, C., 153–4
logic, 31, 50–1, 135; logical eloquence, 134–5; logical subjects, 51; logicians, 73
love, 6, 68, 89–90, 91, 97; of humanity and usefulness of power, 104; Platonic, Hobbes' doubts about genuineness, 97
Lukes, S., 146
lust, 90

Macpherson, C. B., 145
madness, 140
magnitude(s), 37, 49, 52, 54, 60, 62, 64, 76, 79
manners, 103, 106
mark, 38
martyrdom, 131
materia prima, 57
mathematics, 8, 58; demonstrations of, 8; mathematical facts, 58; mathematical sciences, 7; mathematical truth, 45; mathematici, 38, 44
matter, 56, 77; animate, 74; see also body
McNeilly, F. S., 150
mean (doctrine of), 106–7
means, 30, 34, 111, 152
measurement, 27, 54
mechanics, 5–6, 22, 24, 25, 48–9; and first part of philosophy, 8; mechanistic explanation, 58; mechanistic physics, 12; mechanistic psychology, 11, 68; pure, 1, 47, 138
metaphysics, 4, 8, 59, 140
method, 11, 16, 18, 26, 50, 66–7, 146; analytical/, of analysis 10, 18; of civil philosophy, 22; of dissolution, 21, 146; of exposing and calculating quantity, and geometry, 67; of natural philosophy, 22–3; of resolution, 18, 19; resolutive-comparative, 16; of teaching, 11; see also analysis; dissolution; synthesis
methodological individualism, 146
Mill, J. S., 22, 146
mind, 52, 53, 66, 68, 70, 74, 79–80, 81, 82, 89, 92
monarchy, 119, 127
money, 120, 122, 131
morality/morals, 2, 4, 5, 23, 32, 33, 77, 108–10, 130, 143
moral philosophy, 2, 6–7, 12, 24, 42, 44, 106, 107, 110, 135, 136, 143
Mother Teresa, 104
motion(s), 15, 23, 24, 25, 26, 27, 37, 48, 49, 52, 54, 57, 59–61, 63–6, 72, 73, 74, 75, 76, 77, 78, 79, 82–3, 87; animal, 87, 88–9; in brain, 90–1; circular, 78; continual, 62; direction of, 66; as efficient causes, 53; internal, of sentient, 87, 88; measurable, 66–7; of the mind, 6, 68; of parts of body, 25; physicist's study of, 67; simple, 66; vital, 87; voluntary, 92

Nagel, T., 99, 100, 151, 152

names, 27, 31–2, 38–41, 44, 45, 49–50, 52, 56, 57, 61–2, 85–6, 89; capacity to name things, 29; general, 27; imposition of, as first step in preferred method of science, 38; naming, 27, 38, 52; power of, 27; proper, 39; universal, 39–41, 56, 61
natural philosophy/science, 3–6, 12–13, 14–15, 17, 18, 21–2, 23–4, 26, 33, 53–4, 57, 59, 60, 61, 145; Aristotle's, suited to human condition before the Fall, 54; benefits of, 31–3; books of, 5; categories of, 51–4; and civil philosophy, 4–5, 6–7, 12–13, 14–17, 22–4, 137–40; modest development of before Hobbes's day, 44; and motion, 25, 59–60; and power, 35, 36–7; and quantity, 66–7; see also method; philosophy; science
nature, 29, 37, 41–2, 49, 52, 54, 56, 64, 68, 122; author of, 24
necessity, 71, 150; necessary connections, 93–4; necessities of life, 32
nerves, 20, 88
Nozick, R., 141, 146, 151
numbers, 60, 75
numeral words, 85–6

Oakeshott, M., 148
obedience, 131, 134, 136, to Christ or God, 131; civil, 19; to civil law, 9; to king's commands, 19; to sovereign, 121; unconditional, 107; see also duty; civil; quiescence; subject
obligation(s), 118–20, 141; binding, 119; moral, 26, 109; sovereign's, 119; see also duty
optics, 2, 77–8
Oxbridge/Oxford, 4–5, 145

pact, 138; see also covenant
pain, 30, 88–9, 91, 93
panpsychism, 74, 149
passion(s), 7, 8, 10, 12, 25, 33, 56, 87, 89–92, 98, 100, 102, 113, 134, 136, 141–2, 148, 153; passion words, 91, 98; simple, 89
past, 93, 100
peace, 2, 8, 10–11, 27, 32, 97, 104, 106, 107, 108, 109, 112, 119–20, 134, 152, 153; arts of, 104; rules of, 142
person, 90; def., 120
Peters, R., 145, 150
phantasm(s), 24, 62, 69, 70, 73, 75, 77, 78–9, 80, 81, 82–4, 85, content of, 70; differences in, 83–4; discrete, 83; individual, 83; of the lucid body, 77–8
phenomena, 53–4, 60, 69, 77, 78, 79, 139; mental, 68; of nature, 23, 42, 137–8
philosophy, 14, 18, 46, 51, 56, 57–9, 64–5, 72, 140–1, 148; civil, see under civil philosophy; coercive, 141; elements of, 22; experience not a part of, 87; first part of, 15; 'in general', 22; moral, see under moral philosophy; parts of, 5, 14, 25–7;

philosophia prima (first philosophy), chapter 5 *passim*; revisionary, 143; sideral, 76; *see also* civil philosophy; natural philosophy; science

physics, 4, 5, 6, 7, 8, 22, 25, 47, 59, 61, 66–7, 69, 138, 139–40, 143, 148, 153; as contributing to first part of philosophy, 7, 8; elements of, 56

physiology, 74, 77

pia mater, 78

pity, 97–8, 135

place, 23, 59, 60, 62; difficulties with definition of, 62

Plato, 7

pleasure, 12, 29–30, 88, 89, 91, 93, 150; *see also* pain

politics, 2, 5, 23, 77, 140, 145, 148; *see also* civil philosophy

possibility, 94, 113

potentialities, 61

poverty, 122, 151

power, 25, 32, 37, 54, 55, 77, 100 (def.), 103, 104, 112, 119, 134, 142, 150, 153; civil, 127; coercive, 10, 113; common, 101; of commonwealth, 20; of comparing and distinguishing ideas, 82; delivered by science, 37; desire for, 100; detachment of legislative from executive, misconceived, 131–2; division of between king and parliament, 140; ecclesiastical, 131; of sovereign, excessive? 120; God's, 37, 77, 139; kingly, 19; love of, 97; of making war, 131; natural advantages in, 101; over natural effects, 35, 36, 37; persuasive, of civil science, 133; protective, 147; of raising taxes, 120; reserves of, 123; of sovereign, 21, 105, 108, 117, 121–2, 128, 131–2, 137, 153; sovereign's, of life and death, 120; surplus, 150; of written or spoken things, 38–9

practical deliberation, 10, 12, 16, 30, 92

practical reasoning, 135

predicate(s), 39, 46, 50, 141

prediction(s), 27

pride, 37; *see also* glory

primitives, 31–3, 35

principles, 10, 11, 59, 68, 70, 71, 139, 143; first, 57; of motion, 65, 68, 71; of nature, 68; about passions, 26; of politics, 1, 25; of ratiocination, 23; of things themselves, 69

promise/promising, 112, 113, 115, 118

proof, 73

properties, 15, 31, 41, 48–50, 51–2, 53, 57, 64–5, 66, 79–80, 138; geometrical, 63–4; non-determinate, 63; primary/secondary, 79

proportion, 55, 60

proposition(s), 46, 50, 141, 149; affirmative, 47; definitionally true, 45; externally true, 39; general, 27; of geometry and mechanics, 47–8; non-evident, 42; of

physics, 47; of science, 45, 46; singular, 39, 47; significant, 31; types of, 42; universals, 39, 41, 47

protestant sects, 128

prudence, 10, 31, 58, 134; civil and moral, 11

punishment, 18, 34, 122; Christ's, 131; sovereign's, 131

qualities, 75, 78–9, 107; primary/secondary, 79–80; sensible, 75

quiescence, 137

Quine, W. V. O., 40

race metaphor, 97, 98

ratiocination/reasoning, 2, 7, 10, 16, 18, 23, 26, 33, 37, 38, 39–40, 44, 46, 51, 54, 56, 69, 73, 80, 107, 108, 139, 143, 149; capacity for, 29, 148; methodical, 26

reaction, 69, 70, 74, 81, 83; sensory, 83, 84

rebellion, 125, 128, 133, 134, 136, 137, 147

refraction, 78

Reid, T., 149

religion, 128, 140

resolution, 10, 14, 18, 19, 56–7, 146; continual, 46; into definitions, 46; resolutive method, 10

responsibility, 8

rewards, 120, 134–5, 146–7

rhetoric, *see* counsel, eloquence

right(s), 19, 112, 113, 119, 146; distribution of, 20–21; of nature, def., 111–12, 113, 116, 121, 128, 137, 152; of ownership, 132; of self-governance, 119; of sovereigns, 1, 19, 20; of states, 18–19

Robertson, G. C., 145

Rorty, R., 148, 153

Rousseau, J. J., 33, 36

Ryan, A., 147–8

safety, 108, 116, 121, 122, 123, 151

salvation, 124, 125

savage(s), 31–2, 35, 37, *see also* primitives

scarcity, 8, 32, 36, 37

scepticism, 65–6

Schneider, H., 153

schoolmen, 4, 5, 80, 140

science(s), 27, 28, 29, 32, 33, 34, 35, 36, 37, 38, 39, 40, 41–2, 43–45, 46, 50, 57, 58–59, 68, 77, 86, 102, 106, 128, 134, 135, 137–8, 139–40, 141, 145, 148, 149, 152, 153; applied, 27; civil, *see* civil philosophy; supposed conventionalist theory of, 45; deductive, 42, 143; demonstrative, 42, 45; elements of, 3; natural, *see* natural philosophy/science; normative, 17, 18; parts of, 7, 26; prior, 25, 27; product of reason, 26, 31; science-worship, 35–6; second class, 139; unified, 3–4; *see also* philosophy

scripture, 35, 75, 129, 130, 131

security, *see* peace, safety

sedition, 2, 3, 19, 127, 128, 132, 133, 134, 135
self-defence, 109, 112, 120
self-interest, 96, 108–9
semantics, 90; semantic ascent, 40; semantic information, 41; *see also* names; proposition; speech
sense/sensation, 6, 15, 37, 51, 52, 53, 58, 63, 68, 69–70, 71, 73–4, 75, 77, 78, 79, 80, 82–4, 87, 90, 149; sense-content, 53, 63; *see also* experience
sense-organs, 69, 73–4, 75, 78–9, 82, 83, 84
sentient, 70–1, 75, 79, 84
servants, 102
shapes, 49, 79, 80
signification(s), 45, 48, 56, 135
simplicity, 34
Sin, 118, 124
Skinner, Q., 153, 154
smell, 78, 83
social sciences, 22
sound, 78, 81, 83, 88
sovereign/sovereignty, 7, 17, 105, 116–17, 119–23, 125, 126, 132–3, 135, 137, 143; authority of, 19; coercion, 115–16; commands of, 10, 117, 128; dependence on subjects, 121–3; judgements of, 132; laws, 105, 117, 131; law-maker, 132; power of, 21, 108, 116, 121–2, 127–8, 133, 137, 150; rights of, 19, 20
space, 14, 49, 60, 62, 63, 63–4, 66
species, 50, 80
speech, 31, 37, 86, 134, 137; prescriptive vs fact-stating, 135–6
Spinoza, B., 144
square, 56
stars, 70, 76
state, *see* commonwealth
state of nature, 8, 11, 12, 19, 24, 36, 96, 102, 103–4, 112, 112–17, 125–6, 128, 137, 146–7, 153
subject (vs predicate), 46, 48, 51
subjectivity, 53, 75, 79–80, 80–1
subjects (citizens), 7, 9, 19, 20, 119, 121, 122–3, 126, 127, 135, 143, 153
submission, 21, 119, 127
substance, 51–2, 57
sun, 51; 77; sunlight, 78
survival, 54, 96, 101, 109, 126
syllogism(s), 27, 38, 39, 41, 43, 45, 46, 50, 51, 52, 141, 149
synthesis, 10–11, 72, 138; *see also* analysis; demonstration; method

taxes, 18, 122, 131
Taylor, A. E., 151
teaching, 43–4, 50, 57, 92
technology, 36
terms, 50, 59, 61
temperate men, 103
Thomas, K., 148, 152
thought(s), 31, 37, 38, 41, 63; nature of thinking, 85–7
tidal activity, 76
time(s), 23, 37–8, 56, 59, 60, 62, 66, 71, 84, 146
toil, 34
touch, 79, 83
trade, 123
triangle, 40, 138–9
trust, 113, 114
truth(s), 38, 41, 43, 45, 46, 47, 125–6, 134, 139, 144, 146, 149

understanding, 138, 142
universal, conceptions, 56; efficient cause, 23; name(s), 39–41; propositions, 39–40, 42, 46; rules, 40, 41; things, 49, 52, 59, 146
universities, 4, 20

vacuum, 76
vainglory, *see* glory
valuation(s), 30, 88, 91–2, 123
vice, 3, 9, 106
vital organs, 20
virtue(s), 3, 9, 106, 107, 108, 114, 117–18, 124, 151; virtue words, 136
vision, 69, 77

Waldman, T., 153
war(s), 10, 27, 101–2, 104, 118, 122, 134, 137, avoidability of, once state exists, 104–5; avoidance of, as moral requirement, 9; cold, 102; inevitability of, in state of nature, 101–2
Warrender, H., 151
Watkins, J. W. N., 146, 151
Wilkes, K., 151
will(s), 92, 94, 107, 118–19, 123, 132, 139, 152; free, 92–3; God's, 105; power of, 95
wisdom, 10, 124, 128, 134–5, 151
Wittgenstein, L., 86, 140
wolfishness, 125–6
words, *see* names
world, 76, 80
wrong, 30, 101, 127